Metaphors Used on Polish and American Internet Forums for Mothers

GDAŃSK STUDIES IN LANGUAGE

Edited by Danuta Stanulewicz

VOLUME 11

Advisory Board

Tadeusz Danilewicz (University of Gdańsk, Poland)
Laura A. Janda (UiT The Arctic University of Norway)
Roman Kalisz (Wyższa Szkoła Języków Obcych, Świecie, Poland)
Ewa Komorowska (University of Szczecin, Poland)
Wojciech Kubiński (University of Gdańsk, Poland)
Ronald Langacker (University of California, San Diego, USA)
Elżbieta Mańczak-Wohlfeld (Jagiellonian University, Poland)
Galina Paramei (Liverpool Hope University, UK)
Małgorzata Rocławska-Daniluk (University of Gdańsk, Poland)
Olga Sokołowska (University of Gdańsk, Poland)
Kazimierz A. Sroka (Polonia University in Częstochowa, Poland)
Maria Wysocka (University of Silesia, Poland)

Marta Gierczyńska-Kolas

Metaphors Used on Polish and American Internet Forums for Mothers

A Comparative Analysis

Bibliographic Information published by the Deutsche Nationalbibliothek
The Deutsche Nationalbibliothek lists this publication in the
Deutsche Nationalbibliografie; detailed bibliographic data is
available in the internet at http://dnb.d-nb.de.
Library of Congress Cataloging-in-Publication Data
Names: Gierczynska-Kolas, Marta, author.
Title: Metaphors used on Polish and American internet forums for mothers : a comparative analysis / Marta Gierczynska-Kolas.
Description: Frankfurt am Main ; New York : Peter Lang, [2017] | Series: Gdansk studies in language; vol. 11 | Includes index.
Identifiers: LCCN 2017002916| ISBN 9783631673935 (Print) | ISBN 9783653067224
(E-PDF) | ISBN 9783631709078 (EPUB) | ISBN 9783631709085 (MOBI)
Subjects: LCSH: Metaphor--Usage. | Electronic discussion groups--Social aspects--Poland. | Electronic discussion groups--Social aspects--United States. | Mothers--Social networks--Poland. | Mothers--Social networks--United States. | Language and the Internet--Poland. | Language and the Internet--United States. | Comparative linguistics.
Classification: LCC P301.5.M48 G55 2017 | DDC 808/.032--dc23 LC record available at
https://lccn.loc.gov/2017002916

This publication was financially supported by the Institute of
English and American Studies of the University of Gdańsk.

ISSN 2196-016X
ISBN 978-3-631-67393-5 (Print)
E-ISBN 978-3-653-06722-4 (E-Book)
E-ISBN 978-3-631-70907-8 (EPUB)
E-ISBN 978-3-631-70908-5 (MOBI)
DOI 10.3726/978-3-653-06722-4

© Peter Lang GmbH
Internationaler Verlag der Wissenschaften
Frankfurt am Main 2017
All rights reserved.

Peter Lang – Frankfurt am Main · Bern · Bruxelles · New York ·
Oxford · Warszawa · Wien
All parts of this publication are protected by copyright. Any
utilisation outside the strict limits of the copyright law, without
the permission of the publisher, is forbidden and liable to
prosecution. This applies in particular to reproductions,
translations, microfilming, and storage and processing in
electronic retrieval systems.

This publication has been peer reviewed.

www.peterlang.com

This book is dedicated to two important Danutas –
my mother and my mentor

Contents

List of tables 11

Introduction 13

Chapter One Theoretical overview of cognitive linguistics and various theories of metaphors 17

   1.1   Introductory remarks 17
   1.2   Cognitive Linguistics 17
   1.3   Cognitive semantics 19
         1.3.1 Conceptual structure is embodied 20
         1.3.2 Semantic structure is conceptual structure 20
         1.3.3 Meaning representation is encyclopedic 21
         1.3.4 Meaning construction is conceptualisation 21
   1.4   The Conceptual Metaphor Theory 21
         1.4.1 Hiding and highlighting 25
         1.4.2 The cognitive processes in metaphor understanding 26
         1.4.3 The experiential basis of metaphor 27
         1.4.4 The Invariance Hypothesis and asymmetrical directionality 28
         1.4.5 Classification of metaphors 29
               1.4.5.1 The conventionality of metaphors 29
               1.4.5.2 The cognitive function of metaphor 30
               1.4.5.3 The nature of metaphor 33
               1.4.5.4 Levels of generality of metaphor 34
   1.5   The Context-Limited Simulation Theory of Metaphor 34
   1.6   The Discourse Dynamics Framework for Metaphor 37
   1.7   The Theory of Lexical Concepts and Cognitive Models 39
   1.8   Metonymy and metaphtonymy 41
   1.9   Research on the subject 43
   1.10 Concluding remarks 44

Chapter Two Communication in the Internet 47

   2.1   Introductory remarks 47
   2.2   The Internet as a unique environment for communication 48
           2.2.1 Asynchronous communication 50
           2.2.2 Synchronous communication... 52
           2.2.3 Active communication 53
           2.2.4 The Internet as a medium stimulating communication................. 54
   2.3   The forum as a form of communication medium 54
   2.4   Features of language used in online communication...............................57
   2.5   Research on the subject..67
   2.6   Concluding remarks 68

Chapter Three Metaphors employed by Polish users of Internet forums for mothers 69

   3.1   The aims of the research...69
           3.1.1 Data collection 69
   3.2   An analysis of selected examples of conceptual metaphors 73
           3.2.1 Metaphors of emotions.. 74
                  3.2.1.1 Metaphors of anger.. 74
                  3.2.1.2 Metaphors of aggitation and nerves................................... 75
                  3.2.1.3 Metaphors of depression 77
                  3.2.1.4 Metaphors of happiness and sadness 80
                  3.2.1.5 Metaphors of other feelings and emotions........................ 81
           3.2.2 Metaphors of relationships... 83
           3.2.3 Metaphors of sex.. 87
           3.2.4 Metaphors of conception... 88
           3.2.5 Metaphors of bringing up children 89
           3.2.6 Metaphors of children's progress 89
           3.2.7 Metaphors of the human body 90
                  3.2.7.1 Metaphors of parts of the body.. 90
                  3.2.7.2 Metaphors of teeth... 92

		3.2.8	Metaphors of illnesses 93
		3.2.9	Metaphors of everyday life 95
		3.2.10	Metaphors of shopping 99
		3.2.11	Metaphors of problems and hardship 100
		3.2.12	Metaphors of people, their behaviour and attitudes 105
		3.2.13	Metaphors of time 106
		3.2.14	Other metaphors 107
			3.2.14.1 Metaphors of weather 107
			3.2.14.2 Metaphors of computers and Internet-related phenomena 108
			3.2.14.3 Metaphors of the world, life, fate and nature 109
			3.2.14.4 Metaphors of freedom and patience 112
	3.3	Concluding remarks 113

Chapter Four Metaphors employed by American users of Internet forums for mothers 115

4.1	Introductory remarks 115
	4.1.1 Data collection 115
4.2	An analysis of selected examples of conceptual metaphors 121
	4.2.1 Metaphors of emotions 121
	4.2.1.1 Metaphors of anger 121
	4.2.1.2 Metaphors of happiness and sadness 122
	4.2.1.3 Metaphors of other feelings and emotions 124
	4.2.2 Metaphors of relationships 125
	4.2.3 Metaphors of sex 125
	4.2.4 Metaphors of pregnancy 126
	4.2.5 Metaphors of everyday life 126
	4.2.6 Metaphors of people, their actions and attitudes 127
	4.2.7 Metaphors of the human body 131
	4.2.8 Metaphors of experiences 132
	4.2.9 Metaphors of criticism 133
	4.2.10 Metaphors of choosing an option 134

      4.2.11 Metaphors of time 135
            4.2.11.1 Metaphors of time in general.. 135
            4.2.11.2 Metaphors of future.. 135
      4.2.12 Metaphors of weapons 136
  4.3 Concluding remarks 136

Chapter Five A comparative analysis of metaphors used on Polish and American Internet forums 139

  5.1 Introductory remarks 139

  5.2 A qualitative analysis of metaphorical language used on various discussion threads... 140

  5.3 A quantitative analysis of metaphorical expressions............................ 149

  5.4 Concluding remarks 163

Conclusions 165

Author index 185

Subject index 189

List of tables

Table 1:	Mappings for POLITICS IS A PLAY	25
Table 2:	Mappings for TIME PASSING IS MOTION OF AN OBJECT	30
Table 3:	Ontological metaphors	31
Table 4:	Orientational metaphors UP-DOWN	32
Table 5:	Image-schemas	33
Table 6:	A summary of synchronous and asynchronous forms of CMC.	49
Table 7:	List of topics taken from the Internet forum BabyBoom	55
Table 8:	Written language criteria applied to Netspeak	57
Table 9:	Spoken language criteria applied to Netspeak	58
Table 10:	Classification of word-formation processes of Internet neologisms	61
Table 11:	Classification of blending neologisms	61
Table 12:	Basic abbreviations based on pronunciation	62
Table 13:	Acronyms in Netspeak	62
Table 14:	Top 20 emoticons according to Twitter users	64
Table 15:	Emoticons	65
Table 16:	Abbreviations used on American forums for mothers	116
Table 17:	Corresponding discussion threads	140
Table 18:	Metaphorical expressions: Thematic areas	150
Table 19:	Use of metaphors in thematic areas: Ranking lists	152
Table 20:	Use of metaphors in thematic areas: Ranking lists (2)	154
Table 21:	Target domains of the most popular metaphors	156
Table 22:	Source domains of the most popular metaphors	160

Introduction

The last decades in the field of linguistics are characterized not only by the development of many new disciplines within it but also by an increased interest in interdisciplinary research. Multidimensional phenomena include metaphor which has been studied by linguists, psychologists, sociologists, educators and philosophers.

> The most sustained and innovative recent work on metaphor has occurred in cognitive science and psychology. Psycholinguistic investigation suggests that novel, poetic metaphors are processed differently than literal speech, while relatively conventionalized and contextually salient metaphors are processed more like literal speech. This conflicts with the view of "cognitive linguists" like George Lakoff that all or nearly all thought is essentially metaphorical. There are currently four main cognitive models of metaphor comprehension: juxtaposition, category-transfer, feature-matching, and structural alignment. Structural alignment deals best with the widest range of examples; but it still fails to account for the complexity and richness of fairly novel, poetic metaphors (Camp 2006: 154).

Stanulewicz (2009: 474) sums up Lakoff and Johnsons's approach to metaphors. According to these researchers and their associates, "metaphor should be treated not only as a figure of speech used in poetry [...] because they are also employed – frequently unconsciously – in 'ordinary' spoken and written texts". What is more, "the metaphors we utilize not only shape our perception of the world, but also influence our personal decisions, including those of utmost importance, and even construct our social reality" (Stanulewicz 2009: 474). Sokołowska (2008: 37) states that metaphor is "a powerful cognitive tool".

Understanding that metaphors are omnipresent in people's lives was one of the reasons that motivated me to choose Internet forums designed for parents as sources of data for analysis of conceptual metaphors. The language used in threaded online discussions is specific because it shares features of written and spoken language. The topic of conscious parenting is constantly gaining popularity, also in the media. Breakfast TV shows invite specialists, like physiotherapists, psychologists and medical doctors, to give advice on how to raise children. Celebrities who are also parents advocate for various causes, like singing to babies, reading to children, ecological parenting etc. There are various magazines on the Polish market dedicated to parents, discussing topics such as giving birth, parenting, education of children etc.; newspapers issue extra material on problems connected with raising children. Finally, mothers themselves take the initiative and open clubs for young parents promoting healthy and active lifestyles, encouraging hobbies, organizing meetings with celebrities and various specialists. Also, the popularity of community portals and forums promoting conscious parenting has been constantly growing since 2009. According to the second largest website analyzing web traffic and web page statistics, Alexa (www.alexa.com, accessed on the 25th of May 2011), the community portal "BabyBoom" was ranked as number 787 among all Polish websites based on website traffic (the number of people visiting the website). The Internet forum of "BabyBoom" is extremely popular with mothers, which can be easily noticed by analyzing their statistics. In 2011 there were over 400 community groups, 23,300 topics, almost 75,500 users and nearly 7 million comments (data gathered on 20th of May 2011 on www.babyboom.pl) (Gierczyńska-Kolas 2013: 56). In 2015 there were over 29,000 topics, almost 115,000 users and nearly 11 million comments (data gathered on 7th of February 2015 on www.babyboom.pl) – a vast repository of linguistic data.

This study is an attempt to analyze the language of Internet forum users, especially the conceptual metaphors they employ. It offers an analysis of the material collected from various Polish and American Internet forums for mothers which are an ever-growing inexhaustible source of spontaneously used ordinary language.

The purpose of this study is to analyze conceptual metaphors used on Polish and American Internet forums for mothers.

Additional objectives of the thesis are the following: to present what thematic areas require the use of metaphors, to show what topics of Internet discussions cannot be expressed metaphorically and to examine the differences and similarities between the metaphors used by Polish and American parents.

Achieving the objectives of this study required performing some specific tasks:

- developing a theoretical base of the study, in this case, considering the main objectives of the Conceptual Metaphor Theory;
- selecting topics of Internet forums which provided versatile material for the analysis;
- identifying conceptual metaphors in the analyzed material;
- classifying metaphors by thematic areas, and more narrowly, by their target domains;
- translating Polish metaphorical expressions into English, with special emphasis on cultural information;
- comparing Polish and American metaphors in many respects.

It is hoped that this study will be a useful contribution to the better understanding of conceptual metaphors used in online discussions as this is an interesting and still not fully described topic, especially from a comparative perspective.

This work consists of five chapters: "Theoretical overview of cognitive linguistics and various theories of metaphors", "Communication in the Internet", "Metaphors in the language of Polish users of Internet forums for mothers", "Metaphors in the language of American users of Internet forums for mothers" and "A comparative analysis of conceptual metaphors used on Polish and American Internet forums for mothers".

Chapter One, as its title suggests, focuses on Cognitive Linguistics itself. It provides a short overview of this approach, a history of its emergence and it also contains an overview of cognitive semantics, a branch of Cognitive Linguistics that deals with word and sentence meaning. Chapter One also presents the theory of Conceptual Metaphor proposed by George Lakoff and Mark Johnson (1980), as well as the Context-Limited Simulation Theory of Metaphor elaborated by Lawrence Barsalou (1999), the Lexical Concepts and Cognitive Models Theory introduced by Lynne Cameron (2009) and a Discourse Dynamics Framework for Metaphor developed by Vyvyan Evans (2006).

The second chapter, entitled "Communication in the Internet", provides a brief review of synchronous, asynchronous and active forms of communication on the Internet as well as a description of features of the language used in online communication which is specific because of the fact that it has features of both written and spoken communication at the same time. The second chapter also sets out to demonstrate that an Internet forum is a unique communication medium because it facilitates online threaded discussions with multiple users.

Chapters Three and Four present a broad selection of metaphorical expressions and the most popular mappings in the language of Polish and American users of Internet forums for parents, especially mothers. Metaphors used in various thematic areas are described in individual subsections.

The conclusions emerging from the analysis are provided in Chapter Five. The aims of the chapter are to present which topics were discussed with metaphorical language and to demonstrate to what extent the used metaphors differ or show similarities.

Chapter One Theoretical overview of cognitive linguistics and various theories of metaphors

1.1 Introductory remarks

Chapter One attempts to provide a brief overview of Cognitive Linguistics, a history of its emergence and main assumptions, as well as of cognitive semantics and four principles that characterize this area of Cognitive Linguistics. This chapter aims to review four most important theories of metaphor: the Conceptual Metaphor Theory with its main assumptions, notions and classifications of metaphors according to their conventionality, function, nature and level of generality; the Context-Limited Simulation Theory of Metaphor, the Lexical Concepts and Cognitive Models Theory and the Discourse Dynamics Framework for Metaphor.

1.2 Cognitive Linguistics

Cognitive Linguistics is a modern school of linguistic thought which came to existence in the 1970s to oppose Generative Grammar which developed within formal linguistics and had its roots in twentieth-century Anglo-American analytic philosophy. Nerlich and Clarke (2007: 590) state that cognitive linguistics "emerged from […] dissatisfaction with dominant orthodoxies in twentieth-century linguistics". Among these orthodoxies they list the generative/formalist approach to syntax in North America, the formalist/computational tradition in research into semantics in North America and Europe and the structuralist/formalist approach to semantics that prevailed in Europe.

Cognitive Linguistics did not emerge from one source only or at any precise moment. It was in 1975, however, that George Lakoff used the term *cognitive linguistics* for the first time. At roughly the same time, Leonard Talmy introduced principles of Gestalt psychology into linguistic analysis and Ronald W. Langacker incorporated Talmy's concepts into the theory of Cognitive Grammar. These three figures are considered the founding fathers of Cognitive Linguistics.

From 1980 onwards, research within the framework of Cognitive Linguistics came to the fore. George Lakoff and Mark Johnson worked on the categorization of metaphors and Ronald W. Langacker on Cognitive Grammar, Gilles

Fauconnier and Mark Turner on blending theory and Dirk Geeraerts on diachronic prototype semantics (Nerlich and Clarke 2007: 591).

In 1989 the First International Conference on Cognitive Linguistics was organized by René Dirven in Duisburg, Germany. According to Langacker, the establishment of the International Cognitive Linguistics Society and the first issue of the journal *Cognitive Linguistics* in 1989/1990 "marked the birth of cognitive linguistics as a broadly grounded, self-conscious intellectual movement" (Langacker, in Evans and Green 2006: 3). Since that time, the number of followers has been growing, various national cognitive linguistics associations have emerged, and, according to Nerlich and Clarke (2007: 592), "Cognitive Linguistics may now be said to be one of the major popular frameworks within theoretical linguistics at large".

Cognitive Linguistics focuses foremost on the experiential and environmental background of linguistic structures, as opposed to the assumptions of traditional approaches to linguistics, such as the search for regularities and monosemy, the rejection or downplaying of disciplines such as pragmatics, sociolinguistics and semantics; the distinction between literal and figurative language and the separation of conceptual processes from linguistic processes.

The main focus of cognitive linguistics lies in the relationship between language and thoughts, thoughts and mental processes involving background knowledge as well as psychological, physiological and cultural factors.

> Because Cognitive Linguistics sees language as embedded in the overall cognitive capacities of man, topics of special interest of Cognitive Linguistics include: the structural characteristics of natural language categorization (such as prototypicality, systematic polysemy, cognitive models, mental imagery, and metaphor); the functional principles of linguistic organization (such as iconicity and naturalness); the conceptual interface between syntax and semantics (as explored by Cognitive Grammar and Construction Grammar); the experiential and pragmatic background of language-in-use; the relationship between language and thought, including questions about relativism and conceptual universals (Geeraerts and Cuyckens 2007: 4).

The fact that numerous different subjects are being explored within Cognitive Linguistics does not make it a homogenous approach but rather a framework. However, there are underlying assumptions shared by cognitive linguists.

Lakoff argued that there were two key commitments that made Cognitive Linguistics a distinctive enterprise, namely the Generalization Commitment and the Cognitive Commitment. The first commitment is based on the assumption that there are common principles that link all the different aspects of language. In other words, according to this assumption, an important function of linguistics is the identification of the common principles that hold across different areas of linguistic studies, namely phonology, semantics, morphology, syntax and others (Evans and Green 2006: 28). The view that the second commitment – the Cognitive Commitment – represents is that the "language and linguistic organization should reflect general cognitive principles rather than cognitive principles that are specific to language" (Evans and Green 2006: 41). What this means is that the common principles should demonstrate the knowledge of human cognition coming from other disciplines of cognitive science, such as sociology, philosophy, psychology, neuroscience and others.

Geeraerts and Cuyckens (2007: 6–15) provide an overall summary of overriding features and perspectives of Cognitive Linguistics. According to them, because "Cognitive Linguistics is the study of language in its cognitive function, where *cognitive* refers to the crucial role of intermediate informational structures in our encounters with the world", language is considered to be "a repository of world knowledge, a structured collection of meaningful categories that help us deal with new experiences and store information about old ones" (Geeraerts and Cuyckens 2007: 5). Cognitive Linguistics stresses the importance of semantics and its study of meaning as a basic linguistic phenomenon, which comes from the assumption that categorization is one of the primary functions of language. The conceptualizations expressed in language structures are based on the ways in which people experience the world from the physiological, cultural and social perspectives (Geeraerts and Cuyckens 2007: 5). Cognitive Linguistics appreciates the fact that cultures and individuals do not share the same background knowledge that is why the language will reflect different experiences of different people and groups of people.

1.3 Cognitive semantics

Cognitive semantics is the branch of Cognitive Linguistics that deals with word and sentence meaning. According to Evans and Green (2006: 153), cognitive semantics "represents an approach to the study of mind and its relationship with embodied experience and culture. It proceeds by employing language as a key methodological tool for uncovering conceptual organization and structure".

Evans and Green (2006) present the guiding principles of cognitive semantics. The four principles that characterize cognitive semantics are the following:

1. Conceptual structure is embodied.
2. Semantic structure is conceptual structure.
3. Meaning representation is encyclopedic.
4. Meaning construction is conceptualization.

1.3.1 Conceptual structure is embodied

The first main assumption of cognitive semantics relates to "the relationship between conceptual structure and the external world of sensory experience" (Evans and Green 2006: 157). In other words, cognitive semantics explores how human sensory-perceptual experiences make conceptual structure meaningful. The embodied cognition thesis states that "the nature of conceptual organization arises from bodily experience (Evans and Green 2006: 157). This idea can be illustrated by an example of a man closed in a room. The room, in this case, has properties of a *bounded landmark* as well as *containment* (Evans and Green 2006: 157). The man is aware of the properties of his body, like the lack of ability to leave the room through a tiny gap under the door or a key hole. In other words, this man experiences a physical relationship between his body and the interior, which is why the concept of containment is meaningful.

> The fact that our experience is embodied – that is, structures in part by the nature of the bodies we have and by our neurological organization – has consequences for cognition. In other words, the concepts we have access to and the nature of the 'reality' we think and talk about are a function of our embodiment: we can only talk about what we can perceive and conceive, and things that we can perceive and conceive derive from embodied experience (Evans and Green 2006: 46).

1.3.2 Semantic structure is conceptual structure

First of all, the semantic structure is a set of meanings which are commonly associated with words (Evans and Green 2006: 159). Secondly, people have concepts because they are useful or necessary to understand the external world. Concepts can also differ depending on the cultural background. The second principle states that "language refers to concepts in the mind of the speaker rather than to objects in the external world" (Evans and Green 2006: 158). In other words, the meanings associated with words create a subset of possible concepts (Evans and Green 2006: 159) which always refer to human experiences. The concept of BACHELOR used by Evans and Green (2006) to illustrate this principle is an extensively discussed example in works concerning semantics. The traditional definition of *bachelor* is an "unmarried adult male" (Evans and Green 2006: 160). Because of the background knowledge people have about the world, a priest or a homosexual would not be called *bachelors*, even though they do fit the definition of this term.

1.3.3 Meaning representation is encyclopedic

As opposed to the dictionary view of meaning – that words represent "neatly packaged bundles of meaning" (Evans and Green 2006: 160) – cognitive semanticists state that words "serve as 'points of access' to vast repositories of knowledge relating to a particular concept or conceptual domain" (Evans and Green 2006: 160). What this means is that words do not have encoded meanings; they only prompt us to construct the meaning. The example of the aforementioned *bachelor* shows that the encyclopedic definition (i.e. 'unmarried adult male') cannot be applied to all instances of male adults who, for different reasons, are unmarried. Evans and Green (2006) argue that there is a cultural stereotype regarding *bachelors*, namely that they are 'sexual predators'. Because of it, understanding of the sentence below is not problematic, even though this sentence contains contradictory information: *Watch out Jane, your husband's a right bachelor!* (Evans and Green 2006: 161).

1.3.4 Meaning construction is conceptualisation

The fourth principle is closely related to the third one. Since words serve only as prompts for the construction of meaning, that means that this process takes place at the conceptual level. That is why, "meaning construction is equated with conceptualization, a dynamic process whereby linguistic units serve as prompts for an array of conceptual operations and the recruitment of background knowledge" (Evans and Green 2006: 162).

1.4 The Conceptual Metaphor Theory

"A metaphor (from the Greek *metapherein*, meaning "transference") is a figure of speech in which a word or phrase is used to describe something it does not literally denote, e.g., *This journal is a gem*" (McGlone 2007: 109–110).

Metaphor has been studied for over 2000 years. As Ortony (1979: 3) states, "any serious study of metaphor is almost obliged to start with the works of Aristotle". In ancient Greece, metaphor was described by rhetoricians as the *master trope* – a rhetoric device of the highest importance that helped in persuading people. That is why Aristotle stated that metaphors are not only present in poetic language, but also in the language of politics, law and everyday speech. According to Hiraga (2005: 23), Aristotle regarded metaphor as "substitution of words, as completely paraphrasable into a nonmetaphorical expression by means of an analogy between the substitution word and the word being substituted". That is why a metaphor can be treated as an ornament of language which conveys no new information. McGlone states that

> Aristotle considered metaphor a sign of language mastery and genius, but he also deemed it ornamental, appropriate for poetry but too enigmatic for philosophical or scientific discourse. Few contemporary language scholars agree with his limited view of metaphor's utility, although many still endorse his account of metaphor understanding (McGlone 2007: 110).

In his works, such as *Poetics* and *Rhetoric*, Aristotle characterized metaphor with the formula *A is B*, as in a common example of everyday language: *He is a pig*. As a consequence, since that time, the metaphor has been treated as an implicit comparison of two categories. A metaphor like *He is a pig* is called a *resemblance metaphor* (Evans and Green 2006: 293). It is not the physical appearance that is assigned to the person called a pig, but rather the qualities of the pig, like being dirty, smelly or messy. There are also *image metaphors*, described by Lakoff and Turner (1989), "which are based on conceptual relationships which can be reversed and still be meaningful: we refer to lions as the 'kings of beasts' and might even equate a particular lion with a particular human exemplar of stoutheartedness" (Grady 2007: 193).

A simile, like a metaphor, compares two objects or ideas. However, it should be emphasized that metaphors and similes are not interchangeable figures of speech. McGlone (2007: IX), describes them metaphorically as "the salt and pepper on your linguistic spice shelf, each with its own distinct flavor". A simile is signaled by *as* or *like*. For example, *he is as dirty as a pig* or *he is dirty like a pig* are similes. Metaphor, on the other hand, "implies the comparison by substituting something or the attributes of something with another" (McGlone 2007: IX), as in the sentence *he became a pig when she dumped him*.

Metaphor has been one of the central topics of cognitive linguistics since its emergence in the 1970s. The major claim of cognitive linguistics in this field of study is that metaphor is primarily an issue of conceptualization, a cognitive process, and not merely a linguistic ornament. What is more, according to this approach, metaphor can be expressed in nonverbal ways, such as gestures or pictures. This is possible because "*metaphor* is understood to refer to a pattern of conceptual association, rather than to an individual metaphorical usage or a linguistic convention" (Grady 2007: 188).

According to Grady (2007: 189), "Cognitive Linguistics' unique contribution has been to treat metaphorical language as data to be examined systematically and to be considered in connection with other basic aspects of mental activity".

In 1980 George Lakoff and Mark Johnson proposed the Conceptual Metaphor Theory in their book *Metaphors We Live By*. In this work they (1980: 5) state that "the essence of metaphor is understanding and experiencing one kind of thing in terms of another". The main assumption of this theory is that "metaphor is not simply a stylistic feature of language, but that thought itself is fundamentally metaphorical in nature" (Evans and Green 2006: 286). In other words, according to Lakoff and Johnson, people do not only speak in metaphors, also they think in metaphors. "Conventional metaphors [...] are usually *automatic, unconscious* mappings, *pervasive* in everyday language [...]. Literary metaphors are [...] normally just creative extensions and elaborations of these conventional mappings" (Lakoff and Turner 1989: 67–72).

Numerous concepts, such as time, quantity and emotions, are comprehended through metaphorical mappings. They derive from the concrete experiences and knowledge of the world. Without metaphors, the possibilities to communicate would be severely limited.

> Metaphor is a tool so ordinary that we use it unconsciously and automatically, with so little effort that we hardly notice it. It is omnipresent: metaphor suffuses our thoughts, no matter what we are thinking about. [...] It is conventional: metaphor is an integral part of our ordinary everyday thought and language. And it is irreplaceable: metaphor allows us to understand ourselves and our world in ways that no other modes of thought can (Lakoff and Turner 1989: XI).

Seeing that metaphors are omnipresent in people's lives was the reason why Lakoff and Johnson did not focus on poetic or figurative language but they presented examples of metaphors from everyday language. The examples below, selected from articles featured on the website http://www.gover.pl/ accessed in August 2008, show popular manifestations of the metaphor POLITICS IS A PLAY.

(1) a. Na firmamencie polskiej *sceny medialnej* pojawiła się *nowa gwiazda*.
 'A *new star* appeared on the *political stage* in the media'.

 b. *Polityczny spektakl* się zakończył.
 'The *political performance* finished'.

 c. Próbują kreować i tworzyć różnego rodzaju *scenariusze* polityczne.
 'They try to create various kinds of *political scenarios*'.

 d. Było łzawe tłumaczenie w TVN24, był festiwal Nelly w TV, były *czarne charaktery*, jest też *happy end*.
 'There was a tearful explanation in TVN24, Nelly's festival on TV, there were *bad characters*, there is also a *happy end*'.

> f. Aby zrobić prawdziwe *polityczne show*, nie trzeba do tego zawodowych rozbawiaczy tłumu, można je zrealizować w świątyni polskiej polityki, czyli w gmachu sejmowym, który dzisiaj przypomina trochę *teatr, ze sceną, widownią i aktorami.* Ostatnim arcydziełem *komedii polskiej, wystawionej „na deskach"* naszego sejmu był *spektakl* pt. „Debata i głosowanie nad votum nieufności dla VI kadencji parlamentu".
>
> 'To make a real *political show*, we do not need professional comedians, it can be made in the temple of Polish politics, namely in the building of the Parliament, which today resembles *a theatre with a stage, audience and actors.* The last masterpiece of Polish *comedy staged* in our Parliament was a *show* under the title "The debate and voting on the vote of no confidence for the sixth tenure of Parliament".'

The mappings between politics and film/theatre show the following features of the Conceptual Metaphor Theory. Firstly, the systematicity is easily noticeable between the concepts of politics and theatre. Secondly, all the metaphors have an experiential basis – cultural knowledge. The similarities between the two domains are not hard to identify because people have background knowledge of the film or theatre. Because of this knowledge, conceptual linkings of politicians and actors, the public and audience, the Parliament and a theatre are well justified.

Conceptual domain is one of the most important and most frequently used notions in discussions of metaphors. "This is our conceptual representation, or knowledge, of any coherent segment of experience. We often call such representations concepts, such as the concepts of BUILDING or MOTION" (Kövecses 2002: 249). Such a conventional association of two domains – like the domain of POLITICS with the domain of PLAY – at the conceptual level is called a *conceptual metaphor*. According to this view, the basic concepts based on cultural experiences are called source domains (e.g. PLAY). These are simply structured and concrete concepts in terms of which the other domain is described. The more abstract and complex concepts to which the words refer are called target domains (e.g. POLITICS). In other words, the domain of PLAY is mapped (i.e. projected) onto the domain of POLITICS. Metaphorical mapping links two different domains: the source and target domains. Kövecses claims that

> Both source and target domain are characterized by a number of different dimensions of experience, such as purpose, function, control, manner, cause, shape, size, and many others. I call these 'aspects of domains'. Each such aspect consists of elements: entities and relations. Metaphorical mappings between a source and a target obtain between these elements (Kövecses 2002: 247).

According to Grady (2007: 190), *mapping* is the most fundamental notion of the Conceptual Metaphor Theory. "This term borrowed from mathematics refers to systematic metaphorical correspondences between closely related ideas" (Grady 2007: 190). Table 1 illustrates the idea proposed by Lakoff and Johnson that source and target domains have various roles.

Table 1: Mappings for POLITICS IS A PLAY

Source: PLAY	Target: POLITICS
NEW (MOVIE) STAR	NEW POLITICIAN
POLITICAL SCENE	POLITICS
PERFORMANCE	POLITICAL ACTION
POLITICAL SCENARIOS	POLITICAL PLANS
BAD CHARACTERS	OPPONENTS
HAPPY ENDING	SOLVED PROBLEM
AUDIENCE	PUBLIC
THEATRE	PARLIAMENT
ACTORS	POLITICIANS
A SHOW	A DEBATE

Metaphorical mappings are conventional; they are a fixed part of the human cognitive system. Mappings in metaphorical processes occur in an automatic and unconscious way. Accordingly, in the conceptual metaphor POLITICS IS A PLAY, the knowledge of a play is mapped onto the knowledge about politics. In this mapping process, the source domain PLAY reconceptualises the abstract meaning of POLITICS.

1.4.1 Hiding and highlighting

There are two processes closely related to the notion of source and target domains, namely *hiding* and *highlighting*, which presuppose each other. "When a target is structured in terms of a particular source, this highlights certain aspects of the target while simultaneously hiding other aspects" (Evans and Green 2006: 303–304). In other words, when a source domain is mapped onto a target domain, only some aspects of the target domain are highlighted, or brought into focus, while other aspects are hidden or suppressed.

To illustrate how the processes of hiding and highlighting work, Kövecses (2010: 92) gives following examples:

(2) AN ARGUMENT IS A CONTAINER: Your argument has *a lot of content*. What is the *core* of his argument?
AN ARGUMENT IS A JOURNEY: We will *proceed in a step-by-step* fashion. We have *covered a lot of ground*.
AN ARGUMENT IS WAR: He *won* the argument. I couldn't *defend* that point.

AN ARGUMENT IS A BUILDING: She *constructed a solid* argument. We have got a *good foundation* for the argument.

Taking into consideration the examples presented above, Kövecses (2010: 92) states the following:

> The CONTAINER metaphor highlights the content of basicness of an argument.
> The JOURNEY metaphor focuses on progress and content.
> The WAR metaphor's main focus seems to be the issue of control over the argument.
> The BUILDING metaphor captures the aspects of the construction of an argument and its strength.

On the basis of these examples, it can be stated that each of the metaphors highlights some aspects of arguments, while simultaneously hiding their other aspects. While the CONTAINER metaphor brings into focus the content and basicness of the argument, it hides other aspects, such as progress, control and construction. It can be concluded that "different metaphors highlight different aspects of the same target concept and at the same time hide its other aspects" (Kövecses 2002: 81) or, as Evans and Green (2006: 304) put it, "metaphors can perspectivise a concept or conceptual domain".

1.4.2 The cognitive processes in metaphor understanding

Following the statement of conceptual metaphor theorists that metaphor is an issue of conceptualization, McGlone (2007) states that the metaphor LOVE IS A JOURNEY plays two distinct roles in the human conceptual system.

> Firstly, it has a representational role by structuring peoples' understanding of love. This claim derives from the rhetoric of "cognitive economy" (Miller and Johnson-Laird, 1976), according to which the mind borrows the semantic structure of simple concepts to organize aspects of complex concepts that might be too computationally expensive to represent in a stand-alone fashion (McGlone 2007: 111).

Secondly, the metaphor LOVE IS A JOURNEY is presumed "to play a process role in that it mediates our use and understanding of certain metaphoric expressions pertaining to love" (McGlone 2007: 111). In other words, to interpret the sentence *our marriage is on the rocks*, the conceptual correspondences between love and journey must be retrieved from semantic memory. McGlone states that

> [...] the metaphor's hypothesized process role appears to be economical from a cognitive standpoint, in that (a) metaphoric meanings may be retrieved from memory rather than constructed, and (b) the meanings of several metaphoric expressions (dead end, spinning our wheels, etc.) may be generated from a single semantic structure (the LOVE IS A JOURNEY schema) (McGlone 2007: 111).

The way in which people interact with the environment, comprehend certain things and situations, and perceive the world in general plays an important role in defining everyday reality. Consequently, the human conceptual system is based on the acquired experience. Taking into consideration that people frequently perceive and comprehend specific things and situations in terms of others – as already shown in example (1) –Lakoff and Johnson claim that the human "conceptual system is metaphorical in nature" (Lakoff and Johnson 1980: 3). Accordingly, people use metaphorical concepts for thinking and understanding reality. What is more, people make use of metaphorical thinking in language-based communication processes.

1.4.3 The experiential basis of metaphor

According to Grady (2007), one of the central principles of Lakoff and Johnson's theory that "sharply distinguishes the approach from alternative theories" is *experiential motivation*. Experiential motivation justifies the reasons why people see similarity between source and target domains which may frequently be hard to identify. In *Metaphors We Live By* the authors state that "no metaphor can ever be comprehended or even adequately represented independently of its experiential basis" (Lakoff and Johnson 1980: 19).

For instance, Grady explains the experiential basis of the metaphor MORE IS UP as follows:

> […] elevation and quantity are conceptual domains closely related in experience, since whenever we see a pile of objects or liquid in a contained space, we are aware of the connection between the height which the pile (or whatever) reaches and the number of objects or amount of the liquid. In this way, the mapping between quantity and height is well motivated, rather than arbitrary, but does not depend on similarity per se (Grady 2007: 192).

Kövecses explains the experiential basis of metaphor in the following words:

> […] we experience the interconnectedness of two domains of experience and this justifies for us conceptually linking the two domains. For example, if we often experience anger as being connected with body heat, we will feel justified in creating and using the conceptual metaphor ANGER IS A HOT FLUID IN A CONTAINER. The experiences on which the conceptual metaphors are based may be not only bodily but also perceptual, cognitive, biological, or cultural (Kövecses 2002: 249).

The statement made by the conceptual metaphor theorists that metaphor reflects correspondences in peoples' conceptual system leads to investigating what other –nonlinguistic – evidence exists to prove this thesis. Evans and Green (2006: 303) claim that the metaphorical basis of various nonlinguistic phenomena has been extensively investigated. This basis includes the social organization, politics, foreign policy, advertisements, mathematical theories and even myths, dreams, gestures and morality. As an example, they mention a hierarchical organization of a business institution which can be represented by a diagram with the most important person at the top of it and the rest of the personnel placed at lower points. What is more, even sentence structure can have a metaphorical basis. Sentences can be represented by *tree diagrams*, "structures that are hierarchically organized so that the sentence 'dominates' or 'contains' phrases, which in turn 'dominate' or 'contain' words" (Evans and Green 2006: 303).

1.4.4 The Invariance Hypothesis and asymmetrical directionality

As stated beforehand, *mapping* is one of the most significant notions of the Conceptual Metaphor Theory. It is important to mention constraints on mappings. The main constraint on mappings between domains is the Invariance Hypothesis or Invariance Principle (Lakoff and Turner 1989: 82–83). Its main point is that the mapping cannot contravene the basic topological structure of the source domain. Barcelona (2000: 4) explains this concept on the basis of the example TIME IS MONEY. This metaphor allows people to treat time as a commodity which one can spend and which is valuable, but not as a commodity one can give or get back. This limitation which comes from "the inherent structure of the target domain" (Barcelona 2000: 4) is, according to Barcelona, the reason why most metaphors are only partial.

Grady comments on *asymmetrical directionality* as follows:

> This directionality is more than an interesting and characteristic feature of metaphorical conceptualizations; it is evidence against a traditional and still common view of metaphor, in which a metaphorical usage is most fundamentally a reflection of 'similarity' between the source and target ideas (Grady 2007: 191).

Asymmetrical directionality occurs because metaphorical substitution is not valid in both directions between the source and target domains. While the term *open* – which is a synonym to *not secretive* and *honest* – can refer to a person, describing a door or window as *honest* or *not secretive* would be completely devoid of sense. Likewise, it is possible to say *foundations of a theory* but *postulates of a building* is meaningless.

This feature sharply distinguishes the Conceptual Metaphor Theory from the theory proposed by Max Black who states that there exists interaction between domains.

1.4.5 Classification of metaphors

Various classifications of metaphors – according to their conventionality, function, nature and level of generality – have been introduced by Lakoff and Johnson (1980), Lakoff and Turner (1989) as well as by Lakoff (1987). An overview of each class of metaphors illustrated with examples provided by Kövecses (2002) is included in the next four subsections.

1.4.5.1 The conventionality of metaphors

The first aspect according to which Kövecses (2002: 29–41) divides metaphors is their degree of conventionality, in other words, "how deeply entrenched a metaphor is in everyday use by ordinary people for everyday purposes" (Kövecses 2002: 29). Although much of what people say is metaphorical, a majority of metaphors are used automatically and unconsciously. Most people are not aware of the metaphorical character of their utterances; their metaphorical use remains virtually unnoticed since many metaphorical expressions are deeply embedded in our everyday language and thought.

Kövecses provides examples of metaphors that are highly conventionalized, or as he puts it, "well worn or even cliched" (Kövecses 2010: 34).

> (3) ARGUMENT IS WAR: I *defended* my argument.
> LOVE IS A JOURNEY: We'll just have to *go our separate ways*.
> THEORIES ARE BUILDINGS: We have *to construct* a new theory.
> IDEAS ARE FOOD: I can't *digest* all these facts.
> SOCIAL ORGANIZATIONS ARE PLANTS: The company *is growing fast*.
> LIFE IS A JOURNEY: He had a *head start* in life.

These metaphors are put at one end of what Kövecses calls "scale of conventionality". At the other end of the scale the researcher places metaphors which are highly unconventional or novel, frequently encountered in literature. Kövecses, however, points out that the appearance of novel metaphors is not restricted only to works of art. He states that there are "many creative speakers who can produce novel linguistic metaphors based on conventional conceptual metaphors" (Kövecses 2002: 31). Among the "creative speakers" he lists sports journalists, politicians, priests, users of slang, writers of song lyrics and graffiti writers (Kövecses 2002: 31). Examples of original metaphorical usages can be multiplied but let the following two quotations suffice to illustrate the point. The first one is a famous quotation from Karl Marx, who described religion "as the opium of the people" (Steen 2006: 54), the second one is a line from a song entitled "Baptism" by Lenny Kravitz: "I want to be baptized in your love".

1.4.5.2 The cognitive function of metaphor

The cognitive function of metaphor is the role that metaphor plays in peoples' thinking and perceiving the world. On the basis of cognitive functions, three kinds of metaphors were distinguished: structural, ontological and orientational.

Structural metaphors enable speakers to understand the target domain A in terms of the structure of the source domain B because the source domain "provides a relatively rich knowledge structure for the target concept" (Kövecses 2002: 33).

As an example of structural metaphor, Kövecses (2010: 38) provides TIME PASSING IS MOTION OF AN OBJECT.

(4) The time will *come* when...
The time has long since *gone* when...
The time for action has *arrived*.
In the weeks *following* next Tuesday...
On the *preceding* day...
I'm looking *ahead* to Christmas.
Thanksgiving is *coming up* on us.
Time is *flying by*.

Table 2 presents mappings in the metaphor TIME PASSING IS MOTION OF AN OBJECT.

Table 2: Mappings for TIME PASSING IS MOTION OF AN OBJECT (based on the examples discussed by Kövecses 2010: 38)

Target: TIME		Source: OBJECT
TIME	....	OBJECT
THE PASSING OF TIME	....	MOTION
FUTURE TIME	....	IN FRONT OF OBSERVER
PAST TIME	....	BEHIND THE OBSERVER

Metaphors like TIME PASSING IS MOTION OF AN OBJECT are called structural metaphors because they make use of a highly structured and definite concept like MOTION OF AN OBJECT to structure a less definite one like PASSING TIME. On the basis of the aforementioned phrases, it can be concluded that speakers understand time in terms of physical objects, their location and their motion. As Kövecses (2002: 34) comments on the subject, "without the metaphor it would be difficult to imagine what our concept of time would be. Most structural metaphors provide this kind of structuring and understanding for their target concepts".

Lakoff and Johnson (1980: 52–55) highlight the importance of the fact that the metaphorical structuring, involved in metaphors like TIME PASSING IS MOTION OF AN OBJECT, is partial. It cannot be total because it would mean that passing time is really a moving object.

Ontological metaphors, unlike structural metaphors, fail to provide elaborate cognitive structuring for the target domain. Nevertheless, the cognitive function of these metaphors is also significant. "They enable speakers to conceive of their experiences in terms of objects, substances, and containers in general, without specifying further the kind of object, substance, or container" (Kövecses 2002: 251). Table 3, taken from Kövecses (2002: 35), illustrates how ontological status is given to general categories of target domains.

Table 3: Ontological metaphors (Kövecses 2002: 35)

Source domains	Target domains
PHYSICAL OBJECT →	NONPHYSICAL OR ABSTRACT ENTITIES (e.g., *the mind*)
PHYSICAL OBJECT →	EVENTS (e.g., *going to the race*)
PHYSICAL OBJECT →	ACTIONS (e.g., *giving someone a call*)
SUBSTANCE →	ACTIVITIES (e.g., *a lot of running in the game*)
CONTAINER →	UNDELINEATED PHYSICAL OBJECTS (e.g., *a clearing in the forest*)
CONTAINER →	PHYSICAL AND NONPHYSICAL SURFACES (e.g., *the visual field*)
CONTAINER →	STATES (e.g., *in love*)

The author claims that *personification* (i.e. describing nonhuman entities as human beings) is a form of ontological metaphor, which he illustrates with the following examples (Kövecses 2010: 39):

(5) Life has *cheated* me.
　　Inflation is *eating up* our profits.
　　Cancer finally *caught up* with him.
　　The computer *went dead* on me.

Lakoff and Johnson (1980: 26–29) claim that people use ontological metaphors for various purposes; among them they list referring, quantifying, identifying aspects, identifying causes, setting goals and motivating actions. The authors provide numerous examples. Let the metaphor INFLATION IS AN ENTITY suffice to illustrate the point.

(6) INFLATION IS AN ENTITY
Inflation is lowering our standard of living.
If there's much *more inflation,* we'll never survive. We need to *combat inflation.*
Inflation is hacking us into a corner.
Inflation is taking its toll at the checkout counter and the gas pump.
Buying land is the best way of *dealing with inflation. Inflation makes me sick.*

Orientational metaphors provide even less cognitive structuring for the target concept than the ontological ones. Instead, their role is "to make a set of target concepts coherent in our conceptual system" (Kövecses 2002: 35). "The name 'orientational metaphor' derives from the fact that most metaphors that serve this function have to do with basic human spatial orientations" (Kövecses 2002: 35–36), such as UP–DOWN, IN–OUT, FRONT–BACK, CENTER–PERIPHERY, NEAR–FAR etc. Because orientational metaphors are based on physical and cultural experiences of the speakers, they are not arbitrary. Table 4 illustrates concepts characterized by the "upward" orientation and concepts opposite to them, characterized by the "downward" orientation.

Table 4: Orientational metaphors UP–DOWN (Kövecses 2002: 36)

MORE IS UP Speak *up*, please.	LESS IS DOWN Keep your voice *down*, please.
HEALTHY IS UP Lazarus *rose* from the dead.	SICK IS DOWN He *fell* ill.
CONSCIOUS IS UP Wake *up*.	UNCONSCIOUS IS DOWN He *sank* into a coma.
CONTROL IS UP I'm *on top* of the situation.	LACK OF CONTROL IS DOWN He is *under* my control.
HAPPINESS IS UP I'm feeling *up* today.	SAD IS DOWN He's really *low* these days.
VIRTUE IS UP She's an *upstanding* citizen.	LACK OF VIRTUE IS DOWN That was a *low-down* thing to do.
RATIONAL IS UP The discussion *fell* to an emotional level.	NONRATIONAL IS DOWN He couldn't *rise above* his emotions.

The physical basis of the given examples of metaphors should be obvious. Taking as an example the metaphors CONSCIOUS IS UP and UNCONSCIOUS IS DOWN, it is clear that they derive from the fact that humans sleep lying down and when awaken they change the position from the horizontal to vertical one.

Lakoff and Johnson clarify that

> The division of metaphors into three types – orientational, ontological, and structural – was artificial. All the metaphors are structural (in that they map structures to structures); all are ontological (in that they create target domain entities); and many are orientational (in that they map orientational image-schemas) (Lakoff and Johnson 2003: 264).

1.4.5.3 The nature of metaphor

Kövecses (2002: 36–38) discusses the nature of metaphors. According to him, some metaphors are based on peoples' basic knowledge of concepts or images. There is also another kind of metaphors which he calls *image-schema metaphors*. They are "based on 'skeletal' image-schemas, such as the path-schema, the force-schema, the contact-schema, etc. They are skeletal in the sense that these source domains do not map rich knowledge onto the target" (Kövecses 2002: 250). Image-schemas are based on the physical experiences people have while interacting with the world. Table 5 shows how the image-schemas structure abstract concepts metaphorically.

Table 5: Image-schemas (Kövecses 2010: 43)

IMAGE-SCHEMA	METAPHORICAL EXTENSION
IN–OUT	I'm *out* of money.
FRONT–BACK	He's an *up-front* kind of guy.
UP–DOWN	I'm feeling *low*.
CONTACT	Hold *on*, please. ('Wait')
MOTION	He just *went* crazy.
FORCE	You're *driving* me insane.

Gibbs, Costa Lima and Francozo (2004: 1192) state the following:

> Image schemas differ from the notion of schemata traditionally used which are abstract conceptual and propositional event structures (see Rumelhart, 1980). By contrast, image schemas are imaginative and nonpropositional in nature and operate as organizing structures of experience at the level of bodily perception and movement. Empirical evidence from cognitive and developmental psychology is consistent with the idea that sensorimotor representations of imagery are essential to many forms of higher-order perception and thought (Intos-Peterson and Roskos-Ewoldsen, 1987; Jeannerod, 1999; Mandler, 1992; Spelke et al., 1992).

These authors also claim that image schemas are characterized by an internal structure and "can serve as the embodied basis for many abstract, metaphorical concepts" (Gibbs, Costa Lima and Francozo 2004: 1193). To illustrate the point, they provide examples of the image schema of MOMENTUM as it is pervasive in daily life. The authors differentiate visual momentum – when we see moving objects, kinesthetic momentum – when we are moving and when we are moved by other things, auditory momentum – "as a correlate of visual and kinesthetic momentum and independently as when thunder builds up to a crescendo" and internal momentum – "when certain bodily functions build up in such a way that they cannot be stopped" (Gibbs, Costa Lima and Francozo 2004: 1193).

(7) I was bowled over by that idea.
We have too much momentum to withdraw from the election race.
I got carried away by what I was doing.
We better quit arguing before it picks up too much momentum and we can't stop.
Once he gets rolling, you'll never be able to stop him talking.

1.4.5.4 Levels of generality of metaphor

Kövecses (2002) employs another scale to show different metaphors. This time, it is a scale of generality. He divides the metaphors into generic-level and specific-level metaphors.

Generic-level metaphors are placed on a high level and the specific-level metaphors occupy a low level on a scale of generality. The difference between them lies in the source and target domains they are composed of, that is to say, generic-level metaphors are composed of generic-level source and target domains, while specific-level metaphors are composed of specific-level domains. Kövecses (2002: 250) states that "generic-level metaphors are instantiated, or realized, by specific-level ones". To illustrate this point, he gives an example of a generic-level metaphor EMOTIONS ARE FORCES, which is realized by the specific-level metaphor ANGER IS A HOT FLUID IN A CONTAINER (Kövecses 2002: 250).

1.5 The Context-Limited Simulation Theory of Metaphor

The Context-Limited Simulation (CLS) Theory was proposed by Lawrence Barsalou (1999). In his research, Barsalou addresses the nature of human knowledge and its roles in language, thought, and memory. He focuses specifically on the perceptual basis of knowledge, concepts and their structural properties as well as on their dynamic representation. What the Context-Limited Simulation Theory is based on is a perceptual simulation model of language use and interpretation (Barsalou 1999).

In the perceptual neural system, perceptions, including perceptions of language and other communicative acts, are filtered, combined, and aggregated at a series of levels, beginning with raw perceptions, all the way up to the coherent multi-sensory objects we experience. Only these, the most highly aggregated and unitary perceptions, are ordinarily accessible to conscious attention. Barsalou (1999) argues that a *conceptual* neural system parallels and is capable of partially simulating – and interacting with – the functions of the perceptual neural system at every level. The perceptual neural system includes states and experiences internal to the body as well as cognitive states such as abstract reasoning and emotions; the conceptual neural system includes simulators that generate simulations of the same full range of experience, including thoughts, internal body states, muscular action, and emotions (Ritchie 2008).

Barsalou (1999: 600) argues that the Conceptual Metaphor Theory and its idea of concrete domains representing abstract concepts are actually not sufficient for representing such concepts. As an example, Barsalou mentions the metaphor ANGER IS LIQUID EXPLODING FROM A CONTAINER.

> Instead, a direct, nonmetaphorical representation of an abstract domain is essential for two reasons: first, it constitutes the most basic understanding of the domain. Knowing only that *anger* is like *liquid exploding from a container* hardly constitutes an adequate concept. If this is all that people know, they are far from having an adequate understanding of *anger*. Second, a direct representation of an abstract domain is necessary to guide the mapping of a concrete domain into it. A concrete domain cannot be mapped systematically into an abstract domain that has no content. […] Furthermore, metaphorical language may often indicate polysemy rather than metaphorical conceptualization (Barsalou et al. 1993). For example, when someone says, "John exploded in anger," the word "explode" may function polysemously. "Explode" may have one sense associated with heated liquid exploding in containers, and another associated with the rapid onset of angry behavior. Rather than activating conceptual knowledge for *liquid exploding from a container*, "explode" may simply activate a perceptual simulation of angry behavior directly (Barsalou 1999: 600).

Barsalou suggests three key mechanisms essential for proving that perceptual accounts of abstract concepts are possible. He describes them as follows:

> First, an abstract concept is framed against the background of a simulated event sequence. Rather than being represented out of context in a single time slice, an abstract concept is represented in the context of a larger body of temporally extended knowledge, […] it is possible to simulate event sequences perceptually, and it is possible for a simulator to frame more specific concepts. Thus, perceptual symbol systems can implement the framing that underlies abstract concepts. Second, selective attention highlights the core content of an abstract concept against its event background […]. An abstract concept is not the entire event simulation that frames it but is a focal part of it. […] It is possible to focus attention on a part of a perceptual simulation analytically. In this way, perceptual symbol systems capture the focusing that underlies abstract concepts. Third, perceptual symbols

for introspective states are central to the representation of abstract concepts. If one limits perceptual symbols to those that are extracted from perception of the external world, the representation of abstract concepts is impossible. [...] The same symbol formation process that operates on the physical world can also operate on introspective and proprioceptive events. As a result, the introspective symbols essential to many abstract concepts can be represented in a perceptual symbol system. Although many different introspective events enter into the representation of abstract concepts, propositional construal appears particularly important (Barsalou 1999: 600).

Basing on the success in formulating accounts of *truth* and *disjunction* (Barsalou 1999), the author suggests a general strategy for interpreting metaphors. What comes first is the identification of an event sequence in which the abstract concept is framed. The second step is the characterization of the "multimodal symbols that represent not only the physical events in the sequence but also the introspective and proprioceptive events" (Barsalou 1999: 600). The third step is the identification of "the focal elements of the simulation that constitute the core representation of the abstract concept against the event background" (Barsalou 1999: 600). The core element in metaphor interpretation is suppressing the context-irrelevant perceptual simulators, also those associated with the literal meaning of the *vehicle* – the metaphorically used word or phrase, activating the context-relevant simulators, and linking them to the topic of the metaphor to form its meaning. The activation of the context-relevant secondary simulators in a particular context is also of great importance in the CLS theory. It helps in identifying the nuances of thoughts and feelings expressed by metaphors in *particular* contexts. Ritchie highlights the importance of secondary stimulators in following words:

> The expressive power of metaphor derives from the fact that the "defining" attributes of the vehicle are suppressed as contextually irrelevant, leaving the context-relevant "secondary" attributes, those that express the nuances of thought and feeling experienced by the originator of a message, activated in the hearer's working memory where they may receive more cognitive processing and become more strongly associated with the topic (Ritchie 2008).

Ritchie (2008) provides an example of an analysis of a speech given by Tony Blair in 2005 at the conference of the Labour Party at Gateshead.

> Blair uses the metaphor, "*back*," drawn from the party slogan, "*Forward – not back*" in at least five distinct ways within the first five minutes or so of the speech; all of them contradict the negative implications of the word as used in the slogan. At least one of these ("*I'm back*") is literal in at least two senses as well as metaphorical in yet another sense (Gateshead is in his home district, and he has recently returned from travels outside the UK; but he is also "*back*" from his extended preoccupation with international issues

related to the Iraq war to the more traditional Labour preoccupation with domestic issues – and to a focus on the coming election). Classifying or labeling these metaphors in terms of systematic or conceptual metaphors (for example, *DOMESTIC ISSUES IS HOME* and *INTERNATIONAL ISSUES IS AWAY FROM HOME*) can be instructive but to capture the nuances of meaning accomplished by Blair's multiple use of this metaphor in the speech, we need to examine the perceptual simulators that are activated by the vehicle and left in a heightened state of activation *in each particular context* in which the metaphor appears.

Barsalou states that the Context-Limited Simulation Theory "demonstrates that perceptual symbol systems have the expressive power to represent abstract concepts" (Barsalou 1999: 600). According to Ritchie, the most important feature of the CLS theory which distinguishes it from other theories of metaphors is the emphasis on the subtle nuances of expression and feeling.

1.6 The Discourse Dynamics Framework for Metaphor

The Discourse Dynamics Framework theory (DDF for short) is based on two principles, the inseparable inter-connectedness of language, thought and culture, and their dynamic natures. In view of DDF, metaphor has multiple inter-connected and dynamic dimensions – linguistic, cognitive, affective, physical and cultural – unfolding in real time.

Cameron states that

> Human systems satisfy criteria for being complex dynamic systems broadly interpreted. Like complex dynamic systems, human systems are comprised of different types of agents or elements, which interact through different types of relations. Examples of elements include language items that people use and the meanings they construct for them, or neural synapses in the brain; in social systems, agents can be individual people or groups. Agents and elements (people, words and meanings, synapses etc.) are continuously changing but, and this is what makes a system non-linear and complex, the relations between agents or elements are also continuously changing. Like complex dynamic systems, human systems are open to new energy (in the form of technical innovation, ideas, etc.) from outside, rather than closed. As with complex dynamic systems, the connections among elements or agents of human systems make the context or environment part of the system, rather than a separate background against which the system operates. Metaphor, in all its manifestations, can then be seen as a part of the continuously changing and interconnected systems of language, thinking, affect, physicality and culture (Cameron 2009).

Cameron proposed various scales and levels on which complex dynamic systems operate. There are different types of elements and agents and various types of relations between them. The focal level is the face-to-face conversation because at this particular level meanings of words and phrases are negotiated. "As a result of this dialogic process, words and phrases – and metaphors – are not 'owned' by the individuals who produce them, but are 'interindividual', belonging to both speaker and listener and intrinsically connected to the specific context of use" (Cameron 2009).

According to Cameron various types of metaphor phenomena may be, organized by their discourse dynamics on different time scales and levels:

- on the microgenetic timescale and individual level:
    - process metaphor – metaphorically-processed language
    - linguistic metaphor – language that has the potential for metaphorical processing
- between the microgenetic and the discourse event timescales:
    - metaphor clusters
    - metaphor shifting
- on the discourse event timescale:
    - systematic metaphor – set of connected linguistic metaphors
    - interplay of metaphor, metonymy and other figures, literal language
- at the socio-cultural group / speech community level:
    - within-group metaphor
    - metaphoreme
    - conceptual metaphor
    - primary metaphor
- on the phylogenetic timescale of socio-cultural history:
    - conventionalized metaphors (Cameron 2009)

A process metaphor is an empirical phenomenon evidenced by neurological activity. It is a linguistic expression processed metaphorically "in production and / or in comprehension, through mental activation of two distinct ideas and some transfer, interaction or blend of meaning between them in order to make sense and contribute to the building of coherence in the discourse context" (Cameron 2009). A linguistic metaphor, on the other hand, is a textual phenomenon, rather than neurological, and it appears when two distinct ideas can be linked metaphorically to make sense and build coherence in the context of the discourse. Cameron states that "Linguistic metaphors may or may not be processed metaphorically by the speakers" and she provides an example of such a metaphor: *there is no way of purging that debt* (Cameron 2009).

A discourse event is described by Cameron as lasting for an hour or so "coherent activity involving the use of language", such as a lesson, lecture, conversation, interview or a meeting. Metaphor clusters "are a self-organizing phenomenon, emergent on the discourse event level, that seem to signal intensive discourse work of some sort" (Cameron 2009).

Systematic metaphors differ from conceptual metaphors in the direction from which they emerge. Systematic metaphors emerge from the microgenetic dynamics of conversation upwards and conceptual metaphors act downwards from the phylogenetic scale and socio-cultural group level. Systematic metaphors are "sets of semantically-connected linguistic metaphors, collected together across one or more discourse events. The accumulated set of connected metaphors is an emergent phenomenon" (Cameron 2009).

At the socio-cultural group level, four different metaphoric phenomena can be noticed. One of them is within-group metaphors which serve to mark the identity of groups and sustain intimacy, as in a prison talk. Primary metaphors, as described by Grady (1999), highlight the influence of embodied action on language and thinking and are more abstract from than conceptual metaphor. The metaphoreme, as described by Cameron, is "a bundle of stabilized but flexible, patterns of word-meaning links underlying the use of semi-fixed metaphorical expressions in the language of a group" (Cameron 2009).

Conventionalized metaphors once novel on a phylogenetic timescale, "can 'come alive' again, or be 'unfrozen', in the sense that, although conventionalized phylogenetically, individuals may interpret them as process metaphors on the microgenetic timescale" (Cameron 2009).

To summarize, the production and interpretation of metaphors is, according to the Discourse Dynamics Framework for Metaphor, achieved on a level of a face-to-face conversation between individuals and it is always connected with a specific discourse context.

1.7 The Theory of Lexical Concepts and Cognitive Models

The Theory of Lexical Concepts and Cognitive Models (LCCM Theory for short) was developed by Vyvyan Evans (2006). As Evans puts it, it is a "cognitively realistic theory of lexical representation and a programmatic theory of lexical concept integration" (Evans 2006: 491). The key assumption of this theory is that

> [...] there is a basic distinction between lexical concepts and meaning. While lexical concepts constitute the semantic units conventionally associated with linguistic forms, and form an integral part of a language user's individual mental grammar, meaning is a property of situated usage-events, rather than words. That is, meaning is not a function of language per se, but arises from language use (Evans 2006: 491).

Evans puts his theory in opposition to the traditional, formal approaches of meaning-construction based on the assumption that words have encoded meanings. He claims that the meanings of words depend largely on the contexts in which they appear. "In other words, words don't have 'meanings' in and of themselves. Rather meaning is a function of the utterance in which a word is embedded, and the complex processes of lexical concept integration [...]" (Evans 2006: 492). To illustrate the point, the author provides an example of different uses of the word *fast*.

(8) a. That parked BMW is a *fast* car.
 b. That car is traveling *fast*.
 c. That doddery old man is a *fast* driver.
 d. That's the *fast* lane (of the motorway).

In each of these examples, the meaning of *fast* is different. In (a) *fast* refers to the potential for rapid locomotion. In (b) it relates to rapid locomotion. In (c) it relates to motion beyond an established norm. In (d) *fast* describes a venue for rapid locomotion. "Examples such as these show that the view of open class words, as possessing fixed meanings, is untenable on closer scrutiny" (Evans 2006: 492).

In the LCCM Theory, figurative language involves an access route that is based on primary and secondary cognitive models. The use of metaphoric language is seen as a "function of the meaning construction processes of activation of cognitive models (an access route), thus achieving an interpretation for the lexical concept" (Evans 2008).

> In LCCM theory, metaphor constitutes an 'aboutness' relation. That is, metaphoric language involves a **vehicle lexical concept** that says something about a **target lexical concept**. What makes such instances of language use metaphoric is that there is a **clash** in the primary cognitive model profiles of the target and vehicle lexical concepts (Evans 2008).

Evans employs an example of the sentence *The time seemed to whiz by*. In this sentence, *time* is the target lexical concept and *whiz by* is used figuratively. The clash in the primary cognitive models of time and whiz appears because time is not an artifact and thus it does not have the ability to undergo rapid locomotion. However, the general knowledge that artifacts undergoing rapid motion are not perceptually accessible forms a secondary cognitive model. The clash in the primary cognitive models profiles of whiz and time leads to a situation in which "an access route to the secondary cognitive model of 'perceptual access' is activated giving rise to an interpretation of 'whiz' which is compatible with 'time'" (Evans 2008).

> In view of this, the utility of metaphor, from the perspective of LCCM theory, is that it facilitates activation of a range of cognitive models, and thus increases the range of information provided. That is, activation of an extended access route involving secondary cognitive models provides a greater degree of information (**resonance**), and does so by providing the requisite propositional content (**the target cognitive model**). Resonance

affords a greater affective response than merely providing the requisite propositional content, which is to say, providing similar content as a literal paraphrase.

To summarize, the interpretation of metaphors – in view of the LCCM Theory – is achieved by exploiting clashes in primary cognitive model profiles, which leads to activation of secondary cognitive models. This process gives rise to resonance and thus affective responses.

1.8 Metonymy and metaphtonymy

According to *The Oxford Dictionary of Pragmatics*, metonymy (in Greek *metōnymia*, in Latin *denominatio*) is "a figure of speech in which linguistic expression denoting one entity is used to refer to another entity that is associated with it in one way or another. Therefore, metonymy is a variety of figurative (non-literal) use of language" (Huang 2012: 193). Lakoff and Johnson state otherwise, that similarly to metaphors,

> [...] metonymic concepts structure not just our language but our thoughts, attitudes, and actions. And, like metaphoric concepts, metonymic concepts are grounded in our experience. In fact, the grounding of metonymic concepts is in general more obvious than is the case with metaphoric concepts, since it usually involves direct physical or causal associations. The PART FOR WHOLE metonymy, for example, emerges from our experiences with the way parts in general are related to wholes. PRODUCER FOR PRODUCT is based on the causal (and typically physical) relationship between a producer and his product. THE PLACE FOR THE EVENT is grounded in our experience with the physical location of events (Lakoff and Johnson 1980: 39–40).

Lakoff and Johnson claim that metonymy is "not merely a referential device. It also serves the function of providing understanding" (1980: 36). As an example, the authors provide the metonymy THE PART FOR THE WHOLE, to show that "there are many parts that can stand for the whole. Which part we pick out determines which aspect of the whole we are focusing on" (1980: 36). For instance, the expression *good heads* refers to intelligent people and *face* refers to a person.

Metonymy is also encountered in religious and cultural symbolism. For instance, the metonymy DOVE FOR HOLY SPIRIT is "grounded in the conception of the dove in Western culture and the conception of the Holy Spirit in Christian theology. [...] The dove is conceived of as beautiful, friendly, gentle, and, above all, peaceful" (Lakoff and Johnson 1980: 40). According to Lakoff and Johnson,

> The conceptual systems of cultures and religions are metaphorical in nature. Symbolic metonymies are critical links between everyday experience and the coherent metaphorical systems that characterize religions and cultures. Symbolic metonymies that

are grounded in our physical experience provide an essential means of comprehending religious and cultural concepts (Lakoff and Johnson 1980: 40).

Kövecses (2002: 173) claims that "metonymy is a cognitive process in which one conceptual entity, the vehicle, provides mental access to another conceptual entity, the target, within the same domain, or idealized cognitive model (ICM)". As examples the author provides numerous instances of the metonymies THE PRODUCER FOR THE PRODUCT (*I'm reading **Shakespeare***), THE PLACE FOR THE EVENT (***Watergate** changed our politics*), THE PLACE FOR INSTITUTION (***Washington** is negotiating with **Moscow***), THE CONTROLLER FOR THE CONTROLLED (***Ozawa** gave a terrible concert last night*) and AN OBJECT USED FOR THE USER (*We need a better **glove** at third base*) (Kövecses 2002: 172).

Kövecses states that there are certain linguistic expressions which are not clearly either metaphors or metonymies. "Often, what we find is that an expression is both; the two figures blend in a single expression. In these cases, we have individual examples where metaphor and metonymy interact" (Kövecses 2002: 188). This particular phenomenon, metaphtonymy, was studied by Goossens (1990). *The Oxford Dictionary of Pragmatics* provides the following definition of metaphtonymy:

> A blended term used to refer to the figure of speech in which metaphor and metonymy interconnect with each other. Two types of metaphtonymy are found to be particularly commonly used: metaphor from metonymy and metonymy within metaphor. The first subtype can be illustrated by considering *The prisoner is often close-lipped*. In this example, the metaphoric interpretation that the prisoner often speaks but gives little away is based on the metonymic interpretation that the prisoner is often silent. A good example of the second subtype is *Mary has finally caught her boss's ear*, in which the metonymic reading 'ear for attention' is placed within the metaphoric reading 'attention is a moving physical entity' (Huang 2012: 192).

According to *The Bloomsbury Companion to Cognitive Linguistics*, Goossens identified four interaction patterns between metaphor and metonymy. "The role of metonymy in these examples is not to make metaphor possible, but to assist in constructing the metaphor or in shaping its range of meaning effects" (Taylor and Littlemore (eds.) 2014: 153).

(i) Metaphor from metonymy, which takes place when an original metonymy develops into a metaphor. For example, beating one's breasts stands for the open show of sorrow associated with this action. […] *He beat his breast about his infidelity*.
(ii) Metonymy within metaphor, as in *I wanted to argue but I had to bite my tongue*. Here the tongue stands for a person's ability to speak and biting one's tongue is a metaphor for 'refraining from speaking'.

(iii) Demetonymization inside a metaphor. For example, in English slang 'lip' generally stands for 'dishonest/impudent talk' (e.g. *Don't give me any of your lip*). But in the metaphor *pay lip service* ('give insincere support') 'lip service' means 'service as if with the lips only', so 'lip' no longer stands for 'dishonest/impudent talk'.

(iv) Metaphor within metonymy, which occurs when a metaphor is used to add expressiveness to a metonymy. For example, in *to be on one's hind legs*, 'hind' incorporates the metaphor PEOPLE ARE ANIMALS inside the source of a metonymy whereby standing up invokes the overall scene of a person standing up and saying something publicly, often to defend his views emphatically. (Taylor and Littlemore (eds.) 2014: 153).

In the researched material there are several cases of metonymy and metaphtonymy. They will be analyzed in the following chapters.

1.9 Research on the subject

The academic research of the past few decades has shown a strong commitment to the study of cognitive metaphors. Let us mention selected works of scholars working in the United States of America, Great Britain and other countries: Croft and Cruse (2004), Evans (2010), Gibbs (2008), Glucksberg (2001, 2008), Lakoff (1982, 1990, 1993), Lakoff and Johnson (1990, 1999, 2003), Lakoff and Turner (1989), Langacker (1987, 1999, 2008), Rohrer (2006), Rumelhart (1993), Semino (2008), Sweetser (1989), Taylor (2007) and Turner (1987).

Also in Poland numerous scholars have investigated metaphor, e.g. Bartmiński (2009, 2012), Biel (2010), Jakubowska (2009), Kalisz (2001, 2008), Krzeszowski (1991, 1998), Maćkiewicz (2010), Pajdzińska (1996), Redzimska (2008a, 2008b, 2010), Sokołowska (2008), Stanulewicz (2008), Strugielska and Siek-Piskozub (2008) and Szwedek (2008, 2009).

Works concerning metaphors used in politics were published by Chilton (2006), Chilton and Schäffner (2002), Gierczyńska (2009), Kloch (2006), Lakoff (2002), Musolff (2004), Ożóg (2002), Podracki and Trysińska (2006) and Wilson (1990).

Metaphors of emotions have been analyzed by, inter alia, Apresjan (1997), Bamberg (1997), Cichmińska (2010), Ekman (1992, 1996), Esenova (2008), Goddard (2008), Kövecses (1986, 1990, 1998, 2000, 2002, 2006), Maia (1998), Malewska (2010) Ortony (1980), Oster (2010) and Wierzbicka (1999).

Badyda (2013) researched metaphors of senses and perception, Dixon (2011, 2013a, 2013b) and Kalisz (1999) focused on metaphors of fear, while Chilton (1996), Dixon (2013b), Fabiszak (2007, 2010) and Lakoff (1991) on metaphors of war.

Research into metaphors concerning language and used in linguistics was conducted by, inter alia, Reddy (1979), Stanulewicz (2001, 2008), Elżbieta Wąsik (1999, 2008) and Zdzisław Wąsik (2008); and into metaphors of space and time by Kalisz (1990) and Stanulewicz (2010).

Metaphors used in business were analyzed by Bielenia (2009a, 2009b) and Łuczak (2010, 2011, 2014); metaphors of death by Mazur (2011); metaphors in sports by Dixon (2012) and metaphors in music by Rejniewicz (2010).

The works of Gorczyńska (2002, 2010) and Jindo (2011) focus on metaphors in the Bible and the works of Hiraga (2006), Maćkiewicz (2010), Matuszczyk (2010) and Słoń (2010) on conceptual metaphors in literature.

Cieślicka (2002), Cortazzi and Lixian (1999), Musiał (2002), Stanulewicz (2009) as well as Siek-Piskozub and Srtugielska (2010), Strugielska and Siek-Piskozub (2013) have contributed significantly to the research in metaphors of teaching and learning, and Gabryś (1994), Holme (2004) Rundell (2002), Piechota (2005), Ponterotto (1994) and Wolf (1999) to the research on ELT and teaching metaphors.

1.10 Concluding remarks

The present chapter has attempted to present a brief overview of Cognitive Linguistics, a history of its emergence and main focuses, as well as of cognitive semantics and four principles that characterize this branch of Cognitive Linguistics. The aim of this chapter has been to review four most important theories of metaphors: the Conceptual Metaphor Theory with its main assumptions, notions and classifications of metaphors according to their conventionality, function, nature and level of generality, the Context-Limited Simulation Theory of Metaphor, the Discourse Dynamics Framework for Metaphor and the Lexical Concepts and the Cognitive Models Theory.

A primary tenet of the Conceptual Metaphor Theory is that metaphors are a matter of thought and not merely of language. The mappings of a conceptual metaphor are motivated by image schemas which are pre-linguistic schemas concerning time, space, movement and other core elements of embodied human experience. In opposition to the Conceptual Metaphor Theory, scholars propose the Context-Limited Simulation Theory, the Discourse Dynamics Framework and the Theory of Lexical Concepts and Cognitive Models. The CLS Theory advocates that thanks to the activation of primary simulators, as well as to context-relevant secondary simulators, a particular context helps in identifying the nuances of thoughts and feelings expressed by metaphors. In view of the DDF theory, metaphors have multiple interconnected and dynamic dimensions (linguistic, cognitive, affective, physical and cultural), unfolding in real time and are a part of a complex dynamic system operating on different scales and levels. According to the LCCM theory, the interpretation of metaphors is achieved by exploiting clashes in primary cognitive model profiles, which leads to the activation of secondary cognitive models. This process gives rise to resonance and thus affective responses.

In Chapters Three, Four and Five, we will predominantly employ the Conceptual Metaphor Theory to analyze metaphors extracted from Polish and American Internet forums for mothers.

Chapter Two   Communication in the Internet

2.1 Introductory remarks

The Internet understood as a place where communication takes place is a relatively new medium of information exchange. Due to its continuing growth and development of technologies, it provides vast research material in many areas. For linguists, it is valuable because of the emergence of a number of new phenomena in language. Newly created communities with their own varieties of language can be found. What is more, online communication has unique characteristic elements of language. Let these several examples suffice to illustrate the point: using emoticons and acronyms, modifications of the graphic code with deviations from the code norms, especially in written language (like unconventional spelling, capitalization and punctuation). Crystal (2004) proposes to use the term *Netspeak* for the language used in online communication. Crystal also lists several other names, which he describes as cumbersome, among these are *Netlish, Weblish, Internet language, cyberspeak, electronic discourse, electronic language, interactive written discourse, computer-mediated communication (CMC)* (Crystal 2004: 17).

> As a name, *Netspeak* is succinct, and functional enough, as long as we remember that 'speak' here involves writing as well as talking, and that any 'speak' suffix also has a receptive element, including 'listening and reading'. The first of these points hardly seems worth the reminder, given that the Internet is so clearly a predominantly written medium [...], and yet, as we shall see, the question of how speech is related to writing is at the heart of the matter. But the second point is sometimes ignored, so its acknowledgement is salutary. On the Internet, as with traditional speaking and writing, the language that individuals produce is far exceeded by the language they receive; and as the Internet is a medium almost entirely dependent on reactions to written messages, awareness of audience must hold a primary place in any discussion. The core feature of the Internet is its real or potential interactivity (Crystal 2004: 17–18).

The process of globalization and the development of new technologies which allow communication between people living in far-flung places around the globe have an impact on the process of communication. Castells comments on the importance of the Internet as a communication medium as follows: "The Internet is a means of communication which for the first time allows for communication of many with many in their preferred time and on a global scale" (Castells 2003: 12–13, translation mine).

The Internet is frequently compared with the achievements of humanity as useful as print, railway, telegraph, electricity or television. The Internet is an invaluable source of information and thanks to it, a new communication environment has developed in which different forms of interaction can be found. Information, especially the speed of its acquisition and transmission, is of the highest importance for the functioning of modern society. The Internet plays an important role in society because of its essential characteristics, such as global coverage and interactivity. Along with the development of services available on the Internet, its function in social communication increases.

This chapter attempts to provide an overview of the features of language used on the Internet, in both synchronous and asynchronous forms of communication. It also aims to present an Internet forum as a unique form of communication medium.

2.2 The Internet as a unique environment for communication

Communication and the behaviour of Internet users differ from face-to-face communication in a fairly significant way. The main reasons for this are the lack of direct contact with the partners of interaction, constraints on capacity of the communication channel (especially text messaging) and a sense of anonymity. Wallace (2005: 17) notices that anonymity has an important impact on people's behavior and helps in eradicating inhibitions.

As Szpunar (2006: 219–220) and Zawojski (2002: 428) remark, Computer Mediated Communication (CMC for short) is also referred to as a *face-to (via monitor)-face* communication or a *face-to-monitor* communication. "In CMC man becomes a superfluous element, the interaction with the machine is more important" (Szpunar 2006: 219). Continuing this line of reasoning, Szpunar explains that mediated interaction – as the name suggests – is via external media, such as electronic impulses. This interaction is extended in time and space, reaching beyond the immediate context of regular interaction (Szpunar 2006: 220; Giddens 2006: 487–488). It is worth noting that the new quality of interaction and communication in virtual reality is determined by specific characteristics, such as

- the reduction of sensory experiences – mainly the senses of sight and hearing, and combination of both these senses, an important limitation is still the lack of physical contact;
- textuality – the interlocutors usually communicate only by written texts, which carries certain constraints;

- equalization of statuses – online communication gives equal chances to all users, regardless of their social or economic status;
- overcoming space constraints – the possibility of communicating with people with similar interests and needs, regardless of geographical location;
- stretching and concentration of time – the possibility of synchronous communication where many people are involved in the same conversation at one time;
- the availability of a large number of contacts – the possibility of communicating with a selected large group of people;
- the possibility of a permanent record – documenting and storing virtual communication acts (Suler 1996).

It is easily noticeable that with changing technologies, communication on the Internet is changing as well. Murray singles out following types of CMC: communication based on a written text, audiovisual communication and mixed communication. Text-based communication includes e-mail, mailing lists, teleconferences based on written and graphical interface, e-journals, databases, discussion groups, IRC etc. Audiovisual communication includes applications such as Real Audio, and mixed communication includes all types allowing for simultaneous use of e-mail, voice communication, writing on the bulletin board (such as NetMeeting) etc. (Murray 2009).

The following forms of communication on the Internet are classified in terms of the time dependence of sending and receiving of a message. There are asynchronous forms which are characterized by a shift in time between the sending and receiving of messages and the ones that require presence of both the sender and the receiver at the same time, called synchronous. Table 6 presents forms of CMC.

Table 6: A summary of synchronous and asynchronous forms of CMC

Forms of communication	Synchronous	Asynchronous
WWW (World Wide Web)		✓
E-mail		✓
Discussion groups		✓
Blog		✓
E-newspapers		✓
E-books		✓
Data bases		✓
Maps		✓

Forms of communication	Synchronous	Asynchronous
RSS (Really Simple Sindication)		✓
Radio online		✓
Web TV		✓
Web 2.0		✓
IRC (Internet Relay Chat)	✓	
IM (Instant Messaging)	✓	
MUD (Multi User Dungeon or Multiple User Dimension)	✓	
Video	✓	
Conference	✓	
Audio	✓	
VoIP (Voice over Internet Protocol)	✓	
DAB (Digital Audio Broadcasting)	✓	

2.2.1 Asynchronous communication

The most common form of asynchronous communication on the Internet is the website. It is a document written in a suitable programming language which is downloaded from the server and read by users thanks to an appropriate program called a web browser. Users decide which information they will read first, they can navigate the document as they please. Web pages, whose main advantages are their informative nature, attractive graphics and ease of use, represent – like databases and electronic press – one-sided communication in which the sender does not address the recipient directly and does not expect any answer. According to the analysis of World Wide Web Size, at the end of September 2016, there were approximately 4.95 billion websites in the network (www.worldwidewebsize.com, accessed on 05.11.2016).

Time shifts between the time of sending information and the time it is received also characterize electronic mail (e-mail for short) which is probably the most commonly used service on the Internet. As in the case of postal mail, the sender composes a text message and sends it to the recipient to a specified address. However, e-mail addresses differ significantly from addresses of postal mail. An email address has a personal identifier and the recipient's Internet domain name, separated by the sign @, for example *k_gut@gmail.com*, where *k_gut* is the user's personal ID and *gmail.com* is the domain's name. In addition to transferring text messages, e-mail also allows one to send attachments. One can attach a number of files with an image, text or sound to each e-mail message.

A limitation here may be the size of the transmitted attachment. Other features that also distinguish e-mails from traditional letters sent by post are the speed of their reception, using anaphors (citing long fragments or whole received e-mails), less formal language and deviations from rules of spelling and style.

Among the asynchronous forms of communication on the Internet there are also discussion forums. They resemble websites on which, thanks to browsers users can exchange information with others. The interaction on a discussion forum always starts from the foundation of a new thread. Then users who are interested in it can write back or comment on a topic started in this way, developing individual threads. Each forum is controlled by an administrator, and some also by moderators. In addition to the exchange of information with other people, users can post new threads, delete old threads and delete or edit messages. The aim of the administrator's work is to maintain order and compliance with the accepted rules of behaviour.

Another form of online communication is the blog. Blogs (short for weblogs) are special websites filled with dated texts. Entries in blogs are arranged in reverse chronological order, giving the opportunity to see the latest entries at the top of the page. These entries are usually of personal nature, and therefore blogs are used as online diaries. They can also, like web pages, be enriched graphically and audibly to make them more attractive. An interesting fact about blogs is posting links to other users' blogs and sites recommended by the author. In this way, new communities are formed.

All the texts available online, E-newspapers, E-books, data bases and maps, "use the Internet as an alternative platform for their distribution. […] E-publications use the communicative potential of the net naturally" (Gogołek 2010: 128, translation mine).

RSS – Really Simple Sindication – was developed by the company Netscape in 1997 as a channel of delivering personalized information. The advantage of RSS over traditional ways of delivering information is saving time in the real life thanks to automatic gathering of information from many sources. Information chosen by the RSS user is delivered automatically to his/her computer in the form of feeds (RSS feeds, XML feeds). A feed can be a text, a link to photographs, pictures, the most recent weather forecast, information from blogs and any other forms of information (Gogołek 2010: 138).

Radio and television programs available online are gaining on popularity. They use podcasts as a form of audio or video publication. They were created because of the development of civil journalism and the private initiative; nowadays they are becoming more and more commercial.

The last form of asynchronous communication in the Internet analyzed here is Web 2.0. Web 2.0 is a set of tools which are easy to use and frequently free of charge. It serves communication and autopresentation. Creation of content of Web 2.0 is, in the most part, generated by private individuals, e.g. blogs, active participation in social groups and forums, codevelopment of Wiki, creating websites or common use of online games (Gogołek 2010: 161–162).

In addition to the forms which are characterized by time shift between transmitting the message and receiving it, it is also possible to distinguish forms of synchronous online communication which require the simultaneous presence of both the sender and the recipient.

2.2.2 Synchronous communication

Conversations via the Internet were initiated in 1988 by the creation of the Internet Relay Chat (IRC for short) in Finland. The IRC was created as a tool for communication and it was a starting point for other forms of online communication, like chats, communicators and instant messengers. The most commonly used synchronous online interaction is the chat, an online conversation in real time using written messages. Taking into account the number of interlocutors involved in the conversation in the chat at the same time, online chat can take place in two ways. One possibility is a chat in the so-called *main window*. It is a place visible to all the users of the chat in which everyone can take part in the discussion. This situation can be compared to a debate which is attended by many participants. Another possibility offered by this form of synchronous online interaction is a *private* chat. This option, in contrast to the public discussion, is conducted in a separate chat window to which only two people talking to each other have access.

Regardless of the type of chat, a common feature of these discussions is their linearity. This means that in contrast to face-to-face conversation, messages in chat rooms do not overlap, but appear one after another, in the order they are received by the server. The chat also provides anonymity because the participants of discussions in chat rooms rarely use their real names; they replace them with aliases or nicknames ("nicks").

As a result of the introduction of new features, text-based online communication has been enriched by symbols, graphics and images standing for emotions. Currently, each chat offers a standard set of emoticons, including at least a few emoticons of a "status" (describing the availability of the user). What is more, chats are frequently enriched with the voice communication function for users with microphones and headphones or speakers. Developing technology allows

Internet users to transfer images of chat participants from webcams, giving an opportunity to observe the interlocutor. Such features make synchronous online communication closer to the situation of natural verbal communication.

Other examples of synchronous online communication are so-called MUDs. A Multi User Dungeon or Multiple User Dimension, MUD for short, is a game taking place in a fictional world in real time. Players can communicate with each other by means of text commands, or chat, not just with the characters of the game, but also with characters controlled by other users. More advanced software allows for voice transmissions between users. A MUD provides the following communication options: *Say* – a user addresses all other users, *Page* – talking in private, *Whisper* – a private conversation in the same room, which accommodates other participants of the game. Many MUD programs also enable players an asynchronous form of communication – sending e-mails to each other.

VoIP – Voice over Internet Protocol – is a quickly evolving service of telephone communication via the Internet. The main advantage of VoIP is much lower or no costs of such conversations. An example of using VoIP is also online education taking place in the real time (Gogołek 2012:120).

Instant Messaging (IM for short) is a tool allowing an exchange of information, especially in the work place, in the form of short, understandable for participants, messages. Garrett and Danziger (2007) claim that IM disturbs people at work far less than electronic mail, phone calls or face to face contact.

Lesser technological limitations allow broadcasting live films and audio materials via the Internet. DAB (digital audio broadcasting), whose European equivalent is Eureka, is constantly gaining on popularity.

2.2.3 Active communication

Gogołek (2010) differentiates one more form of online communication beside synchronous and asynchronous, namely active communication. "In this form of communication the net ceases to be a passive participant of information exchange but it actively takes part in the transport, as well as in changing the information between a sender and a receiver" (Gogołek 2010: 170).

As examples of active communication the author lists education portals, search engines, trade and bank services, games, new media (e.g. Last.fm, Tidal) as well as servers which choose the advertisements appearing on the user's screen on the basis of the content of read websites and previously set personal profile.

2.2.4 The Internet as a medium stimulating communication

According to Ben-Ze'ev, the Internet has four key characteristics that make it extraordinarily attractive: imagination (it causes cyberspace to be magical and can free people from physical disabilities or life problems), interactivity (starting an interaction people are more open, it is easier to receive reciprocity (it does not require much effort or real action), availability (the Internet is available almost for all who want to use it; a high level of availability of the network is a result of frequent technological advances) and anonymity (people feel confidently and freely when interacting online because anonymity reduces the susceptibility to injuries and the importance of social norms) (Ben-Ze'ev 2005). Therefore, rather than alienate (as was frequently suggested in the 1990s), the Internet stimulates communication.

According to Grzenia (2006), communication on the Internet allows achieving almost all – important for the participants – objectives of the communication process while providing the opportunity to maintain distance from the other participants in the act of communication. The ability to hide one's identity or even create a new one is not without significance. It is not just about camouflage because the purpose of the sender hiding their "I" can also be fun, not to mention the need to implement different psychological needs (Grzenia 2006). The Internet provides an extremely simple and convenient way to communicate and exchange information. This medium saves time, materials and costs of shipping data. With the use of images, video and graphics, information is provided in a very attractive form.

2.3 The forum as a form of communication medium

Internet forums are Internet applications that allow online discussions, called threaded discussions; there are also information sources for those who do not wish to take part in any discussions. Forum participants can begin, after signing in and logging in, discussion topics (threads) and post replies (posts). The threads and posts cannot be edited by other participants, except for the site administrator and moderators.

> Whether called discussion forums, lists, groups, message boards, or just boards, these online discussion venues predate not only Web 2.0 social networking but also the web itself. In the 1970s, online computer bulletin board participants used their telephones to dial in to the bulletin board system (BBS) and partake of the scintillating conversations. As did so much of the old online, BBS then moved to the web. From the old Usenet discussion groups to Google groups to Yahoo! groups to the many installations of phpBB,

vBulletin, and other specialized web forum software, discussions have been occurring online for decades (Notess 2009: 41).

Posts can be written in response to the topic's opening letter or to the posts of other users. Very frequently such posts contain a quote, extract or a whole post to which one is replying.

Forums, topics and posts come in numerous shapes and sizes. There are topics which have been inactive for years, and those which were started many years ago and still have a large number of participants who write on a daily basis. To illustrate how topics differ in length, time span of their activity and popularity, a list of 15 randomly selected topics from the Internet forum BabyBoom with their starting dates, dates of the last post (which frequently indicates that the topic is no longer active), as well as with the number of posts is provided in Table 7.

Table 7: List of topics taken from the Internet forum BabyBoom www.babyboom.pl/forum/ created 08.09.2012

	Topic / Thread	Starting date	Date of the last post	Number of posts
1	*Babyboomowy nick a profil na FB* 'Babyboom nick versus profile on FB'	12-11-2011	01-02-2012	15
2	*Ból i twardnienie brzucha, skracanie się szyjki macicy* 'Abdominal pain and hardening, the shortening of the cervix'	15-12-2004	5-09-2012	2756
3	*Cukrzyca ciążowa ...i życie po niej* 'Gestational diabetes ... and life after it'	6-01-2005	4-09-2012	18 155
4	*Czy to owsiki?:(* 'Is that pinworms?:('	20-06-2012	23-07-2012	3
5	*i MOJA Nataszka jest z nami* 'and MY Nataszka with us'	10-11-2010	25-11-2011	4
6	*Iui - inseminacja w walce o pierwszą dzidzię* 'IUI – insemination in the fight for the first baby'	19-05-2010	08-09-2012	14 316
7	*JAK ODZWYCZAIC OD SMOCZKA?* 'How to wean from a pacifier?'	1-11-2004	16-08-2012	407
8	*Kto po in vitro?* 'Who after in vitro?'	22-05-2009	08-09-2012	23 720
9	*Pierwsza wizyta u dentysty* 'The first visit to the dentist'	2-07-2005	16-08-2012	25

	Topic / Thread	Starting date	Date of the last post	Number of posts
10	*Pytania do moderatora i uwagi na temat forum* 'Questions to the moderator and comments on the forum'	12-10-2011	7-12-2011	32
11	*Starania po raz pierwszy :)* 'Trying for the first time :)'	30-07-2010	08-09-2012	74 560
12	*Wiarygodność testu ciążowego* 'The credibility of a pregnancy test'	28-06-2005	4-09-2012	2889
13	*Witam wszystkich* 'Hi all'	3-08-2012	6-08-2012	1
14	*Wzrost i waga naszych dzieci* 'Height and weight of our children'	2-08-2005	08-09-2012	391
15	*Żłobek* 'Nursery'	30-07-2012	30-07-2012	1

The first six topics presented Table 7 are examples of the first topics started after the foundation of BabyBoom. Threads 4–5, 13 and 15 are considered extremely short, as opposed to topics 3, 6, 8 and 11. Threads 5 and 10 can be considered inactive, since for over a year nobody has posted a message, but some topics have only occasional activity, that is why it is difficult to judge when the thread becomes inactive for good.

Even though interaction between forum users is so stretched in time, as in the cases of the topics started in 2004 or 2005 and still active, it allows a user to join at any point and express his/her own opinion. One can also, at any point, decide to stop participating in a discussion or just follow the thread without writing new posts.

In the case of an Internet forum, the number of receivers can change even within one message, where a part of the message is addressed to all participants of the discussion, and another part to chosen people.

Not only threads differ in length, but also posts which can be as short as a single word and as long as several dozen sentences.

Notess comments on the importance of Internet forums in the following way:

> [...] forums are the web's workhorse communication medium. As forum search engine Omgili (www.omgili.com) proclaims on its homepage, forums can be used to "tap into personal experiences, solutions to problems, and ideas and opinions." Omgili even gives example search topics under headings such as consumer experiences, personal experiences, troubleshooting, recommendations, and opinions (Notess 2009: 41).

2.4 Features of language used in online communication

The language of online communication is a specific phenomenon, created by Internet users. What visibly distinguishes the language of CMC, called by Crystal (2004) Netspeak, from traditional forms of communication is the fact that it has features of both written and spoken language. Crystal (2004) presents summaries of written and spoken language criteria applied to Netspeak (Tables 8 and 9).

Table 8: Written language criteria applied to Netspeak presented in Crystal (2004: 42)

		Web	E-mail	Chat groups	Virtual worlds
1	space-bound	yes, with extra options	yes, but routinely deleted	yes, but with restrictions	yes, but with restrictions
2	contrived	yes	variable	no, but with some adaptation	no, but with some adaptation
3	visually decontextualized	yes, but with considerable adaptation	yes	yes	yes, but with some adaptation
4	elaborately structured	yes	variable	no	no
5	factually communicative	yes	yes	variable	yes, but with some adaptation
6	repeatedly revisable	yes	variable	no	no
7	graphically rich	yes, but in different ways	no	no	yes, but in different ways

Table 9: Spoken language criteria applied to Netspeak presented in Crystal (2004: 43)

	Web	E-mail	Chat groups	Virtual worlds
1 time-bound	no	yes, but in different ways	yes, but in different ways	yes, but in different ways
2 spontaneous	no	variable	yes, but with restrictions	yes, but with restrictions
3 face-to-face	no	no	no	no
4 loosely structured	variable	variable	yes	yes
5 socially interactive	no, with increasing options	variable	yes, but with restrictions	yes, but with restrictions
6 immediately revisable	no	no	no	no
7 prosodically rich	no	no	no	no

Analyzing the criteria presented by Crystal, it is easily noticeable that websites comply with all the criteria of written language, and on the other hand, e-mail, chat groups and virtual worlds comply with most criteria of spoken language.

> Web page-writers typically have no idea who their readers are going to be, and in their guessing, targeting, and feedback-requesting they display the same behaviour as any paper-bound author or organization might. At the same time, some of the Web's functions (e.g. e-sales) bring it much closer to the kind of interaction more typical of speech, with a consequential effect on the kind of language used, and many sites now have interactive facilities attached, in the form of e-mail and chat group facilities. In contrast to the Web, the situations of e-mail, chat groups, and virtual worlds, though expressed through the medium of writing, display several of the core properties of speech. They are time-governed, expecting or demanding an immediate response; they are transient, in the sense that messages may be immediately deleted (as in e-mails) or be lost to attention as they scroll off the screen (as in chat groups); and their utterances display much of the urgency and energetic force which is characteristic of face-to-face conversation. The situations are not all equally 'spoken' in character. We 'write' e-mails, not 'speak' them. But chat groups are for 'chat', and people certainly 'speak' to each other there – as do people involved in virtual worlds. (Crystal 2004: 29).

Crystal claims, however, that even in those electronic situations which are most speech-like, there are features which significantly differentiate Netspeak from face-to-face conversation. These features include the following:

1. the lack of simultaneous feedback – "messages sent via a computer are complete and unidirectional" (Crystal 2004: 30);
2. the lack of technical solution "allowing the receiver to send the electronic equivalent of a simultaneous nod, an *uh-uh*, or any of the other audio-visual reactions which play such a critical role in face-to-face interaction" (Crystal 2004: 30);
3. messages cannot overlap – "recipients are committed to experiencing a waiting period before the text appears" (Crystal 2004: 30);
4. time delay – "the rhythm of an Internet interaction is very much slower than that found in a speech situation, and disallows some of conversation's most salient properties. With e-mails and asynchronous chat groups, a response to a stimulus may take anything from seconds to months, the rhythm of the exchange very much depending on such factors as the recipient's computer (e.g. whether it announces the instant arrival of a message), the user's personality and habits (e.g. whether messages are replied to at regular times or randomly), the circumstances of the interlocutors (e.g. their computer access). […] bandwidth processing problems, traffic density on the host computer, or some problems in the sender's or receiver's equipment" (Crystal 2004: 31);
5. turn-taking – because of long lags, the conversational situation in CMC becomes "so unusual that its ability to cope with a topic can be destroyed. This is because the turn-taking, as seen on a screen, is dictated by the software, and not by the participants" (Crystal 2004: 33);
6. "formal properties of the medium, such the domain of *prosody* and *paralanguage* – phonological terms which capture the notion of 'it ain't what you say but the way that you say it' – as expressed through vocal variations in pitch (intonation), loudness (stress), speed, rhythm, pause, and tone of voice. As with traditional writing, there have been somewhat desperate efforts to replace it in the form of an exaggerated use of spelling and punctuation, and the use of capitals, spacing, and special symbols for emphasis. Examples include repeated letters (*aaaaahhhhh, hiiiiiii, ooops, soooo*), repeated punctuation marks (*no more!!!!!, whohe????*)" (Crystal 2004: 34).

Bakuła (2008: 186) disagrees with some of Crystal's points. As regards feedback, Bakuła claims that it depends on the means of communication, for example SMS and sending information as a picture, audio or video allow users to give and receive feedback immediately. Gogołek (2010: 22) claims that the rapid development of technologies and communication channels in the Internet make the communication act much more similar to real life face-to-face communication. In the case of videoconference, the only thing that differentiates it from a conventional conference is the distance between speakers. Other informative elements, like mimics, gestures, eye contact, are completely the same. Another point which Bakuła opposes is the use of gestures and other audio-visual reactions which Crystal believes is crucial in face-to-face communication. Frequently they actually disturb or make the communication act unclear, as in the example of lying, covering embarrassment with laughter or keeping a poker face.

Habrajska (2006) claims that the influence of the Internet on language should lead to the revision of so far existing topologization in language which does not consider the specifics of such a medium. "It would be useful to make the notions *written language* and *spoken language* more precise by including the graphic representation of spoken language in typologies" (translation mine). Bakuła (2003, 2008) makes such a revision in his publications. There is no "official" language of the Internet, even though English is the most commonly used; the same elements or features of Netspeak appear in all the languages used in online communication.

As the first core trait of language used on the Internet Crystal (2004) lists the lexicon. The characteristic vocabulary of Netspeak includes terms connected with software or its functions and commands. The author lists several expressions, such as *file, edit, view, insert, paste, format, tools, window, help, search, refresh, address, history, stop, contact, top, back, forward, home, send, save, open, close, select, toolbars, fonts* (Crystal 2004: 82).

The research on the language of the Internet focuses mainly on studying neologisms. Word Spy is a website and a newsletter that was designed in January 1996 for tracking neologisms that occur in Netspeak. The website allows users to search for the meaning and context of use of new words or phrases.

The list of neologisms under the category Language comprises inter alia: *antigram, antilanguage, apostrofly, aptagram, autofail, autological, beforemath, Bubbonics, camouflanguage, Christianese, collabulary, crash blossom, crosswordese, cryptolect, Cupertino effect, deja dit, Denglish, ebonic poetry, Ebonics, forelash, franglophone, frankenword, frequency illusion, frontfire, fruitloopery, fuzzword, globish greengrocers', apostrophe, Greenspeak, guerrilla proofreading, holorime, hyperwhite, inner-capped, invacuate, jamais vu, jingo-jangle, linguistic profiling, logophilia, manual babbling, Menglish, metaphasis, mononymous, Netspeak, noun-banging, oronyms, plastic words, predictionary, protologism, pubilect, slanguist, social swearing, speako, Spinnish, stylometrician, substition, supersize, technopropism, tentafier, triviata, virtue signalling, vocal grooming, weblish, word burst, wordnap, wordrobe* (http://wordspy.com/index.php?tag=language, accessed 20.06.2016).

Liu (2014) carried out a study of word-formation processes in Netspeak neologisms by analyzing 210 neologisms under the category Internet posted by www.wordspy.com. The conclusions are provided in Tables 10 and 11, taken from Liu (2014).

Table 10: Classification of word-formation processes of Internet neologisms (taken from Liu 2014: 29)

	Number	Proportion	Examples
Compounding	153	72.9%	*arachnerd, podcasting, slashdot effect*
Blending	25	11.9%	*altmetrics, collabulary, cybrarian*
Affixation	13	6.2%	*defirend, domainer, ungoogleable*
Acronyms	2	1%	*captcha, MOOC*
Conversion	2	1%	*friend, google*
Clipping	1	0.5%	*blog*
Old words with new meaning	5	2.3%	*bookmark, chiclet, flame, sticky, unstrung*
Hard to define	9	4.2%	*bitcom, folsonomy, gator, Phishing, sextuple-u, Webrarian*
Total	210	100%	

Table 11: Classification of blending neologisms (taken from Liu 2014: 29)

head+word (5)	head+tail (11)	word+tail (9)
altmetrics	*vlog*	*songlifting*
emotags	*collabulary*	*twitterverse*
internot	*cybarian*	*viewser*
e-mentor	*digilante*	*fiberhood*
e-fence	*Gootube*	*Googleganger*
	juvenoia	*webology*
	spime	*web-isode*
	vortal	*knowbie*
	wikiality	*websumer*
	ubiquilink	
	wedsite	

Using acronyms is another characteristic and distinctive feature of language used in online communication. They are used not only because they save time as they are easier and quicker to write than whole words and phrases, but using acronyms also emphasizes belonging to different newsgroups, online forums or chat rooms and indicates the knowledge of the principles of communication and separateness or even uniqueness of their users. What is more, some of the acronyms perform the function of codenames, "by which you can get around some rules of netiquette (that is, a set of rules for proper behaviour in the network), namely those that prohibit the use of vulgar language, see, e.g., NFW – no fucking way" (Gruszczyński 2001: 189, translation mine). Obviously, a disadvantage of these abbreviations – as always in the case of their use – is the lack of their full understanding among some users. On forums there are frequent requests for explanations of abbreviations, which puts into question their effectiveness and functionality. Abbreviations are based on the pronunciation of their corresponding letter or digit (Table 12).

Table 12: Basic abbreviations based on pronunciation

2	to/too
4	for
B	be
C	see
I	eye
O	owe
R	are
U	you
Y	why

There are numerous lists of rapidly evolving acronyms used in Netspeak. Table 13 contains the most common acronyms presented on the website http://www.connexin.net/internet-acronyms.html (accessed 20.06.2016).

Table 13: Acronyms in Netspeak

Acronym	Explanation	Acronym	Explanation
2F4U	too fast for you	NaN	not a number
4YEO FYEO	for your eyes only	NNTR	no need to reply
AAMOF	as a matter of fact	noob n00b	newbie
ACK	acknowledgment	NOYB	none of your business
AFAIK	as far as I know	NRN	no reply necessary
AFAIR	as far as I remember / recall	OMG	oh my God
AFK	away from keyboard	OP	original poster, original post
AKA	also known as	OT	off topic
B2K BTK	back to keyboard	OTOH	on the other hand

Acronym	Explanation	Acronym	Explanation
BTT	back to topic	PEBKAC	problem exists between keyboard and chair
BTW	by the way	POV	point of view
B/C	because	ROTFL	rolling on the floor laughing
C&P	copy and paste	RSVP	repondez s'il vous plait (French: please reply)
CU	see you	RTFM	read the fine manual
CYS	check your settings	SCNR	sorry, could not resist
DIY	do it yourself	SFLR	sorry, for late reply
EOBD	end of business day	SPOC	single point of contact
EOD	end of discussion	TBA	to be announced
EOM	end of message	TBC	to be continued / to be confirmed
EOT	end of thread /text / transmission	TIA	thanks in advance
FAQ	frequently asked questions	TGIF	thanks God, its Friday
FACK	full acknowledge	THX TNX	thanks
FKA	formerly known as	TQ	thank you
FWIW	for what it's worth	TYVM	thank you very much
FYI / JFYI	(just) for your information	TYT	take your time
FTW	fuck the world / for the win	TTYL	talk to you later
HF	have fun	w00t	whoomp, there it is; meaning "hooray"
HTH	hope this helps	WFM	works for me
IDK	I don't know	WRT	with regard to
IIRC	if I recall / remember correctly	WTH	what the hell / what the heck
MMW	mark my words	WTF	what the fuck
N/A	not available / applicable	YMMD	you made my day

An intriguing problem in online communication is the communication of emotions. In direct contact it is done through appropriate mimics, gestures and the tone of voice. According to Wallace (2005), the lack of emotions in online communication was not compensated for initially, that is why communication via the Internet was perceived as cold and impersonal. Till the time of the introduction of characters symbolically depicting faces (in horizontal view) of different states, which were then replaced by small drawings, called smileys or emoticons (blend of *emotion icon* – an image, a symbol of emotions) (Wallace 2005: 20).

> What is interesting to the linguist, of course, is why these novelties have turned up now. Written language has always been ambiguous, in its omission of facial expression, and in its inability to express all the intonational and other prosodic features of speech. Why did no one ever introduce smileys there? The answer must be something to do with the immediacy of Net interaction, its closeness to speech. In traditional writing, there is time to develop phrasing which makes personal attitudes clear; that is why the formal conventions of letter-writing developed. And when they are missing, something needs to replace them. A rapidly constructed Net message, lacking the usual courtesies, can easily appear abrupt or rude. A smiley defuses the situation (Crystal 2004: 38–39).

Emoticons are combinations of punctuation signs (colon, parenthesis, comma, dash), mathematical signs (>, <, =); sometimes letters are also used. Emoticons can replace single words, phrases or whole sentences. They are usually placed at the end of the text, but they can also be an integral part of the message. A research has been carried out among 96,269,892 Twitter users who provided 20 emoticons accounting for 90% of all their occurrences. The total of emoticons listed on www.datagenetics.com is 2242. Table 14 presents the outcomes of the research.

Table 14: *Top 20 emoticons according to Twitter users (http://www.datagenetics.com/blog/october52012/index.html, accessed in April 2015)*

Rank	Emoticon	Usage	Percent	Notes
1	:)	32.115.789	33.360%	happy face
2	:D	10.595.385	11.006%	laugh
3	:(	7.613.014	7.908%	sad face
4	;)	7.238.295	7.519%	wink
5	:-)	4.254.708	4.420%	happy face (with nose)
6	:P	3.588.863	3.728%	tongue out
7	=)	3.564.080	3.702%	happy face
8	(:	2.720.383	2.826%	happy face (mirror)
9	;-)	2.085.015	2.166%	wink (with nose)
10	:/	1.840.827	1.912%	uneasy, undecided, sceptical, annoyed
11	XD	1.795.792	1.865%	big grin
12	=D	1.434.004	1.490%	laugh
13	:o	1.077.124	1.119%	shock, yawn

Rank	Emoticon	Usage	Percent	Notes
14	=]	1.055.517	1.096%	happy face
15	D:	1.048.320	1.089%	grin (mirror)
16	;D	1.004.509	1.043%	wink and grin
17	:]	954.740	0.992%	happy face
18	:-(	816.170	0.848%	unhappy
19	=/	809.760	0.841%	uneasy, undecided, sceptical, annoyed
20	=(	760.600	0.790%	unhappy

Maliszewska (2002) provides some interesting examples of emoticons which are not used to express emotions, but to show features of somebody's look and character, to provide age and position in a family, nationality, profession and belonging to a social group or class. There are also emoticons which – in a form of a joke – portray famous people or replace whole messages about activities or events. The originality of these elements is related to the fact that most people who use them are young people who mainly socialize on the Internet. Examples of emoticons used for different purposes than showing emotions are provided in Table 15.

Table 15: Emoticons not expressing emotions (Maliszewska 2002: 150–155)

Emoticon	Meaning	Emoticon	Meaning
3:-)	I have curly hair	=:-)	a punk
(:I	I am an intellectual	:-%	a bank worker
oO:-)	a grandmother	+-:-)	I am a priest
8:-)	I am a small girl	(Z(:-P	Napoleon
I-)	Chinese	:-OO	I am yawning
*^_^*	a Japanese girl	*I	I love sunsets

Another feature of Netspeak described by Crystal is "distinctive graphology".

> The range extends from an enhanced system (by comparison with traditional writing) with a wide range of special fonts and styles, as in the most sophisticated Web pages, to a severely reduced system, with virtually no typographic contrastivity (not even such 'basic' features as italics or boldface). There is a strong tendency to use lowercase everywhere. […] The 'save a keystroke' principle is widely found in e-mails, chat groups, and virtual worlds, where whole sentences can be produced without capitals (or punctuation) (Crystal 2004: 87).

Because the use of lower-case is regarded as a norm, the use of capital letters is considered to be "a strongly marked form of communication", including shouting (Crystal 2004: 87).

Non-standard spelling and not respecting orthographical rules are very common in Netspeak. Crystal (2004) claims that American spelling is more frequently used than British spelling because of the American origin of the Internet and because American spelling conventions are simpler. He also claims that

> New spelling conventions have emerged, such as the replacement of plural -s by -z to refer to pirated versions of software, as in *warez, tunez, gamez, serialz, pornz, downloadz,* and *filez*. Non-standard spelling, heavily penalized in traditional writing (at least, since the eighteenth century), is used without sanction in conversational settings (Crystal 2004: 88).

In Polish Netspeak, spelling mistakes are made very frequently. There are various reasons for their occurrence. Firstly, they can be caused by pressing the wrong letter on the keyboard, as in an example below, taken from the Internet forum BabyBoom. In example (9) the words *everything* (*wszystko*), was written incorrectly '*wszytsko*'.

(9) *I **wszytsko** w tym temacie:-)* (www.babyboom.pl/żyrafaSophie; 04.07.2009)
 lit. And all in this topic :-)
 'There's nothing left to say:-)'

Secondly, mistakes can be caused by the lack of knowledge of orthographical rules and thirdly, by not using Polish diacritic marks as in the example below, taken from the Internet forum BabyBoom. In (10) the word *to argue* (*kłócić*) was misspelled effecting in an unacceptable form *klucic*.

(10) *Oki rzeczywiscie nie ma sensu sie **klucic**, kazda ma swoje zdanie i niech tak zostanie (ale mi sie zrymowalo :-D) Ide usypiac malca, bo cos ciezko mu to samemu idzie ;-) Spokojnej nocki wszystkim mamuskom i dzieciaczkom zycze :-)* (www.babyboom.pl/żyrafaSophie; 05.07.2009).
 'OK, there is really not point in arguing, everyone has their own opinion and let it stay this way (I got to rhyme the sentence :-D) I am going to put my kids to bed because he [my partner] struggles with it on his own ;-) All mommies and children, I wish you a quiet night :-)'

Lisecki (2001) provides several examples of deliberate use of ungrammatical structures in Polish which are motivated by irony, joke, having fun etc. (11) exemplifies the incorrect spelling in *zla pisofnia* [zła pisownia], incorrect use of spaces between words in *Niewłasci **weod st**epy* [niewłaściwe odstępy] and misplacing of letters in *Przepraszam, dzisiaj cierpie na**ksydlejes*** [Przepraszam, dzisiaj cierpię na dysleksję].

(11) „"To zdanie nie czasownika", „**Zła pisofnia**", „Niewłasci **weod st**epy", „Przepraszam, dzisiaj cierpie na**ksydlejes**"" (Lisecki, 2001: 113). lit. 'This sentence no verb', 'Wron spellin', 'Incorre ctspac esbetwe enwords', 'I'm sorry, today I am suffering fromxiadysle'. 'This sentence has no verb', 'Wrong spelling', 'Incorrect spaces between words', 'I'm sorry, today I am suffering from dyslexia'.

According to Szczepańska (2009: 60), "globalization of the world and culture is accompanied by the globalization of communication". The development of international trade and cooperation in the areas of politics, economy, education, technology and tourism create a need for rapid communication between specialists in various fields. This leads to the unification of language used in CMC. Since English is the native language for 380 million people and a second language for 250 million people (Szczepańska 2009: 60–61), it became the lingua franca of the Internet. Polish used in online communication undergoes changes to look more like English. One such an instance is the use of *q* instead of *ku*, based on the corresponding pronunciation, as in *qrcze* 'gosh' (used as an interjection), *qrwa* 'fuck' (used as an interjection), *domqu* 'little house'. Simple words, like *sorry* instead of *przepraszam*, *hello* instead of *cześć*, *crazy* for *stuknięty*, *thanks* instead of *dzięki* or *cool* for *fajne*, are commonly used in Polish, as well as the stems of some English words which are borrowed and create the bases for whole groups of words with Polish derivational suffixes. An example of this process is the word *hardcore* (*mocny, ostry*). In Polish, there are several words using this stem, for example: *hardkorowe* 'hardcore' (used as an adjective as in a *Ta piosenka jest hardcorowa* 'This song is hardcore'), *hadkorowiec* 'hardcore' (used as a noun describing a person) (Szczepańska 2009: 60).

2.5 Research on the subject

The Internet, as a relatively new environment for communication, has been a popular object of linguistic study in the past few decades. To name just a few among numerous linguists, these are the authors whose works this study acknowledges: Aouil (2008), Aouil and Kajdasz-Aouil (2007), Bakuła (2003, 2008), Baron (1998, 2003), Bralczyk and Mosiołek-Kłosińska (2000), Castells (2003, 2011), Cherny (1999), Collot and Belmore (1993, 1996), Crystal (1995, 2004), Danet (2001), Davis and Brewer (1997), Ess (1996, 2001), Goban-Klas (2001), Golus (2003a, 2003b), Grzenia (2003a, 2003b, 2006), Gruszczyński (2001a, 2001b), Gut (1999), Habrajska (1997, 2002), Hale and Scanlon (1999), Hård af Segerstad (2002), Herring (1999, 2001, 2002), Jagodzińska (2000), Jasińska (2001), Matuszczyk and Stanulewicz (2002), Maynor (1994), Mroczek (2011), Shea (1994), Sutherland

(1997), Taras (2003), Thurlow, Lengel and Tomic (2004), Thurlow and Walther (1996), Warschauer (2000) and Werry (1996).

2.6 Concluding remarks

What the second chapter has attempted to do is to provide a brief overview of asynchronous forms of communication on the Internet which are characterized by time shift between transmitting the message and its reception, such as website, e-mail, Internet forum and blog. An overview of synchronous forms of communication in the Internet has also been provided. These forms share a common feature, namely their linearity; they require simultaneous presence of both the sender and the receiver. Among these forms, conversations in chat rooms and games in MUDs have been described. Active communication, in which the net changes information according to personal profile of the user, has been mentioned as well.

This chapter has aimed to demonstrate that the Internet forum is a unique communication medium because it allows online threaded discussions with multiple users. Interaction between forum users can be stretched in time, as some topics started several years ago are still active. The function of recording the output data from the very first post allows new users to join in at any time.

Chapter Three Metaphors employed by Polish users of Internet forums for mothers

3.1 The aims of the research

The purpose of this research was to gather metaphorical expressions employed by Polish and American Internet forum users in order to examine if they use metaphorical language to talk about the same subjects and to what extent the used mappings differ or show similarities.

Chapter Three contains a classification of metaphorical expressions found on selected Polish Internet forums for mothers. The metaphorical expressions are presented in 24 subsections, depending on target domains.

3.1.1 Data collection

For the purpose of this work, ten thousand posts from various Polish Internet forums in the time frame August 2012 – January 2013 have been analyzed. The topics of threads are various, ranging from giving advice on breastfeeding and complaining about spouses to sex during pregnancy. The reason for choosing so different topics was to check which topics of online discussions contained the biggest number of metaphorical expressions. The titles of the analyzed forums and quoted posts are presented in their original forms altogether with spelling mistakes and smileys. The corrected versions were provided in square brackets. The list of the Internet forums and topics is provided below.

1. DZIECKO PO 30-STCE [DZIECKO PO TRZYDZIESTCE] 'A child after 30'
   http://www.babyboom.pl/forum/staramy-sie-f66/1-dziecko-po-30-stce-7471-print/?pp=40
   1200 posts analyzed and numerous metaphorical expressions found.
2. 13 pytań o antykoncepcję '13 questions about contraception'
   http://www.babyboom.pl/forum/troche-intymnosci-f15/13-pytan-o-antykoncepcje-3119-print/?pp=40
   242 posts analyzed and several metaphorical expressions found.
3. Apel o życzliwość dla małych brzuszków 'Call for kindness for small [pregnant] bellies'

http://mjakmama24.dlarodzinki.pl/threads/157-Apel-o-życzliwość-dla-małych-brzuszków

23 posts analyzed and several metaphorical expressions found.

4. CIĄŻA TO NIE CHOROBA – Ja to wiem!! 'Pregnancy is not a disease – I know that!!'
http://mjakmama24.dlarodzinki.pl/threads/156-CIĄŻA-TO-NIE-CHOROBA-Ja-to-wiem!!

75 posts analyzed and numerous metaphorical expressions found.

5. Czuję że jestem złą matką [Czuję, że jestem złą matką] 'I feel I am a bad mother'
http://www.babyboom.pl/forum/mamuskowo-f313/czuje-ze-jestem-zla-matka-28058-print/?pp=40

90 posts analyzed and numerous metaphorical expressions found.

6. Czy można i jak zaplanować płeć dziecka?? chłopiec/dziewczynka?:) [Czy można i jak zaplanować płeć dziecka? Chłopiec/dziewczynka?] 'How can you plan the baby's sex?? boy/girl?:)'
http://www.babyboom.pl/forum/staramy-sie-f66/czy-mozna-i-jak-zaplanowac-plec-dziecka-chlopiec-dziewczynka-1147-print/?pp=40

525 posts analyzed and no metaphorical expressions found.

7. Czy ochota na seks po porodzie jeszcze kiedys nadejdzie? [Czy ochota na seks po porodzie jeszcze kiedyś nadejdzie?]
'Will the desire to have sex come back after giving birth?'
http://www.babyboom.pl/forum/troche-intymnosci-f15/czy-ochota-na-seks-po-porodzie-jeszcze-kiedys-nadejdzie-11-print/?pp=40

320 posts analyzed and numerous metaphorical expressions found.

8. Czy twój mężczyzna ogląda strony pornograficzne??? 'Does your man watch pornographic websites???'
http://www.babyboom.pl/forum/troche-intymnosci-f15/czy-twoj-mezczyzna-oglada-strony-pornograficzne-1680-print/?pp=40

722 posts analyzed and no metaphorical expressions found.

9. Dotykanie brzuszka 'Touching the [pregnant] belly'
http://mjakmama24.dlarodzinki.pl/threads/1748-Dotykanie-brzuszka

33 posts analyzed and several metaphorical expressions found.

10. dramatyczny powrót do pracy 'dramatic return to work'
http://www.babyboom.pl/forum/mamuskowo-f313/dramatyczny-powrot-do-pracy-43225-print/

17 posts analyzed and one metaphorical expression found.

11. Kiepski małżeński sex... [Kiepski małżeński seks] 'Poor marital sex...'
    http://www.babyboom.pl/forum/troche-intymnosci-f15/kiepski-malzenski-sex-39889-print/?pp=40
    122 posts analyzed and numerous metaphorical expressions found.
12. kolczyki u niemowlaka 'earrings for a toddler'
    http://www.babyboom.pl/forum/mamuskowo-f313/kolczyki-u-niemowlaka-4610-print/?pp=40
    258 posts analyzed and no metaphorical expressions found.
13. Ludzie mnie zaskakują :) Jak traktuje się kobiety ciężarne? 'People surprise me :) How are pregnant women treated?'
    http://mjakmama24.dlarodzinki.pl/threads/867-Ludzie-mnie-zaskakują-)-Jak-traktuje-się-kobiety-ciężarne
    140 posts analyzed and several metaphorical expressions found.
14. maluszki i mamusie z Kaszub 'Babies and mammies from Kaszuby'
    http://www.babyboom.pl/forum/trojmiasto-f199/maluszki-i-mamusie-z-kaszub-31292/
    66 posts analyzed and no metaphorical expressions found. It was simply an informative thread to introduce oneself to the others.
15. Mamusie i ich maleństwa 2009 [Mamusie i ich maleństwa 2009] 'Mammies and their babies 2009'
    http://www.babyboom.pl/forum/mamuskowo-f313/mamusie-i-ich-malenstwa-2009-a-35002-print/?pp=40
    2399 posts analyzed and numerous metaphorical expressions found.
16. Mąż nie ma ochoty na sex [Mąż nie ma ochoty na seks] 'Husband doesn't want sex'
    http://www.babyboom.pl/forum/troche-intymnosci-f15/maz-nie-ma-ochoty-na-sex-33070-print/?pp=40
    236 posts analyzed and several metaphorical expressions found.
17. Najlepsze pozycje, aby zajść w ciąże? [Najlepsze pozycje, aby zajść w ciążę?] 'Best positions to get pregnant?'
    http://www.babyboom.pl/forum/troche-intymnosci-f15/najlepsze-pozycje-zajsc-w-ciaze-13999-print/?pp=40
    122 posts analyzed and no metaphorical expressions found. This thread was purely instructional.
18. sex analny [seks analny] 'anal sex'
    http://www.babyboom.pl/forum/troche-intymnosci-f15/sex-analny-704-print/?pp=40
    292 posts analyzed and no metaphorical expressions found.

19. sex w ciąży [seks w ciąży] 'pregnant sex'
    http://www.babyboom.pl/forum/troche-intymnosci-f15/sex-w-ciazy-59-print/?pp=40
    954 posts analyzed and no metaphorical expressions found. This thread was mainly instructional and for the exchange of experiences.
20. Starania po raz pierwszy :) 'Trying (to conceive) for the first time :)'
    http://www.babyboom.pl/forum/staramy-sie-f66/starania-po-raz-pierwszy-42617-print/?pp=40
    840 posts analyzed and several metaphorical expressions found.
21. Ulubiona pozycja ;-) 'Favourite position ;-)'
    http://www.babyboom.pl/forum/troche-intymnosci-f15/ulubiona-pozycja-1011-print/?pp=40
    180 posts analyzed and no metaphorical expressions found. This thread contained only straightforward answers with names of favorite positions.
22. Wakacje z maluszkiem 'Holidays with the baby'
    http://www.babyboom.pl/forum/mamuskowo-f313/wakacje-z-maluszkiem-27060-print/?pp=40
    84 posts analyzed and no metaphorical expressions found.
23. Więcej życzliwości dla Cycusiów!!! 'More kindness for (feeding) Breasts!!!'
    http://mjakmama24.dlarodzinki.pl/threads/824-Więcej-życzliwości-dla-Cycusiów!!!
    143 posts analyzed and numerous metaphorical expressions found.
24. Więcej życzliwości dla kobiet w ciąży 'More kindness for pregnant women'
    http://mjakmama24.dlarodzinki.pl/threads/24-Więcej-życzliwości-dla-kobiet-w-ciąży
    366 posts analyzed and several metaphorical expressions found.
25. Zakłopotanie… 'Embarrassment…'
    http://mjakmama24.dlarodzinki.pl/threads/223-Zakłopotanie
    56 posts analyzed and several metaphorical expressions found.
26. Zdrada 'Cheating'
    http://www.babyboom.pl/forum/troche-intymnosci-f15/zdrada-5378-print/?pp=40
    373 posts analyzed and numerous metaphorical expressions found.
27. żony marynarzy..integujmy się:) [żony marynarzy.. integrujmy się] 'sailors' wives.. let's get together:)'
    http://www.babyboom.pl/forum/trojmiasto-f199/zony-marynarzy-integujmy-sie-32652/
    81 posts analyzed and no metaphorical expressions found.

28. Życzliwość dla mam z dziećmi - tak czy nie? 'Kindness for mums with children – yes or no?'
http://mjakmama24.dlarodzinki.pl/threads/2356-Życzliwość-dla-mam-z-dziećmi-tak-czy-nie
42 posts analyzed and several metaphorical expressions found.

3.2 An analysis of selected examples of conceptual metaphors

The most frequently used metaphorical expression found on Polish forums was *to be pregnant* (*być w ciąży*), lit. *to be in pregnancy*. Since the analyzed posts were taken from forums for mothers, this particular metaphor, namely PREGNANCY IS A CONTAINER, was used over 20,000 times. Because this metaphorical expression is very conventional, I have decided not to count it in the quantitative analysis of metaphors.

> (11) *Jestem w 25 tygodniu ciąży*, akurat dzisiaj na poczcie spotkała mnie niemiła sytuacja i to ze strony drugiej *kobiety w ciąży*.
> lit. 'I am in the 25th week of pregnancy, just today at the post office met me an unpleasant situation and it was from another *woman in pregnancy*.' 'I am 25 weeks *pregnant*, just today at the post office I had an unpleasant situation and it was with another *pregnant woman*.'
> (Lydak1 18-10-10, 15:46
> http://mjakmama24.dlarodzinki.pl/threads/24-Więcej-życzliwości-dla-kobiet-w-ciąży/index1.html)

An analogous situation applies to other highly conventional metaphorical expressions containing the names of the days of the week, e.g. *on Wednesday* (*w środę*), lit. *in Wednesday*. In Polish, unlike English, A DAY OF THE WEEK IS A CONTAINER. This particular metaphor is also not included in the analysis in Chapter Five.

> (12) *W środę byłam w banku i przychodni*.
> lit. '*In Wednesday* I was in a bank and in doctor's office.'
> '*On Wednesday* I was in a bank and at the doctor's office.' (fresh83 13-02-2010, 21:45, http://www.babyboom.pl/forum/mamuskowo-f313/mamusie-i-ich-malenstwa-2009-a-35002-print/index44.html?pp=38)

It should be noted that months and years are treated as CONTAINERS in both languages.

3.2.1 Metaphors of emotions

3.2.1.1 *Metaphors of anger*

Much research has already been carried out to analyze the metaphor ANGER IS HEATED FLUID IN A CONTAINER. It has been proved that embodied experience, independent of one's knowledge and understanding of language, helps in understanding this metaphor.

Gibbs (2004) conducted a study in which people were asked about their embodied experiences in regard to source domains in various conceptual metaphors. Gibbs comments on the results in the following way:

> For instance, for the conceptual metaphor ANGER IS HEATED FLUID IN A CONTAINER, the participants responded that the explosion of the fluid inside is caused by the increase in the heat of the fluid. They also reported that this explosion is unintentional because containers and fluid have no intentional agency, and that the explosion occurs in a violent manner. These brief responses provide a rough, nonlinguistic profile of the participants' understanding of a particular source domain concept (i.e., heated fluid in the bodily container) (Gibbs et al. 2004: 1195–1196).

Example (13) presents a metaphorical expression which illustrates this metaphor.

(13) ja sobie nie wyobrazam jak mozna będąc w zwiazku a tym bardziej w malzenstwie byc z dwoma mezczyznami, spac z nimi, pozwalac sie dotykac ach nawet mi sie pisac nie chce nie potrafilabym z tym zyc, sumienie by mnie zjadlo. koncze moj wywod bo *az sie zagotowalam*

[Ja sobie nie wyobrażam, jak można będąc w związku, a tym bardziej w małżeństwie, być z dwoma mężczyznami, spać z nimi, pozwalać się dotykać, ach, nawet mi się pisać nie chce, nie potrafiłabym z tym żyć, sumienie by mnie zjadło. Kończę mój wywód, bo *aż się zagotowałam*.]

lit. 'I can't imagine how it is possible to be in a relationship, and more so, a marriage, and be with two men, sleep with them, let them touch you ah I don't even want to write about it. I wouldn't be able to live with it, my conscience would eat me. I'm finishing my argument now because *I am boiling*.'

'I can't imagine how it is possible to be in a relationship, and more so, a marriage, and be with two men, sleep with them, let them touch you ah I don't even want to write about it. I wouldn't be able to live with it, my conscience would eat me. I'm finishing my argument now because *my blood is boiling*'

(Pati26 13-08-2006, 23:35,
http://www.babyboom.pl/forum/troche-intymnosci-f15/zdrada-5378-print/index5.html?pp=40)

Sentence (14) contains the frequently used metaphorical expression *one's blood pours over them* (*krew kogoś zalewa*), which exemplifies the metaphor ANGER IS A FLOOD OF BLOOD.

(14) A jak kiedys uslyszalam, ze „glodze swoje dziecko", to myslalam, *ze mnie krew zaleje...*
[A jak kiedyś usłyszałam, że „głodzę swoje dziecko", to myślałam, *że mnie krew zaleje...*]
lit. 'And when I once heard that "I'm starving my child", I thought that *my blood will pour over me...*'
'And when I once heard that "I'm starving my child", I thought that *my blood would boil...*'
(joklis 05-07-2009, 12:42,
http://www.babyboom.pl/forum/mamuskowo-f313/czuje-ze-jestem-zla-matka-28058-print/index2.html?pp=40)

The metaphorical expression in (15) is not commonly used; however, it shares the same experiential basis as more conventional examples presented in this subsection. It is common knowledge that the albumen sets because of high temperatures, so does the white in the eye.

(15) A z chrapaniem to serdecznie współczuję bo wiem co to znaczy. Jeszcze w ciąży wysłałam drania na operację przegrody nosowej, bo nie wyobrażałam sobie, że on będzie tak koncertował przy małym dziecku... Wiem, że to nie jego wina, ale nie macie pojęcia jaką agresję wywołuje we mnie dźwięk chrapania, aż się *białko w oku ze złości ścina.*
[A z chrapaniem, to serdecznie współczuję. bo wiem, co to znaczy. Jeszcze w ciąży wysłałam drania na operację przegrody nosowej, bo nie wyobrażałam sobie, że on będzie tak koncertował przy małym dziecku... Wiem, że to nie jego wina, ale nie macie pojęcia, jaką agresję wywołuje we mnie dźwięk chrapania, aż się *białko w oku ze złości ścina.*]
'I heartily sympathize with you about the snoring because I know what it means. When I was still pregnant I sent the wretch for an operation on his nasal septum because I couldn't imagine that he would perform his concert in front of a small child... I know that it's not his fault, but you have no idea what kind of aggression the sound of snoring arouses in me, it makes *the white in my eye coagulate.*'
(saly 06-07-2009, 12:42,
http://www.babyboom.pl/forum/mamuskowo-f313/czuje-ze-jestem-zla-matka-28058-print/index2.html?pp=40)

3.2.1.2 Metaphors of aggitation and nerves

Example (16) contains several figurative expressions. In one of them, nerves are treated as an object with which one can *be hit*. Another metaphorical expression, *jest cyrk* 'it is a circus', is quite popular in Polish as a comment on surprising situations, and situations in which babies cry, misbehave and act up.

(16) Jeszcze żeby chociaż mama mi radziła faktycznie w sprawach trudnych których nie wiem, a ona mi w kółko powtarza straszne historie klientek ze sklepu no i oczywiściesię nakręca.. A najgorsze jest to że jakich argumentow nie użyję, to ona jak katarynka bedzie powtarzać swoje...a *mnie nerwa tłucze* że chyba tych dwoch miesiecy niew ytrzymam i zwariuję. bo ja to zauważyłam, że jak przegapie i Mały pózniej idzie spać to *jest cyrk*.

[Jeszcze, żeby, chociaż mama mi radziła faktycznie w sprawach trudnych, których nie wiem, a ona mi w kółko powtarza straszne historie klientek ze sklepu, no i oczywiście się nakręca... A najgorsze jest to, że jakich argumentów nie użyję, to ona jak katarynka będzie powtarzać swoje... A *mnie nerwa tłucze*, że chyba tych dwóch miesięcy nie wytrzymam i zwariuję, bo ja to zauważyłam, że jak przegapię i Mały później idzie spać, to *jest cyrk*.]

lit. 'If only mum gave me advice on difficult issues that I don't know, but she always repeats horrible stories from customers in the shop and of course she winds herself up. And the worst is I have no arguments and she, like a music box, just repeats herself... *the nerves hit me*, I think that I will not survive these two months and I'll go crazy because I noticed that if I miss it and the little one goes to bed later, *it becomes a circus*.'

'If only mum gave me advice on difficult issues that I don't know, but she always repeats horrible stories from customers in the shop and of course she winds herself up. And the worst is I have no arguments and she, like a music box, just repeats herself...and *I get so angry* that I think that I will not survive these two months and I'll go crazy because I noticed that if I miss it and the little one goes to bed later, *it becomes a circus*.'

(kerna 05-07-2009, 22:52,

http://www.babyboom.pl/forum/mamuskowo-f313/czuje-ze-jestem-zla-matka-28058-print/index2.html?pp=40)

An interesting example of a metaphorical expression is presented in (17). The phrase *zjechać kogoś* (lit. to go down somebody) means to 'tell somebody off' or even 'to scream at somebody'.

(17) jamajka też tak myślałam...jak mała płakała i ktoś z rodziny powiedział „Saruś co Ci mama robi?" *byłam w stanie tak zjechać* że ludzie odemnie odchodzili i się bali cokolwiek powiedzieć.

[Jamajka, też tak myślałam... Jak mała płakała i ktoś z rodziny powiedział „Saruś, co Ci mama robi?", *byłam w stanie tak zjechać*, że ludzie ode mnie odchodzili i się bali cokolwiek powiedzieć.]

lit. 'Jamajka I also thought that...when the little one was crying and someone from the family said "Saruś what's mum doing to you?" *I could go downhill on them* and people left and were afraid to say anything.'

'Jamajka I also thought that... when my daughter was crying and someone from the family said "Saruś what's mum doing to you?", *I could tell them off* and people left and were afraid to say anything.'

(dib2 24-06-2009, 21:17,
http://www.babyboom.pl/forum/mamuskowo-f313/czuje-ze-jestem-zla-matka-28058-print/?pp=40)

In example (18) the nerves are treated as objects one can put into a drawer.

(18) *Nerwy do szuflady* i do pracy!
'[Put] *Nerves into the drawer* and get to work!'
(fresh83 30-01-2010, 22:39,
http://www.babyboom.pl/forum/mamuskowo-f313/mamusie-i-ich-malenstwa-2009-a-35002-print/index13.html?pp=40)

Sentence (19) makes use of the metaphor NERVES ARE FOOD as one can *eat them* (*zjeść nerwy*).

(19) Jak nie wrócili do pory karmienia to *zdążyłam zjeść pełno nerwów*.
lit. 'When they didn't come back for feeding time *I managed to eat a lot of nerves.*'
'When they didn't come back for feeding time *I was a bundle of nerves.*'
(lagajka 14-04-2010, 10:10,
http://www.babyboom.pl/forum/mamuskowo-f313/mamusie-i-ich-malenstwa-2009-a-35002-print/index39.html?pp=40)

Sentence (20), on the other hand, pictures nerves as an animated being which can *get* (*dopaść*) a person.

(20) widze ze *nerwówka cię dopadła* przed chrztem i slubem:-(
[Widzę, że *nerwówka cię dopadła* przed chrztem i ślubem:-(]
lit. 'I see that *the nerves got you* before the Christening and wedding:-('
'I see that *you're getting stressed* before the Christening and wedding:-('
(fresh83 13-05-2010, 23:05,
http://www.babyboom.pl/forum/mamuskowo-f313/mamusie-i-ich-malenstwa-2009-a-35002-print/index44.html?pp=40)

Most of the expressions presented in this subsection are commonly used in Polish and they present no difficulty in understanding the meaning of the messages.

3.2.1.3 *Metaphors of depression*

The most frequently used metaphorical expression presented in this subsection is *to mieć doła* (lit. to have a pit) which means 'to be depressed, to feel low'. The experiential basis for such an expression is physical experience. Examples below show that depression is "gradable". An interesting fact is that the Polish do not use the adjective *głęboki* (deep) to describe *a pit*, meaning depression. Instead, they use the words *mały* 'small' and *duży* 'big'. On the other hand, the phrases *być w głębokiej depresji* 'to be in deep depression' and *być w głębokiej rozpaczy* 'to be in deep despair', are commonly used in Polish.

The author of (21) responds to a previous post in which a woman complained about a hard situation she was in. She used the word *kupa* 'shit' to describe the general state of matters. The author of example (21) cheers her up by saying that it is not as bad as she is saying, it is just *a low* (*niż*). There are certain degrees of depression. Starting from the "smallest" depression one can have:

niż – a low (21)
dołek – a little pit (22)
dół – a pit (23)
dół bez dna – a bottomless pit (24)
czarna rozpacz – black despair (25)
dolina – valley (26)

(21) Asik, nie jest kupa, tylko… *jest niż, który zdarza się każdemu*. Wdech i wydech… to kiedyś minie, musi.
'Asik, it's not poo, just…*it's a low that happens to everyone*. Inhale and exhale… it'll pass, it has to.'
(saly 26-06-2009, 22:36,
http://www.babyboom.pl/forum/mamuskowo-f313/czuje-ze-jestem-zla-matka-28058-print/?pp=40)

(22) czasem *dolek przylazi, ale wychodze z niego* i znow mam nadzieje ze sie uda
[Czasem *dołek przyłazi, ale wychodzę z niego* i znów mam nadzieję, że się uda.]
lit. 'sometimes *a pit comes, but I walk out of it* and again I hope that it will work'
'sometimes *depression comes, but I get out of it* and again I hope that it will work'
(amalfi 26-10-2010, 19:42,
http://www.babyboom.pl/forum/staramy-sie-f66/starania-po-raz-pierwszy-42617-print/index13.html?pp=40)

(23) Dziękuje za wsparcie w dzień jeszcze jakoś funkcjonuje ale wieczorami *czuję potężnego doła* tak jak by mi się życie wymykało z rąk.
[Dziękuję za wsparcie; w dzień jeszcze jakoś funcjonuję, ale *wieczorami czuję potężnego doła*, tak jakby mi się życie wymykało z rąk.]
lit. 'Thank you for your support. During the day I function somewhat but in the evenings *I feel a great pit* just as if my life is out of control.'
'Thank you for your support. During the day I function somehow, but in the evenings *I feel a great depression* just as if my life is out of control.'
(jamajka* 24-06-2009, 22:24,
http://www.babyboom.pl/forum/mamuskowo-f313/czuje-ze-jestem-zla-matka-28058-print/?pp=40)

(24) Dodam jeszcze że mały jest skrajnym wcześniakiem, więc dodatkowo miałam zrycie totalne. Po prostu *dół bez dna*

[Dodam jeszcze, że mały jest skrajnym wcześniakiem, więc dodatkowo miałam zrycie totalne. *Po prostu dół bez dna.*]
lit. 'I should add that the child is an extreme premature, so additionally I had a total massacre. *Simply a bottomless pit*'
'I should add that the child is an extreme premature, so additionally I had a total massacre. *Simply depression without end*'
(kerna 28-06-2009, 00:22,
http://www.babyboom.pl/forum/mamuskowo-f313/czuje-ze-jestem-zla-matka-28058-print/?pp=40)

(25) ASIEŃKA WIDOCZNIE TO TEN WIEK BO iWA TEZ TAK ROBI A JAK JEJ NIE POZWOLE TO *WPADA W CZARNA ROZPACZ*:-)
[Asieńka, widocznie to ten wiek, bo Iwa też tak robi, a jak jej nie pozwolę to *wpada w czarną rozpacz.*]
lit. 'Asienka it's obviously that age because Iwa does that too and if I don't allow her, she *falls into a black despair*:-)'
'Asienka it's obviously that age because Iwa does that too and if I don't allow her *she despairs*:-)'
(WIOLKA1509 12-01-2011, 15:22,
http://www.babyboom.pl/forum/mamuskowo-f313/mamusie-i-ich-malenstwa-2009-a-35002-print/index57.html?pp=40)

(26) u mnie ogolnie *dolina*...oboje myslimy nad rozstaniem...
[U mnie ogólnie *dolina*... Oboje myślimy nad rozstaniem.]
lit. 'and with me it's generally *a valley*...we're both thinking about splitting up...'
'and with me it's *just depression*...we're both thinking about splitting up...'
(natalya 02-08-2006, 12:56,
http://www.babyboom.pl/forum/troche-intymnosci-f15/zdrada-5378-print/index5.html?pp=40)

Example (27) makes use not only of the metaphorical expression *mieć doła* (lit. to have a pit) but also presents a very interesting comparison. *Dół* 'pit', standing for depression, is not described as deep but compared to Kościuszko Mound which is 34.1 meters high. One can *have a pit* (*mieć doła*), but also *catch a pit* (*złapać doła*). The *pit* is something one can *come out of* (*wyjść z*).

(27) tuśka uwierz mi *doła miałabyś jak kopiec kościuszki w Krakowie*
[Tuśka, wierz mi, *doła miałabyś jak Kopiec Kościuszki w Krakowie.*]
lit. 'tuśka believe me *you'd have a pit like Kościuszko Mound in Kraków*'
'tuśka believe me *you'd be so down*'
(jus20sto 30-12-2005, 14:24,
http://www.babyboom.pl/forum/troche-intymnosci-f15/13-pytan-o-antykoncepcje-3119-print/?pp=40)

The author of (28) tells how tired and depressed she was when her baby was born. *Byłam wymięta* 'I was creased' corresponds to 'I was tired' and it exemplifies the metaphor PEOPLE ARE CLOTHES. The second metaphorical expression used in (28) shows the psyche as an animated being with legs, so PSYCHE IS A LIVING CREATURE. The "upright or standing position" of the psyche means that a person is well. *Moja psychika leży* 'my psyche is lying down' is used to express the feeling of being depressed.

(28) Nie widziałam ludzi, nikt nie przychodził. kupa, żygi, cholernie bolące piersi z zapaleniem ropnym, godziny płaczu, noszenie na rękach...w kółko to smo. mąż wracał po 20 a *ja byłam tak wymieta*.... Było coraz gorzej. Jakoś na szczescie udało mi *postawić psychikę na nogi* i funkcjonowałam jakoś, zaczęłam się uśmiechac i minęło.
[Nie widziałam ludzi, nikt nie przychodził. Kupa, rzygi, cholernie bolące piersi z zapaleniem ropnym, godziny płaczu, noszenie na rękach... W kółko to samo. Mąż wracał po 20, a *ja byłam tak wymięta*... Było coraz gorzej. Jakoś, na szczęście, udało mi *postawić psychikę na nogi* i funkcjonowałam jakoś, zaczęłam się uśmiechać i minęło.]
lit. 'I didn't see people, no one came by. Poop, vomit, damn painful breasts with purulent inflammation, hours of crying, carrying the child in arms...all the time the same. Husband came back after 8 pm and *I was so creased*....It got worse. Somehow, luckily I managed to *put my psyche on its legs* and I functioned, I started to smile and it passed.'
'I didn't see people, no one came by. Poop, vomit, damn painful breasts with purulent inflammation, hours of crying, carrying the child in arms...all the time the same. Husband came back after 8pm and *I was ragged*... It got worse. Somehow, luckily I managed to *get on my feet* and I functioned, I started to smile and it passed.'
(kerna 28-06-2009, 00:22,
http://www.babyboom.pl/forum/mamuskowo-f313/czuje-ze-jestem-zla-matka-28058-print/?pp=40)

3.2.1.4 Metaphors of happiness and sadness

Sentences (29) and (30) exemplify the metaphor HAPPY IS UP. This metaphor presupposes another metaphor, namely SAD IS DOWN.

(29) Czasem jest mi bardzo ciężko i wtedy staram się sobie przypomnieć te słowa- niech i *one podniosą cię na duchu.*
'Sometimes it's very hard and then I try to remember those words – let them *lift your spirits up.*'
(AgaMP 31-12-2005, 11:22,
http://www.babyboom.pl/forum/troche-intymnosci-f15/13-pytan-o-antykoncepcje-3119-print/?pp=40)

(30) Czesc dziewczyny :) Wszystkie starajace sie 30-latki – *głowy do góry*!!!!
[Cześć dziewczyny :) Wszystkie starające się trzydziestolatki – głowy do góry!!!!]
lit. 'Hi girls :-) All those 30-year-olds who are trying – *heads up*!!!!'
'Hi girls :-) All those 30-year-olds who are trying – *chins up*!!!!'
(Klaudia 15-11-2005, 10:16
http://www.babyboom.pl/forum/staramy-sie-f66/1-dziecko-po-30-stce-7471-print/index3.html?pp=40)

3.2.1.5 Metaphors of other feelings and emotions

In example (31) *panic* is treated as a seed one can sow, hence the metaphor PANIC IS A PLANT.

(31) nie podejrzewałam ze to cos tak poważnego w tvn24 uspokajali ze to nic takiego, ale pewnie zeby *nie siac paniki*
[Nie podejrzewałam, że to coś tak poważnego. W TVN24 uspokajali, że to nic takiego, ale pewnie, żeby *nie siać paniki*.]
lit. 'I haven't suspected that it was something so serious. In TVN24 they calmed the fears, that it's nothing serious but probably not to *sew a panic*.'
'I never suspected that it was something so serious. In TVN24 they calmed the fears, that it's nothing serious but probably not to *start a panic*.'
(fresh83 16-04-2010, 22:37,
http://www.babyboom.pl/forum/mamuskowo-f313/mamusie-i-ich-malenstwa-2009-a-35002-print/index40.html?pp=40)

In examples (32) and (33) emotions are associated with temperature. In (32) the relationship between people before childbirth is described as *hot* (*gorący*), but lack of sex after giving birth caused *an ice age* (*epoka lodowcowa*) in the marriage. This is an example of the metaphor LACK OF EMOTIONS IS ICE.

(32) A ja długo nie mogłąm dojść do siebie…długo…nawet teraz średnio mi się chce. *U nas chłód a nawet epoka lodowcowa*…:sorry:NA początku bałam się pierwszego razu po porodzie. Potem jakoś to przełknęłam i było ok. Ale mimo to sex jest raz na 2,3 tyg, a nawet miesiąc. Co najgorsze ja wyrabiam i mąż też!!!! To mnie zastanawia. *Koniec gorącego związku…*
[A ja długo nie mogłam dojść do siebie… Długo… Nawet teraz średnio mi się chce. *U nas chłód, a nawet epoka lodowcowa…* Na początku bałam się pierwszego razu po porodzie. Potem jakoś to przełknęłam i było ok. Ale mimo to, seks jest raz na 2, 3 tygodnie, a nawet miesiąc. Co najgorsze, ja wyrabiam i mąż też!!!! To mnie zastanawia. *Koniec gorącego związku…*]
'And I couldn't get over it for a long time… long… even now I really don't want to. *With us it's cold, even an ice age…* At the beginning I was afraid of the first time after giving birth. After that somehow I got past that and it was okay. But despite that, we have sex once every 2, 3 weeks, even a month. What's worse is that I'm

doing fine with this and my husband too!!!! It makes me think. *The end of a hot relationship…*'
(kerna 12-11-2009, 22:47,
http://www.babyboom.pl/forum/troche-intymnosci-f15/maz-nie-ma-ochoty-na-sex-33070-print/?pp=40)

(33) Myślę, że istotą tutaj są powody, dla których doszło do zdrady, o ile łatwiej wybaczyć komuś kto np. "zbłądził", kto po próbach walki o związek trafił na "okazję", niż komuś kto *zrobił to na zimno*, z nudów, bez dania szansy swojemu związkowi…
'I think that important here are the reasons for betrayal, how easy it is to forgive someone who, e.g. "went astray", who having previously fought for the relationship, came across an "opportunity", than someone who *did it in cold blood*, out of boredom, without giving the relationship a chance…'
(Tygrynka 21-02-2011, 14:31,
http://www.babyboom.pl/forum/troche-intymnosci-f15/zdrada-5378-print/index8.html?pp=40)

In (34) the love *has burned out* (*wypaliła się*), so the lack of love makes the relationship cold. This is an instance of the metaphor LOVE IS FIRE.

(34) no wlasnie,zycie jest starsznie kruche.W kazdym zwiazku sa lepsze i gorsze chwile,ale nie mozemy pozwolic,by te zle przytumily nasze uczucia.Oczywiscie sa przypadki,gdzie ta *milosc sie wypalila* i nie ma juz co do ratowania.
[No właśnie, życie jest strasznie kruche. W każdym związku są lepsze i gorsze chwile, ale nie możemy pozwolić, by te złe przytłumiły nasze uczucia. Oczywiście są przypadki, gdzie ta *miłość sie wypaliła* i nie ma juz co do ratowania.]
'Exactly, life is horribly fragile. In every relationship there are good and bad moments, but we can't allow those bad moments to smother our feelings. Of course, there are cases where *love has burned out* and there is nothing to save.'
(Kopka 10-03-2012, 09:49,
http://www.babyboom.pl/forum/troche-intymnosci-f15/maz-nie-ma-ochoty-na-sex-33070-print/index6.html?pp=40)

The phrase *brać sobie coś do serca* 'to take something to heart' in (35) has a similar English equivalent and the meaning is exactly the same, namely 'to worry about something'. Here the metaphors THE HEART IS A CONTAINER and PROBLEMS ARE OBJECTS are employed. The use of the noun *serce* 'heart' may be treated as an example of metonymy as well because the heart is associated with emotions.

(35) My kobiety mamy ciezko wszystko strasznie *bierzemy sobie do serca* i potem cierpimy zamiast olac sprawe i zapomniec dziwne z nas stworzenia
[My kobiety mamy ciężko, wszystko strasznie *bierzemy sobie do serca* i potem cierpimy zamiast olać sprawę i zapomnieć, dziwne z nas stworzenia.]

lit. 'We women have it tough, we *take everything to heart* and then we suffer instead of *peeing on the matter* and forgetting what strange creatures we are'
'We women have it tough, we *take things to heart* and then we suffer instead of *ignoring the matter* and forgetting what strange creatures we are'
(olka21 01-07-2006, 10:53,
http://www.babyboom.pl/forum/troche-intymnosci-f15/zdrada-5378-print/index3.html?pp=40)

In example (36) the heart is animated because it is supposed to find space and to love a child, but it is also treated as a building or container in which there is enough space.

(36) Fresh83, NO CO TY????????? na pewno *twoje serducho znajdzie wystarczająco duzo miejsca na pokochanie drugiego dziecka*!!!
[Fresh83, NO CO TY????????? Na pewno *twoje serducho znajdzie wystarczająco dużo miejsca na pokochanie drugiego dziecka*!!!]
lit. 'Fresh83, NO WAY?????????? I'm sure *that your heart will find enough space to love another child*!!!'
'Fresh83, NO WAY?????????? I'm sure *that in your heart there is enough room to love another child*!!!'
(Anna28 09-06-2010, 12:32,
http://www.babyboom.pl/forum/mamuskowo-f313/mamusie-i-ich-malenstwa-2009-a-35002-print/index49.html?pp=40)

The clause *twoje serducho znajdzie wystarczajaco dużo miejsca na pokochanie drugiego dziecka* 'your heart will find enough space to love another child' may be treated as a case of metaphtonymy which combines the metonymy THE HEART FOR THE HUMAN BEING and the metaphor THE HEART IS A CONTAINER.

3.2.2 Metaphors of relationships

This section contains metaphors of relationships. In examples (37) and (38) relationships between people are described as *sick* (*chore*) which gives rise to the metaphor RELATIONSHIPS ARE LIVING ORGANISMS.

(37) a co do fascynacji innymi facetami/kobietami... ja uwazam, ze to absolutnie normalne. i nie znaczy to, ze *zwiazek jest chory*...
[A co do fascynacji innymi facetami / kobietami... Ja uważam, ze to absolutnie normalne i nie znaczy to, że *związek jest chory*...]
'and when it comes to fascination in other man/women... I think that this is absolutely normal and doesn't mean that the *relationship is sick*...'
(marianeczka 10-09-2006, 01:31,
http://www.babyboom.pl/forum/troche-intymnosci-f15/zdrada-5378-print/index6.html?pp=40)

(38) Kto ukrywa chorobę ten nie znajdzie lekarstwa - *niestety zdrada częstokroć dotyczy choroby ogólnoustrojowej związku..*
'He who hides an illness will not find a cure – *unfortunately cheating often concerns systemic relationship illnesses..*'
(Agawa 28-07-2006, 17:48,
http://www.babyboom.pl/forum/troche-intymnosci-f15/zdrada-5378-print/index4.html?pp=40)

Example (39) presents two different metaphorical expressions. In the first case, the author describes her broken marriage as *ruins* (*ruiny*), which shows the metaphor RELATIONSHIPS ARE BUILDINGS. In the second case, the author is talking about feelings which she does not have any more, and she says *uczucia wyparowały* 'feelings evaporated' which exemplifies the metaphor FEELINGS ARE FLUIDS.

(39) Codziennie wieczorem pytał, potem zamęczał, dręczył, ja płakałam, on mówił, że już go nie kocham, zaczął odwalać straszne rzeczy, ogólnie *ruina z naszego związku pozostała*. Powoli *odparowują ze mnie resztki miłości, namiętności i dawnych uczuć*.
'Every evening he asked, then he tormented, I cried, he said that I don't love him anymore, he started to say terrible things, *our relationship turned to ruins*. Slowly all the rest of love, passion and old feelings evaporated.'
(singing_mama 15-06-2009, 16:24,
http://www.babyboom.pl/forum/troche-intymnosci-f15/czy-ochota-na-seks-po-porodzie-jeszcze-kiedys-nadejdzie-11-print/index4.html?pp=40)

The phrase *iść łatwiejszą drogą* 'to walk the easier way' in example (40) is used to describe situations in which people do not make any effort or try hard enough to be happy in their relationships. It means 'to give up', 'to choose a solution which is the easiest and the least troublesome', like cheating or divorce for instance.

(40) Bo teraz ludzie o wiele szybciej się poddają, nie walczą o swoje i drugiej osoby szczęście, *tylko idą łatwiejszą drogą.*
lit. 'Because now people give up too quickly, they don't fight for their or the other person's happiness, *they walk the easy way.*'
'Because now people give up too quickly, they don't fight for their or the other person's happiness, *they choose the easy way.*'
(Tygrynka 21-02-2011, 14:31,
http://www.babyboom.pl/forum/troche-intymnosci-f15/zdrada-5378-print/index8.html?pp=40)

Other metaphorical expressions are used in example (41). The first one represents the metaphor LIFE IS A PATH. The verb *zbłądzić* 'to go astray' means 'to make mistakes or bad decisions'. The expression *przyprawiać komuś rogi* (lit. to give horns to someone) meaning 'to cheat oa partner or a spouse', this expression exemplifies the metaphor MAN IS AN ANIMAL. The third metaphorical expression, *szukać ze świecą w ręku* 'to look for somebody/something with a candle in one's hand', means 'to look for something precious, extraordinary and uncommon'.

> (41) święta napewno nie jestem, *kazdy moze w zyciu zbłądzic* ale trzeba miec jakies zasady a nie byc dumnym z tego ze sie *rogi mezowi przyprawialo*. a i jeszcze jedno,moze i *szukac ze swieca w reku mezczyzn* ktorzy wybaczaja zdrade swoim zonom…
> [Święta na pewno nie jestem, *każdy może w życiu zbłądzić*, ale trzeba mieć jakieś zasady, a nie być dumnym z tego, że się *rogi mężowi przyprawiało*. A i jeszcze jedno, może i *szukać ze świecą w ręku mężczyzn*, którzy wybaczają zdradę swoim żonom…]
> lit. 'I'm certainly no saint, *everyone can go astray* but you have to have rules and not be proud of the fact that *the husband has been given horns*. And one more thing, maybe *you have to look with a candle in your hand for a man* who would forgive his wife for cheating…
> 'I'm certainly no saint, *everyone makes mistakes* but you have to have rules and not be proud of the fact that *you cheated on your husband*. And one more thing, maybe *you have to look far and wide to find a man* who would forgive his wife for cheating… (Pati26 13-08-2006, 23:35,
> http://www.babyboom.pl/forum/troche-intymnosci-f15/zdrada-5378-print/index5.html?pp=40)

The phrase *iść przez życie* 'to go through life' in (42) used in describing relationships exemplifies the highly conventionalized and frequently used metaphor LIFE IS A PATH which shows considerable similarities with the metaphor LIFE IS A JOURNEY.

> (42) Pomimo wszystko nadal go kocham, nie zdradza mnie (tego nie powinno się być pewnym, ale ja jestem, bo *łatwiej przez życie iść u boku kogoś* komu się ufa), jest wspaniałym ojcem, a to jest na prawdę ważne.
> 'In spite of everything I still love him, he doesn't cheat on me (I shouldn't be sure of that but I am because *it's easier to go through life* with someone at your side who you trust), he is a wonderful father, and that is really important.'
> (singing_mama 17-06-2009, 13:47,
> http://www.babyboom.pl/forum/troche-intymnosci-f15/czy-ochota-na-seks-po-porodzie-jeszcze-kiedys-nadejdzie-11-print/index5.html?pp=40)

References to war are numerous in comments about relationships. Considering the experiential basis of such metaphorical expressions, it seems that the interconnectedness between the source and target domains is based on cultural experiences. Especially metaphorical expressions containing words for fight are widely used in everyday language. One can *fight* for the other person (43), children can *fight* with their parents, employees can *fight* for a pay rise, or a wife can *fight* with her husband for a remote control, all without the actual use of violence.

In examples (43) and (44), highly conventionalised metaphorical expressions are presented. People who try to *fix* their marriages and relationships with other people *fight*. This suggests that it is not easy to achieve the goal and that there are many obstacles to overcome.

In example (43) the husband *fought* (*walczył*) for his wife and marriage when problems occurred.

(43) Ale dzięki mojemu mężowi to pokonaliśmy, bo *walczył o mnie* i będę mu za to wdzięczna do końca życia.
'But thanks to my husband we beat it because *he fought for me* and I will be grateful to him forever.'
(Mamcia Paulinki 08-03-2012, 12:57,
http://www.babyboom.pl/forum/troche-intymnosci-f15/maz-nie-ma-ochoty-na-sex-33070-print/index6.html?pp=40)

Example (44) depicts a situation in which a woman was trying to fix her marriage and forgave her husband cheating on her because she did not want the other woman to *win* (*wygrać*) and be with her husband.

(44) Ja wybaczylam i *zawalczylam*.Bo *nie chcialam zeby ta suka wygrala*.Tu na poczatku chodzilo o urazona ambicje,ale po dlugim czasie nauczylam sie go na nowo kochac.
[Ja wybaczyłam i *zawalczyłam*, bo *nie chciałam żeby ta suka wygrała*. Tu na początku chodziło o urażoną ambicję, ale po długim czasie nauczyłam sie go na nowo kochać.]
'I forgave and I *fought*. Because *I didn't want that bitch to win*. At the beginning it was about hurt ambitions but after a long time I learned to love him again.'
(karolina1978 11-04-2011, 20:09,
http://www.babyboom.pl/forum/troche-intymnosci-f15/zdrada-5378-print/index9.html?pp=40)

The author of (45) describes a situation in which her husband is having an affair. She suggests that there are three ways of dealing with the situation. The author chooses the second option, which is trying to fix the marriage by engaging in a conflict with the other woman. In example (45), the Polish fixed phrase *zacisnąć zwieracze* 'to tighten one's sphincter' corresponds to the English expression *to clench one's teeth*. Both of them mean 'to accept the current situation without complaining'.

(45) Kopka – w takich jak i innych przypadkach kobieta ma 3 wyjścia: 1 pogodzić sie z rzeczywistością, *zacisnąć zwieracze* i żyć z dnia na dzień, 2 *użyć tej samej broni co przeciwnik lub większego kalibru*, 3 rozwód.
Ja postanowiłam że wybiorę wariant 2 z tym, że *użyję bazuki* :-)

'kopka – in situations like that a woman has three choices: 1 deal with reality, clench your teeth and live day by day, 2 *use the same weapon as your opponent but with a higher calibre*, 3 divorce.
I decided to choose number 2 but I'll *use a bazooka* :-)'
(K@m@ 30-11-2011, 22:02,
http://www.babyboom.pl/forum/troche-intymnosci-f15/maz-nie-ma-ochoty-na-sex-33070-print/index5.html?pp=40)

3.2.3 Metaphors of sex

This section presents two metaphors of SEX. Discussion threads connected with sex are quite popular on forums for parents, but the language used there is rather simply informative, not metaphorical.

An interesting example of a novel metaphor is presented in (46), namely LIBIDO IS A HUMAN BEING. The author describes a situation in which she does not feel like having sex during pregnancy. Her libido is not only animated but personified as well because it *has gone on vacation* (*poszło na urlop*).

(46) Mnie to się nie chce teraz w ciąży, *libido poszło na urlop i nie chce wrócić*.
'I don't want to do it being pregnant now, *my libido has gone on vacation and doesn't want to return.*'
(kbetina 22-07-2010, 18:31,
http://www.babyboom.pl/forum/troche-intymnosci-f15/kiepski-malzenski-sex-39889-print/index3.html?pp=40)

In sentences (47) sperm is described as *ammunition*. In sentence (47) *armed ammunition* is connected with the state of erection. This metaphorical expression exemplifies the general metaphor SEX IS WAR, and a more specific one, THE PENIS IS A GUN.

(47) nie znam innych mężczyzn, ale u mnie tak jest, że gdy już się nastawimy i żona w trakcie przestanie, bo sama jest zaspokojona, czy w trakcie jej się odechce, to jestem troszkę "napęczniały" i jest to troszkę flustrujące, a i sam sprzęt troszkę doskwiera od *"nabicia amonicją"*.
[Nie znam innych mężczyzn, ale u mnie tak jest, że gdy już się nastawimy i żona w trakcie przestanie, bo sama jest zaspokojona, czy w trakcie jej się odechce, to jestem troszkę „napęczniały" i jest to troszkę frustrujące, a i sam sprzęt troszkę doskwiera od „*nabicia amonicją*".]
'I don't know other men, but with me it's like when the wife stops because she has been satisfied, or when during she doesn't want any more, I'm a little "swollen" and it's a little frustrating and the equipment itself suffers from "*armed ammunition*".'
(mazitatus 19-08-2010, 00:18,
http://www.babyboom.pl/forum/troche-intymnosci-f15/kiepski-malzenski-sex-39889-print/index3.html?pp=40)

3.2.4 Metaphors of conception

Three metaphors of CONCEPTION are presented in this section. Similarly to discussion threads about sex, conceiving is not a topic in which people use numerous metaphorical expressions. Nevertheless, the metaphor TRYING TO CONCEIVE A CHILD IS GOING TO WAR can be noticed.

The author of example (48) gives advice to another woman still trying to conceive. The sperm is *soldiers* (*żołnierzyki*) which must be strong and of a good quality in order to make the woman pregnant.

(48) Dzialaj, dzialaj.kacha Nie ważne kiedy owulacja przyjdze oby tylko *zolnierzyki były w pogotowiu zwarte i gotowe* na nadchodzace jajeczko no i pamiętaj żeby *zmieniać armie* co drugi dzień :)))))
[Działaj, działaj Kacha. Nieważne kiedy owulacja przyjdzie, oby tylko *żolnierzyki były w pogotowiu zwarte i gotowe* na nadchodzące jajeczko no i pamiętaj, żeby *zmieniać armie* co drugi dzień :)))))]
'Act, act kacha. It doesn't matter when ovulation will come as long as the *soldiers are on standby and ready* for the upcoming egg and don't forget to *change the army* every other day :)))))'
(Nadzieja:) 07-10-2010, 19:48,
http://www.babyboom.pl/forum/staramy-sie-f66/starania-po-raz-pierwszy-42617-print/index8.html?pp=40)

In (49), getting pregnant after the first try is described as 'hitting the target'.

(49) dzięki, dzięki, miałyście jakieś problemy z zajściem bo ja żadnego-*stzał celny* za pierwszym razem!
[dzięki, dzięki, miałyście jakieś problemy z zajściem, bo ja żadnego – strzał celny za pierwszym razem!]
lit. 'Thanks, thanks, did you have any problems with falling pregnant because I didn't – *hit the target* first time!'
'Thanks, thanks, did you have any problems with falling pregnant because I didn't – *bull's eye* the first time!'
(ewan 21-11-2005, 22:03,
http://www.babyboom.pl/forum/staramy-sie-f66/1-dziecko-po-30-stce-7471-print/index3.html?pp=40)

In (50) the noun *ślepak* 'blank' (in the plural) is used to describe sperm which is not of good quality and strong enough to make a woman pregnant.

(50) Zgadzam się-co drugi dzień-nie częściej… żeby *ślepaków nie było* ;)
'I agree – every other day – not more often… *so there are no blanks* ;)'
(Martusia85 07-10-2010, 18:51,
http://www.babyboom.pl/forum/staramy-sie-f66/starania-po-raz-pierwszy-42617-print/index8.html?pp=40)

3.2.5 Metaphors of bringing up children

In following examples the process of bringing up children is described as fighting (51) and battles (52), which exemplifies the metaphor BRINGING UP CHILDREN IS WAR. The verb *walczyć* 'fight' in (51) means 'to try with all might'.

> (51) probowalam wprowadzic smoczek zaraz po urodzeniu i *walczylam* codziennie gdzies do 3 miesiaca a teraz dalam sobie już spokoj....
> [Próbowałam wprowadzić smoczek zaraz po urodzeniu i *walczyłam* codziennie gdzieś do 3. miesiąca, a teraz dałam sobie już spokój....]
> 'I tried to introduce the dummy right after the birth and *I fought* every day for about 3 months and now I've just given up...'
> (WIOLKA1509 06-02-2010, 15:58,
> http://www.babyboom.pl/forum/mamuskowo-f313/mamusie-i-ich-malenstwa-2009-a-35002-print/index16.html?pp=40)

In example (52) *battles* (*boje*) correspond to everyday dilemmas and problems connected with bringing up children.

> (52) w sierpniu urodzilam „lwiatko", ktoremu na imie dalismy Milan (taki sentiment do czeskich imion;-)) i zapraszam do *wspolnych bojów*
> [W sierpniu urodziłam „lwiątko", któremu na imię daliśmy Milan (taki sentyment do czeskich imion;-)) i zapraszam do *wspólnych bojów*.]
> 'In August I gave birth to a little "lion cub", who we called Milan (such a sentiment to Czech names ;-)) and I invite you to *common battles*.'
> (fresh83 11-03-2010, 15:25,
> http://www.babyboom.pl/forum/mamuskowo-f313/mamusie-i-ich-malenstwa-2009-a-35002-print/index31.html?pp=40)

3.2.6 Metaphors of children's progress

This subsection presents metaphorical expressions used to talk about children's progress.

To show how rapid and quick the development of a child was, the author of (53) uses the phrase *eksplodowała z dalszym rozwojem* '(she) exploded with further development'.

> (53) Mariczka przez święta *eksplodowała z dalszym rozwojem*. Potrafi już podpełznąć do zabawki i zaczyna stawać na kolankach.
> 'Through the holidays Mariczka *exploded with further development*. She can crawl to toys and get on her knees.'
> (lagajka 07-04-2010, 08:49,
> http://www.babyboom.pl/forum/mamuskowo-f313/mamusie-i-ich-malenstwa-2009-a-35002-print/index38.html?pp=40)

The author of (54) comments on the progress her child (*Zu* is a clipped form of *Zuzia*, a diminutive of *Zuzanna*) made in a short time using the metaphor PROGRESS IS GOING UP. Her conclusion is that this is happening thanks to the fact that her older siblings help her in gaining new skills and stimulate her progress.

> (54) Nie no Zu jest mega fantastyczna!! Myślę że po części *starsze rodzeństwo ciągnie ją w górę* :)
> [Nie, no Zu jest mega fantastyczna!! Myślę, że po części *starsze rodzeństwo ciągnie ją w górę* :)]
> 'Well Zu is mega fantastic!! I think that the *older siblings are pulling her up with them* :)'
> (lagajka 17-05-2010, 22:11,
> http://www.babyboom.pl/forum/mamuskowo-f313/mamusie-i-ich-malenstwa-2009-a-35002-print/index46.html?pp=40)

Example (55) contains one of the most cliched metaphorical expressions in Polish. *Coś idzie* 'something goes/walks' means 'something makes progress'. Various things can *go/walk* (*iść*), one can ask both in Polish and English: *Jak ci idzie praca?* / *How is your work going?*, *Jak ci idzie w pracy?* / *How are the things going at work?*, *Jak ci idzie z partnerem/rodzicem/szefem/etc.?* / *How is it going with your partner/parent/boss/etc.?*

> (55) ciezko jej idzie chodzenie ale przy meblach sie przesowa
> [Ciężko jej idzie chodzenie, ale przy meblach się przesuwa.]
> lit. '*walking is going hard for her* but she can move holding on to the furniture'
> '*she's finding it difficult to walk* but she can move holding on to the furniture'
> (porzeczkas 24-09-2010, 11:48,
> http://www.babyboom.pl/forum/mamuskowo-f313/mamusie-i-ich-malenstwa-2009-a-35002-print/index55.html?pp=40)

3.2.7 Metaphors of the human body

3.2.7.1 Metaphors of parts of the body

Four metaphors of PARTS OF THE BODY are presented in this section.

The author of (56) treats her spine as an animated being which *calls for help* (*woła o pomoc*) because of the pain.

> (56) Gabi też jest ostatnio mamusiowa... nic tylko wszędzie ze mną, na ręce... a *mój kręgosłup teraz jak jeszcze śpi mi na rękach woła o pomoc* ;)
> 'Gabi is being a mummy's girl lately... everywhere with me, in my arms... and when she is sleeping in my arms, *my spine is calling for help* ;)'
> (karlita 16-04-2010, 19:13,

http://www.babyboom.pl/forum/mamuskowo-f313/mamusie-i-ich-malenstwa-2009-a-35002-print/index40.html?pp=40)

The phrase *rzucić na kogoś/coś okiem* 'to throw one's eye on somebody/something' employed in (57) is one of the most commonly used and most cliched metaphorical expressions in Polish. The meaning of this phrase is 'to take a look, to glance'. The eye is treated as an object separated from the body.

(57) lekarz uspokajal mnie ze to napewno nic takiego i z czasem zniknie ale zawsze lepiej jak *specjalista rzuci okiem*
[Lekarz uspakajał mnie, że to na pewno nic takiego i z czasem zniknie, ale zawsze lepiej jak *specjalista rzuci okiem*.]
lit. 'the doctor assured me that it's nothing serious and it will disappear with time but it's always better to get a *specialist to throw his eye*'
'the doctor assured me that it's nothing serious and it will disappear with time but it's always better to get a *specialist to take a look*'
(fresh83 20-04-2010, 13:12,
http://www.babyboom.pl/forum/mamuskowo-f313/mamusie-i-ich-malenstwa-2009-a-35002-print/index40.html?pp=40)

Post (58) exemplifies the metaphor HEADS ARE CONTAINERS INTO WHICH ONE CAN PUT OBJECTS.

(58) Miłe panie, uważajmy na to, co owe *koleżanki kładą nam do głów*, bo znam przypadki, że jedna drugiej nagadała, że jej syn jest niegrzeczny, bo za mało i słabo go bije..
'Dear ladies, let's be careful about what our friends *put in our heads*, because I know of cases when one tells the other that her son is naughty because she beats him too little and too weakly...'
(singing_mama 17-06-2009, 13:47,
http://www.babyboom.pl/forum/troche-intymnosci-f15/czy-ochota-na-seks-po-porodzie-jeszcze-kiedys-nadejdzie-11-print/index5.html?pp=40)

Example (59) makes use of the metaphors IDEAS/THOUGHTS ARE OBJECTS and HEADS ARE CONTAINERS into which they can be put.

(59) No właśnie!!! A nam czasem *głupoty wpadną do głowy* czy jesteśmy złymi matkami bo po 6 godzinach płaczu, lub 33 zmianie ciuszków od ulewania zaczyna się kurczyć cierpliwość a rosnąć ból głowy;-)
[No właśnie!!! A nam czasem *głupoty wpadną do głowy*, czy jesteśmy złymi matkami, bo po 6 godzinach płaczu, lub 33. zmianie ciuszków od ulewania, zaczyna się kurczyć cierpliwość, a rosnąć ból głowy;-)]
lit. 'Exactly!!! Sometimes *foolish thoughts fall into our heads* that we are bad mothers because after 6 hours of crying or the 33rd change of clothing from bringing up food our patience starts shrinking and the headache starts growing;-)'

'Exactly!!! Sometimes *foolish thoughts come to us* that we are bad mothers because after 6 hours of crying or the 33rd change of clothing from bringing up food our patience is frayed and we get headaches;-)'
(saly 05-07-2009, 00:06,
http://www.babyboom.pl/forum/mamuskowo-f313/czuje-ze-jestem-zla-matka-28058-print/?pp=40)

3.2.7.2 Metaphors of teeth

There are eighteen examples found on the Polish Internet forums for mothers that contain the metaphorical expression *teeth are coming/going/approaching* (*zęby idą*). This particular metaphor depicts teeth as animated beings that are able to move. It is a very frequently used metaphorical expression.

(60) Adasiowi *idzie kilka ząbków* na raz.
lit. 'To Adaś *several teeth are coming at once.*'
'Adaś is *getting several teeth at once.*'
(lenka87 05-07-2010, 18:12,
http://www.babyboom.pl/forum/mamuskowo-f313/mamusie-i-ich-malenstwa-2009-a-35002-print/index52.html?pp=40)

The author of sentence (61) used an uncommon metaphorical expression, *urodził się pierwszy ząbek* 'the first tooth was born'.

(61) a wiecie co w wielkich bólach *urodził nam się PIERWSZY ZĄBEK.*
[A wiecie co? W wielkich bólach *urodził nam się PIERWSZY ZĄBEK.*]
lit. 'Oh and you know that in the great pain, *the first tooth was born.*'
'Oh and you know that in the great pain, the first tooth *came through.*'
(aga_stanczyk 09-03-2010, 22:29,
http://www.babyboom.pl/forum/mamuskowo-f313/mamusie-i-ich-malenstwa-2009-a-35002-print/index30.html?pp=40)

Example (62) is taken from a conversation between several mothers who boasted that their children started teething at the same time. The author of (62) used the expression *zęby się sypnęły* 'teeth sprinkled themselves'.

(62) Widze, ze wszystkim dzieciaczkom *sie zabki sypnely* a Oliwcia dalej nic
[Widzę, że wszystkim dzieciaczkom *się ząbki sypnęły*, a Oliwcia dalej nic.]
lit. 'I see that *teeth have sprinkled themselves* for all the kids, and Oliwcia still nothing'
'I see that *teeth have come through* for all the kids, and Oliwcia still nothing'
(porzeczkas 11-05-2010, 13:18,
http://www.babyboom.pl/forum/mamuskowo-f313/mamusie-i-ich-malenstwa-2009-a-35002-print/index43.html?pp=40)

3.2.8 Metaphors of illnesses

The next set of examples presents, among others, the commonly used and highly conventionalised metaphor ILLNESSES ARE OBJECTS ONE CATCHES as in (63) and (64). In sentence (65), however, it is constipation that catches the person, so illnesses can be animated and can *catch* people as well.

(63) mała mi się gdzieś przeziębiła albo *złapała jakiegoś wirusa* od swoich braci ciotecznych....
'the little one has a cold or she *caught some virus* from her cousins...'
(karlita 14-04-2010, 18:06,
http://www.babyboom.pl/forum/mamuskowo-f313/mamusie-i-ich-malenstwa-2009-a-35002-print/index40.html?pp=40)

(64) witam, *moj synek zalapal katar*.
[Witam, *mój synek załapał katar*.]
lit. 'hello, my son has caught a runny nose.'
'hello, my son has a runny nose.'
(Anna28 08-04-2010, 05:17,
http://www.babyboom.pl/forum/mamuskowo-f313/mamusie-i-ich-malenstwa-2009-a-35002-print/index39.html?pp=40)

(65) A dziś chyba *złapało ją małe zaparcie* – wysilała się nad kupką, a wyszedł tylko kleks na pieluszce.
lit. 'And today I think *small constipation has caught her* – she tried hard to poop, and only a little stain in the nappy.'
'And today I think *she has minor constipation* – she tried hard to poop, and only a little stain in the nappy.'
(lagajka 16-04-2010, 10:23,
http://www.babyboom.pl/forum/mamuskowo-f313/mamusie-i-ich-malenstwa-2009-a-35002-print/index40.html?pp=40)

Fever (*gorączka*) in example (66) is animated and it *is coming* (*nadchodzi*) to a child.

(66) My dzis w domu caly dzien, mala chora byla w nocy i w ciagu dnia jeszcze nie do końca zdrowa, teraz czuje ze *goraczka znowu jej nachodzi*.
[My dziś w domu cały dzień, mała chora była w nocy i w ciągu dnia jeszcze nie do końca zdrowa, teraz czuję, że *gorączka znowu jej nachodzi*.]
lit. 'And we have been at home all day today, the little one was sick last night and during the day she's still not really healthy, now I feel that *fever is coming to her again*'
'And we're at home all day today, the little one was sick last night and during the day she's still not really healthy, now I feel that *she's coming down with fever again*.'
(WIOLKA1509 12-01-2011, 15:22,

http://www.babyboom.pl/forum/mamuskowo-f313/mamusie-i-ich-malenstwa-2009-a-35002-print/index57.html?pp=40)

A highly conventionalised metaphorical expression is presented in (67), namely DISEASE IS AN ENEMY. Diseases and viruses *attack* people.

(67) *grypa zoladkowa zaatakowala* wszystkich, ale juz po chorobie
[*Grypa żołądkowa zaatakowała* wszystkich, ale już po chorobie.]
'*gastric flu has attacked* everyone, but now the illness has passed'
(porzeczkas 10-05-2010, 13:44,
http://www.babyboom.pl/forum/mamuskowo-f313/mamusie-i-ich-malenstwa-2009-a-35002-print/index43.html?pp=40)

In example (68) two different metaphorical usages of the verb *łapać* 'to catch' are shown. A child not only did not *catch* a disease, but also *caught* good immunity.

(68) Mariczka chyba *złapała niezłą odporność* :) Przez weekend była po kilka godzin u Babci, bo musiałam jechać na zajęcia. Była też jej mocno przeziębiona siostra cioteczna, przebywały w jednym pomieszczeniu i nic *Skarbusia nie podłapała*.
lit. 'I think Mariczka *has caugh not a bad immunity* :) Over the weekend she was at grandma's for a few hours because I had to go to classes. Her cousin, who had a very bad cold, was also there and they were in the same room and *the Little Treasure didn't catch anything*.'
'I think Mariczka *has not bad immunity* :) Over the weekend she was at grandma's for a few hours because I had to go to classes. Her cousin, who had a very bad cold, was also there and they were in the same room, but *the Little Treasure didn't pick up anything*.'
(lagajka 12-04-2010, 10:30,
http://www.babyboom.pl/forum/mamuskowo-f313/mamusie-i-ich-malenstwa-2009-a-35002-print/index39.html?pp=40)

Example (69) describes an illness as an animated being able to move, in this case, *to go down* (*zejść*). The experiential basis for such a metaphor is the common knowledge that the bronchi are placed below the throat, that is why the infection goes down, not up.

(69) Milan na nowo kaszle i boje sie ze *zejdzie na oskrzela*
[Milan na nowo kaszle i boję się, że *zejdzie na oskrzela*.]
lit. 'Milan is coughing again and I'm afraid that *it will go down to his bronchi*'
'Milan is coughing again and I'm afraid that *it will move to his bronchi*'
(fresh83 03-03-2010, 13:03,
http://www.babyboom.pl/forum/mamuskowo-f313/mamusie-i-ich-malenstwa-2009-a-35002-print/index26.html?pp=40)

In examples (70) and (71) illnesses are treated as places one must *walk through* (*przejść przez*) or *walk out of* (*wyjść z*) in order to recover, so the metaphor ILLNESSES ARE PLACES is employed here.

(70) Bidulka maleńka… ale niestety nie ma rady, *musi przez to przejść.*
'The poor little thing… but unfortunately you can't do anything *she has to go through it.*'
(lagajka 04-02-2010, 22:31,
http://www.babyboom.pl/forum/mamuskowo-f313/mamusie-i-ich-malenstwa-2009-a-35002-print/index15.html?pp=40)

(71) Owszem, był incydent z tlenkiem węgla, ale *wyszła z tego na zupełną prostą.*
lit. 'Indeed there was the incident with carbon monoxide, *but she went out of it fully straight.*'
'Indeed there was the incident with carbon monoxide, but *she got through that.*'
(lagajka 13-05-2010, 22:22,
http://www.babyboom.pl/forum/mamuskowo-f313/mamusie-i-ich-malenstwa-2009-a-35002-print/index44.html?pp=40)

In example (72) headache has an ability to grow, so the metaphor HEADACHE IS A PLANT is employed.

(72) No właśnie!!! A nam czasem głupoty wpadną do głowy czy jesteśmy złymi matkami bo po 6 godzinach płaczu, lub 33 zmianie ciuszków od ulewania zaczyna się kurczyć cierpliwość a *rosnąć ból głowy*;-)
[No właśnie!!! A nam czasem głupoty wpadną do głowy, czy jesteśmy złymi matkami, bo po 6 godzinach płaczu, lub 33. zmianie ciuszków od ulewania, zaczyna się kurczyć cierpliwość, a *rosnąć ból głowy*;-)]
lit. 'Exactly!!! Sometimes foolish thoughts fall into our heads that we are bad mothers because after 6 hours of crying or the 33rd change of clothing from bringing up food our patience starts shrinking and the *headache starts growing*;-)'
'Exactly!!! Sometimes foolish thoughts come to us that we are bad mothers because after 6 hours of crying or the 33rd change of clothing from bringing up food our patience is frayed and we *get headaches*,-)'
(saly 05-07-2009, 00:06,
http://www.babyboom.pl/forum/mamuskowo-f313/czuje-ze-jestem-zla-matka-28058-print/?pp=40)

3.2.9 Metaphors of everyday life

In (73) one of the most conventionalized metaphorical expressions is used, namely *wyrwać się* 'to tear oneself off' meaning 'to get away'. This particular expression is deeply entrenched in Polish. The example contains another metaphorical expression: remorse is treated like an object with a weight.

(73) A ja dziś na pół dnia *urwałam się na zakupy* i wiecie, co? I powiem, że *nie mam ani grama wyrzutów sumienia*, że wymigałam się od opieki nad Dusią przez tyle czasu.
lit 'Today, for half a day, I *tore myself off for shopping* and you know what? I tell you, *I don't even have a gram of remorse* that I got away from looking after Dusia for so long.'
'Today, for half a day, I *got away shopping* and you know what? I tell you, *I don't even have a gram of remorse* that I got away from looking after Dusia for so long.'
(lagajka 21-03-2010, 21:37,
http://www.babyboom.pl/forum/mamuskowo-f313/mamusie-i-ich-malenstwa-2009-a-35002-print/index34.html?pp=40)

In example (74) stains are animated, they are able to move, in this case *to go down* (*zejść*).

(74) A marchewka no cóż, *plamy prawdopodobnie nie zejdą*
lit. 'Carrots, oh well, *the stains probably won't go down*'
'Carrots, oh well, *the stains probably won't come out*'
(asienka_r 03-03-2010, 12:25,
http://www.babyboom.pl/forum/mamuskowo-f313/mamusie-i-ich-malenstwa-2009-a-35002-print/index26.html?pp=40)

Post (75) presents a highly conventionalized and frequently used metaphorical expression *nie ma wyjścia* (lit. there is no exit), which means 'there is no choice'. This metaphorical expression is deeply entrenched in everyday language.

(75) A niektórzy nie mają rodziny pod bokiem i muszą w dosłownie obce ręce oddać na pół dnia szkraba, *bo nie ma wyjścia*…
[A niektórzy nie mają rodziny pod bokiem i muszą w dosłownie obce ręce oddać na pół dnia szkraba, *bo nie ma wyjścia*…]
lit. 'And some people don't have family at their side and they have to literally put their baby in strangers' arms, *because there is no exit*'
'And some people don't have family at their side and they have to literally put their baby in strangers' arms, *because they have no choice*'
(mmisiak 19-08-2010, 22:06,
http://www.babyboom.pl/forum/mamuskowo-f313/dramatyczny-powrot-do-pracy-43225-print/)

Post (76) depicts a situation in which a woman is so deeply convinced of the competences of her gynecologist in Poland that despite living abroad she always turns to him for help and advice. The metaphorical expression used is *uderzać do kogoś* 'come to ask for help' (lit. hit to somebody). The metaphor used, LOOKING FOR HELP IS KNOCKING TO SOMEBODY'S DOOR, is combined with another metaphor, A PERSON IS A HOUSE.

(76) A prawda jest taka ze lecze sie na odleglosc u gina w Krakowie..Jesli mam jakies pytania to *uderzam do niego* a nie do tego tutaj na miejscu

[A prawda jest taka, że leczę sie na odległość u ginekologa w Krakowie... Jeśli mam jakieś pytania, to *uderzam do niego*, a nie do tego tutaj na miejscu.]
lit. 'But the truth is that I'm getting treated distantly by a gynecologist in Kraków. If I have any questions *I hit to him* and not to the one here.'
'But the truth is that I'm getting treated distantly by a gynecologist in Kraków. If I have any questions *I turn to him* and not to the one here.'
(KINDZIA100 30-03-2006, 00:39,
http://www.babyboom.pl/forum/staramy-sie-f66/1-dziecko-po-30-stce-7471-print/index12.html?pp=40)

In example (77) the phrase *koncertować* 'to perform a concert' is used metaphorically to describe loud snoring.

(77) A z chrapaniem to serdecznie współczuję bo wiem co to znaczy. Jeszcze w ciąży wysłałam drania na operację przegrody nosowej, bo nie wyobrażałam sobie, że on będzie tak *koncertował* przy małym dziecku...
[A z chrapaniem to serdecznie współczuję, bo wiem, co to znaczy. Jeszcze w ciąży wysłałam drania na operację przegrody nosowej, bo nie wyobrażałam sobie, że on będzie tak *koncertował* przy małym dziecku...]
'I heartily sympathize with you about the snoring because I know what it means. When I was still pregnant I sent the wretch for an operation on his nasal septum because I couldn't imagine that he would *perform his concert* in front of a small child...'
(saly 06-07-2009, 12:42,
http://www.babyboom.pl/forum/mamuskowo-f313/czuje-ze-jestem-zla-matka-28058-print/index2.html?pp=40)

In (78) the Health Service is animated and to show how bad it is, the adjective *kulawa* 'limping' is used.

(78) Diablica – zgadzam się w 100%, a myślałam, że *nasza służba zdrowia taka kulawa*.
lit. 'Diablica – I agree with you 100% and I thought that *our health service was limping.*'
'Diablica – I agree with you 100% and I thought that *our health service was so lame.*'
(moniolek 29-03-2006, 17:23,
http://www.babyboom.pl/forum/staramy-sie-f66/1-dziecko-po-30-stce-7471-print/index12.html?pp=40)

The phrase *iść jak po maśle* 'to go like on butter' in (79) is another example of a metaphorical expression deeply entrenched in everyday language. The common knowledge that a surface covered in butter is slippery is the experiential basis for this metaphor.

(79) Dziewczyny nareszcie!!!! Teraz powinno *iść jak po maśle*.
lit. 'Finally girls!!!! Now it should *go like on butter.*'

'Finally girls!!!! Now it should *go smoothly.*'
(aga_stanczyk 09-03-2010, 22:29,
http://www.babyboom.pl/forum/mamuskowo-f313/mamusie-i-ich-malenstwa-2009-a-35002-print/index30.html?pp=40)

In example (80) two different metaphorical expressions are presented. The first one treats the Internet as a place one can enter and in the second one stains are animated.

(80) troszke mnie nie było, jakos nie miałam kiedy *wejsc na neta*... powiedzcie czym mam sprawc marchewke z małej ubranek, śliniaki nie spełniły swojej roli i młoda była ufajtana cała, moczyłam w waniszu pozniej prałam w jej proszku i płynie i niby lepiej ale *do konca nie zeszło*

[Troszkę mnie nie było, jakoś nie miałam kiedy *wejść na net*... Powiedzcie czym mam sprać marchewkę z małej ubranek, śliniaki nie spełniły swojej roli i młoda była ufajdana cała, moczyłam w Vaniszu, później prałam w jej proszku i płynie i niby lepiej, ale *do końca nie zeszło*]

lit. 'I wasn't here for a while, I somehow didn't have time *to enter on the Net*...tell me how I can wash carrot off the little's clothes, the bibs didn't serve their purpose and the little one was completely dirty, I soaked them in Vanish then I washed them in her washing powder and liquid and it's a little better but *didn't completely walked down.*'

'I wasn't here for a while, I somehow didn't have time *to go on the Net*...tell me how I can wash carrot off the little's clothes, the bibs didn't serve their purpose and the little one was completely dirty, I soaked them in Vanish then I washed them in her washing powder and liquid and it's a little better but *didn't completely come out.*'
(marzena.ch 03-03-2010, 13:08,
http://www.babyboom.pl/forum/mamuskowo-f313/mamusie-i-ich-malenstwa-2009-a-35002-print/index26.html?pp=40)

Guzik 'button' in example (81) corresponds to 'nothing'.

(81) *Rozmowa hmmm czasami guzik daje* i nic się nie da zrobić.
lit. 'Talking sometimes *gives a button* and nothing can be done.'
'Talking sometimes *doesn't help* and nothing can be done.'
(amarzena 24-06-2010, 22:46,
www.babyboom.pl/forum/troche-intymnosci-f15/kiepski-malzenski-sex-39889-print/index2.html?pp=40)

In (82) *iść do przodu* 'to go forward' means to 'make progress'.

(82) to ludzkie mieć dość… i również siły odzyskać i *iść do przodu*.
'It's human to be fed up… and also to regain your strength and *go forward*'.
(saly 05-07-2009, 00:06,
http://www.babyboom.pl/forum/mamuskowo-f313/czuje-ze-jestem-zla-matka-28058-print/?pp=40)

Examples (83) and (84) illustrate the metaphor QUEUE IS A CONTAINER. One can be *let into a queue* (*wpuszczony w kolejkę*), *stand in a queue* (*stać w kolejce*), *to get out of the queue* (*wypaść z kolejki*) or *occupy the queue* (*zająć kolejkę*). In English *to stand in a line* is analogous.

>(83) Mnie wielokrotnie *wpuszczono w kolejkę* w sklepie.
>'I have been *let into a queue* at the store repeatedly.'
>(Pandora 23-11-11, 20:30,
>http://mjakmama24.dlarodzinki.pl/threads/2356-Życzliwość-dla-mam-z-dziećmi-tak-czy-nie/index1.html)

>(84) Ja wczoraj w banku stałam chyba ze 40 minut *w kolejce*.
>'I stood yesterday *in a queue* in a bank for 40 minutes'
>(Ola0203 13-01-11, 14:06.
>http://mjakmama24.dlarodzinki.pl/threads/24-Więcej-życzliwości-dla-kobiet-w-ciąży/index5.html)

3.2.10 Metaphors of shopping

Forum users also use metaphors of shopping. Sentences (85) and (86) exemplify the metaphor SHOPPING IS HUNTING/FISHING.

>(85) Ja byłam ostatnio i *upolowałam dla Ani dwa ładne sweterki i dżinsy*
>lit. 'I was recently and *I hunted two lovely sweaters and jeans* for Ania.'
>'I was (shopping) recently and *I bought two lovely sweaters and jeans* for Ania.'
>(asienka_r 26-01-2010, 18:35,
>http://www.babyboom.pl/forum/mamuskowo-f313/mamusie-i-ich-malenstwa-2009-a-35002-print/index10.html)

In example (86) *łowić* 'to fish' corresponds to 'buy'.

>(86) wiecie co musze sie pochwalic!!! bylam dzis w second hand i *zlowilam koszule* z LEE w paseczki za 2,70zl uwielbiam takie zakupy
>[Wiecie co, muszę się pochwalić!!! Byłam dziś w second handzie i *złowiłam koszulę* z LEE w paseczki za 2,70 zł. Uwielbiam takie zakupy.]
>lit. 'You know what I have to boast about!!! I was in a second-hand shop today and I *fished a striped Lee shirt* for 2.70 zl. I love such shopping'
>'You know what I have to boast about!!! I was in a second-hand shop today and I *bought a striped Lee shirt* for 2.70 zl. I love such shopping'
>(fresh83 26-01-2010, 19:32,
>http://www.babyboom.pl/forum/mamuskowo-f313/mamusie-i-ich-malenstwa-2009-a-35002-print/index10.html)

3.2.11 Metaphors of problems and hardship

In this subsection, problems and hardship are pictured mainly by PATH metaphors. PATH metaphors can be categorized according to their level of conventionality. Expressions exemplifying these metaphors appear to be among the most cliched ones. Such metaphors are used in everyday language. Both in Polish and English, one can say that Christmas is *coming*, the spring is *coming*, better times are *coming* etc. In such cases, the events mentioned are understood in terms of animated beings. There is, however, one problematic case, namely the understanding of the word *way*. In English *way* can mean various things, for example:

> manner – *the way he acts is odd*;
> method – *do it your way*;
> style – *a way of dressing*;
> possibility/chance – *it's a good way to relieve pain*.

In Polish, on the other hand, *droga* 'way' is tantamount to a path, road, track or lane.

The author of (87) describes a situation in which she is fighting with her mother-in-law and her husband is not helpful or supportive. The metaphorical expression *przejść przez coś* 'to go through something' means to 'struggle'.

> (87) A moj to nie potrafi zrozumiec, *przez co przechodze* bo „mama tylko zartowala"
> [A mój to nie potrafi zrozumieć *przez co przechodzę*, bo „mama tylko żartowała".]
> 'And mine still can't understand *what I'm going through* because "mum was only joking"'
> (joklis 05-07-2009, 12:42,
> http://www.babyboom.pl/forum/mamuskowo-f313/czuje-ze-jestem-zla-matka-28058-print/index2.html?pp=40)

Example (88) presents two different metaphors. *Wchodzić komuś na głowę* 'to climb somebody's head' means 'to use somebody', 'to have power over somebody' and it exemplifies the POWER IS UP metaphor. *Ciężko mi to przychodzi* 'it comes hard to me' means that a person 'finds something difficult'. This metaphorical expression can be used in various contexts, for instance *asertywność ciężko mi przychodzi* 'assertiveness comes hard to me', *kochanie go ciężko mi przychodzi* 'loving him comes hard to me', *wybaczanie ciężko mi przychodzi* 'forgiving comes hard to me' etc.

> (88) Karolina, rzeczywiście biszkopty to się jeszcze da przeżyć, dobrze czasem powiedzieć, co się myśli, bo wtedy inni tak nie *wchodzą na głowę*, też powinnam, ale mi

to *czasem ciężko przychodzi, ale jak się udaje, że jest wszystko dobrze, jest o wiele gorzej, człowiek dusi to w sobie, a inni robią, co chcą i włażą na głowę.*
lit. 'Karolina, sponge cakes indeed aren't so bad, it's good sometimes to say what you think, because then others don't *climb on your head*, I should too, but it sometimes *comes hard to me* but when I pretend that everything is okay, it's a lot worse. We keep it to ourselves and others so what they want and they *climb on your head*.'
'Karolina, sponge cakes indeed aren't so bad, it's good sometimes to say what you think, because then others don't *run you ragged*, I should too, *but it is sometimes difficult for me*, but when I pretend that everything is okay, it's a lot worse. We keep it to ourselves and others so what they want and they *run you ragged*.'
(calogera 30-08-2010, 10:22,
http://www.babyboom.pl/forum/mamuskowo-f313/czuje-ze-jestem-zla-matka-28058-print/index2.html?pp=40)

In (89), stress is animated and it has an ability to walk.

(89) ale jak sie okazalo ze wszystko jest OK to *stres zszedl* i jakos teraz bardziej mysle o tym ze sie uda byc mama
[Ale jak się okazało, że wszystko jest OK, to *stres zszedł* i jakoś teraz bardziej myślę o tym, że się uda być mamą.]
lit. 'But it turned out that everything is okay and *the stress went down* and now I think I'll manage to be a mother'
'But it turned out that everything is okay and *the stress has gone* and now I think I'll manage to be a mother'
(chori 24-08-2010, 19:04,
http://www.babyboom.pl/forum/staramy-sie-f66/starania-po-raz-pierwszy-42617-print/?pp=40)

The author of (90) is so busy that she *is not making the corners* (*nie wyrabia na zakrętach*). The experiential basis of this metaphor is the common knowledge that when one moves fast, especially driving a car, turning can be difficult.

(90) Długo się nie odzywałam, ale *nie wyrabiam na zakrętach* mój K. wrócił do Holandii a chłopaki dają czadu, starszy ręka w gipsie a młodszy jakoś nie może dojść do siebie po tym szpitalu. Dobrze. że mam Was to mogę się wyżalić:-D:-D:-D, sorry za ponury nastrój ale jakoś tak wyszło.
[Długo się nie odzywałam, ale *nie wyrabiam na zakrętach*. Mój K. wrócił do Holandii, a chłopaki dają czadu, starszy ręka w gipsie, a młodszy jakoś nie może dojść do siebie po tym szpitalu. Dobrze, że mam Was, to mogę się wyżalić :-D:-D:-D, sorry za ponury nastrój, ale jakoś tak wyszło.]
lit. 'I haven't said anything in a while, but *I'm not making the corners* my K. returned from Holland and the boys are acting up, the elder has his arm in plaster and the younger somehow can't come to himself after this hospital. It's good that I have you to complain to :-D:-D, sorry for the depressing mood but just sort of it c ame out.'

'I haven't said anything in a while, but *I'm just not managing*, my K. returned from Holland and the boys are acting up, the elder has his arm in plaster and the younger somehow can't get over his time in hospital. It's good that I have you to complain to :-D:-D sorry for the depressing mood but that's the way it is.'
(tami_dj 17-04-2010, 22:55,
http://www.babyboom.pl/forum/mamuskowo-f313/mamusie-i-ich-malenstwa-2009-a-35002-print/index40.html?pp=40)

The author of (91) comments on her unhappy marriage she would like to end but because of the children it is not possible. A difficult situation is presented as a container one can *be in* or *walk out of*.

(91) ja nie widze *wyjscia z tej sytuacji* jak tylko tkwic w tym i byc poniekad nieszczesliwym...
[Ja nie widzę *wyjścia z tej sytuacji* jak tylko tkwić w tym i być poniekąd nieszczęśliwym...]
lit. 'I don't see any *exit from this situation* but only to sit there and be not really happy...'
'I don't see any *way out of this situation* but only to sit there and be not really happy...'
(mandrzejczuk 18-06-2010, 09:20,
www.babyboom.pl/forum/troche-intymnosci-f15/kiepski-malzenski-sex-39889-print/index2.html?pp=40)

In example (92) two different metaphorical expressions are used. The experiential basis for the first one, *zdarza się wielka kumulacja* 'a great accumulation happens', comes from the National Lottery in which money, when not won, builds up accumulation. In this sentence, however, it is not money, but problems and worries that accumulate. The second metaphorical expression depicts a situation in which a person cannot handle more misfortunes and troubles. The phrase *coś w człowieku pęka* 'something bursts/breaks in a human being' can mean that such a person 'starts crying, screaming, being aggressive or even has a mental breakdown'. This expression exemplifies the metaphor A HUMAN BEING IS A BRITTLE OBJECT.

(92) Ale powiem tak, staram się z tym walczyć, ale czasem *zdarza się wielka kumulacja* kiedy poprostu kilkanaście spraw się nałoży...*i coś w człowieku pęka*.
[Ale powiem tak, staram się z tym walczyć, ale czasem *zdarza się wielka* kumulacja, kiedy po prostu kilkanaście spraw się nałoży... i *coś w człowieku pęka.*]
lit. 'But I will say this, I'm trying to fight with it, but sometimes *a great accumulation happens* when several things happen at once...*and something inside a man bursts.*
'But I will say this, I'm trying to fight with it, but sometimes *a lot builds up* when several things happen at once... *and something inside breaks.*'

(saly 05-07-2009, 00:48,
http://www.babyboom.pl/forum/mamuskowo-f313/czuje-ze-jestem-zla-matka-28058-print/?pp=40)

The experiential basis for the metaphorical expression used in (93) is the physical experience that going up the hill is difficult and coming down is easy. The metaphorical expression *będzie z górki* 'it will be all downhill' is used to show that the situation one faces now is hard but in a few months it will be much easier.

(93) Najwazniejsze to przetrzymac te pare miesiecy i *pozniej juz z gorki*.
[Najważniejsze to przetrzymać te parę miesięcy i *później już z górki*.]
'The main thing is to survive these few months and *then it will be all downhill*.'
(fresh83 05-02-2010, 23:18,
http://www.babyboom.pl/forum/mamuskowo-f313/mamusie-i-ich-malenstwa-2009-a-35002-print/index16.html?pp=40)

Examples (94) and (95) contain highly conventionalized metaphorical expressions depicting problems as logs, stones or burden on the heart. In (95) the Polish metaphorical expression *kamień z serca* 'a stone off my heart' corresponds to the English expression *a weight of my mind*.

(94) A tu cały czas problemy, *same kłody pod nogami...*
lit. 'And here problems all the time, *only logs under our legs...*'
'And here problems all the time, *only stumbling blocks...*'
(fresh83 27-01-2011, 14:52,
http://www.babyboom.pl/forum/mamuskowo-f313/mamusie-i-ich-malenstwa-2009-a-35002-print/index58.html?pp=40)

(95) A u nas goraczka w niedziele znow powrocila:-(znow telefony do lekarzy, nie chcialam isc z Nim na dyzur bo balam sie sie przywleczemy cos gorszego do domu teraz juz jest duuuuuza poprawa trzecia dawka antybiotyku goraczki nie ma:tak:i *kamien z serca!!!!!*
[A u nas gorączka w niedzielę znów powróciła :-(Znów telefony do lekarzy, nie chciałam iść z Nim na dyżur, bo bałam się, że przywleczemy coś gorszego do domu. Teraz już jest duża poprawa, trzecia dawka antybiotyku, gorączki nie ma i *kamień z serca!!!!!*]
lit. 'With us on Sunday the fever came back:-(again calls to the doctors, I didn't want to go with him to the doctor because I was afraid that we would bring something worse home, but now there has been a greeeeeeat improvement, third dose of antibiotic and there is no fever *a stone off my heart!!!!!!*'
'With us on Sunday the fever came back:-(again calls to the doctors, I didn't want to go with him to the doctor because I was afraid that we would bring something worse home, but now there has been a greeeeeeat improvement, third dose of antibiotic and there is no fever, *a weight of my mind!!!!!!*'
(fresh83 16-02-2010, 13:02,

http://www.babyboom.pl/forum/mamuskowo-f313/mamusie-i-ich-malenstwa-2009-a-35002-print/index21.html?pp=40)

Example (96) describes overcoming problems as *fighting* (*walczenie*).

(96) chyba każda z nas ma takie chwile że czuje się "wyrodna matka" i dlatego jamajka nie daj sie otoczeniu, *walcz...*
[Chyba każda z nas ma takie chwile, że czuje się „wyrodną matką" i dlatego jamajka nie daj się otoczeniu, *walcz...*]
'I think all of us have had those moments when we feel like a "bad mother" and jamajka that's why you shouldn't give up, *fight...*'
(szczesliwa 24-06-2009, 23:59,
http://www.babyboom.pl/forum/mamuskowo-f313/czuje-ze-jestem-zla-matka-28058-print/?pp=40)

In (97) problems and concerns are treated as objects one stores inside and in order to de-stress and feel better, one must *throw them out of oneself* (*wyrzucić je z siebie*).

(97) przepraszam ze pisze to tutaj ale nie mialam komu sie wygadac a *musialam to z siebie wyrzucic*:-(
[Przepraszam, że piszę to tutaj, ale nie miałam komu się wygadać, a *musiałam to z siebie wyrzucić*:-(]
lit. 'I'm sorry that I'm writing it here, but I had no one to talk to and I had to *throw it out of myself* :-('
'I'm sorry that I'm writing it here, but I had no one to talk to and I had to *get it off my chest* :-('
(geroland 09-05-2010, 22:38,
http://www.babyboom.pl/forum/mamuskowo-f313/mamusie-i-ich-malenstwa-2009-a-35002-print/index43.html?pp=40)

The author of (98) pictures problems as *rides*.

(98) Czy *macie też takie jazdy z najbliższą rodziną*, widzę, że inne dziewczyny też się zmagają z takim problemem
lit. 'Do you also *have such rides with the closest family*, I can see that other girls also struggle with the same problem'
'Do you also *have such serious problems with the closest family*? I can see that other girls also struggle with the same problem'
(calogera 28-08-2010, 18:01,
http://www.babyboom.pl/forum/mamuskowo-f313/czuje-ze-jestem-zla-matka-28058-print/index2.html?pp=40)

3.2.12 Metaphors of people, their behaviour and attitudes

This section presents metaphorical expressions used to talk about people and their attitudes.

In example (99) the crying and wailing of a child is pictured as a *siren*, which is also loud and unpleasant to listen to. The next two metaphorical expressions picture a person as a machine, in this case, a *perpetual motion machine*.

> (99) Ale dzisiaj to myślałam, że oszaleję. 5 godzin na *syrenie*, bez przerwy, nawet na rączkach nie pomagało. Nie sądzę, po prostu *nie jestem perpetum mobile* i czasem *potrzebuję się wyłączyć* od płaczu, pieluchy, mleka i zupek.
> 'But today I thought that I'd go mad. 5 hours on a *siren*, without a break, even being in my arms didn't help. I don't think, simply *I'm not a perpetual motion* and *I sometimes need to switch off* from crying, nappies, milk and soups.'
> (saly 26-06-2009, 22:36,
> http://www.babyboom.pl/forum/mamuskowo-f313/czuje-ze-jestem-zla-matka-28058-print/?pp=40)

The author of (100) comments on the irrational behaviour of men. The phrase *mieć nasrane w głowie* 'to have shit in one's head' is used in informal Polish to describe a person who is or acts crazy and is not intelligent or rational.

> (100) boże, co niektórzy *faceci naprawde maja nasrane w glowach*
> [Boże, co niektórzy *faceci naprawdę mają nasrane w głowach*]
> lit. 'God, some *guys have shit/crap in their heads*'
> 'God some *guys have shit for brains*'
> (Pati26 06-08-2006, 15:52,
> http://www.babyboom.pl/forum/troche-intymnosci-f15/zdrada-5378-print/index5.html?pp=40)

The phrase *wszystko po kimś spływa* 'everything pours down on somebody' in (101) is used to show the lack of emotional sensitivity or commitment of men.

> (101) dokładnie po facetach niekiedy *wszystko spływu*
> [Dokładnie, po facetach niekiedy *wszystko spływa.*]
> lit. 'exactly, sometimes *everything pours down on men*'
> 'exactly, guys sometimes *don't care, it's like water off a duck's back*'
> (kasiula matula 20-07-2006, 09:56,
> http://www.babyboom.pl/forum/troche-intymnosci-f15/zdrada-5378-print/index3.html?pp=40)

Example (102) contains a metaphorical expression which describes a person as a device with a mechanism which one *winds up*, which means that such a 'person becomes more and more emotional about something'.

(102) Jeszcze żeby chociaż mama mi radziła faktycznie w sprawach trudnych, których nie wiem, a ona mi w kółko powtarza straszne historie klientek ze sklepu no i oczywiście *się nakręca*..
lit. 'If only mum gave me advice on difficult issues that I don't know, but she always repeats horrible stories from customers in the shop and of course *she winds herself up*.'
'If only mum gave me advice on difficult issues that I don't know, but she always repeats horrible stories from customers in the shop and of course *she winds herself up*.'
(kerna 05-07-2009, 22:52,
http://www.babyboom.pl/forum/mamuskowo-f313/czuje-ze-jestem-zla-matka-28058-print/index2.html?pp=40)

3.2.13 Metaphors of time

This subsection presents metaphors of TIME. Time is treated as an animated object which has the ability to move (*fly, come, run away*). It can also be *taken away*.

Post (103) exemplifies the highly conventionalized metaphor of TIME, namely TIME PASSING IS MOTION OF AN OBJECT. This particular metaphor is frequently used in Polish and other languages, including English.

(103) I pyknal Oliwci roczek...Matko jak *ten czas leci*
[I pyknął Oliwci roczek...Matko, jak *ten czas leci*.]
'And Oliwia's one-year birthday has come up... Oh *how time flies*'
(porzeczkas 23-09-2010, 22:47,
http://www.babyboom.pl/forum/mamuskowo-f313/mamusie-i-ich-malenstwa-2009-a-35002-print/index55.html?pp=40)

In examples (104) and (105) time is animated and is able to *come* and *run away*. The time is described as *right* (*odpowiedni*). Such metaphorical expressions are frequently used in Polish.

(104) Mysle ze *na wszystko przychodzi odpowiedni czas* niestety trzeba sie uzbroic w cierpliwosc.
[Myślę, że *na wszystko przychodzi odpowiedni czas*, niestety trzeba się uzbroić w cierpliwość.]
lit. 'I think that *the right time comes for everything*, unfortunately you need to arm yourself in patience.'
'I think that *everything comes at the right time*, unfortunately you need to be patient.'
(Figa 28-10-2004, 15:05,
http://www.babyboom.pl/forum/troche-intymnosci-f15/czy-ochota-na-seks-po-porodzie-jeszcze-kiedys-nadejdzie-11-print/?pp=40)

(105) no ale niedlugo trzeba sie wziac do roboty, *bo czas ucieka* a jutro znow do pracy.
[No, ale niedługo trzeba się wziąć do roboty, *bo czas ucieka*, a jutro znów do pracy.]
lit. 'Well, soon it's time to get down to work, *because time is running away* and tomorrow to work again.'
'Well, soon it's time to get down to work, *because time is running out* and tomorrow to work again.'
(honda 01-02-2010, 12:51,
http://www.babyboom.pl/forum/mamuskowo-f313/mamusie-i-ich-malenstwa-2009-a-35002-print/index13.html?pp=40)

In example (106) the metaphor TIME IS A VALUABLE COMMODITY occurs. Time is treated as a commodity one can *waste* or *take away*.

(106) nasze dzieci tak porzebuja naszej uwagi jednoczesnie *zabierajac nam wolny czas*
[Nasze dzieci tak potrzebują naszej uwagi, a jednocześnie *zabierają nam wolny czas*.]
'our children need our attention, at the same time they *take away our free time*'
(fresh83 07-01-2010, 16:31,
http://www.babyboom.pl/forum/mamuskowo-f313/mamusie-i-ich-malenstwa-2009-a-35002-print/?pp=40)

3.2.14 Other metaphors

3.2.14.1 Metaphors of weather

In example (107) forces of nature are understood as an opponent with whom it is hard to win. This particular metaphor of WAR is highly conventionalized.

(107) kurcze te powodzie sa straszne :-(jak ogladam w tv i widze tych ludzi *walczacych z zywiolem*.......:-(*a z nim ciezko wygrac*:-(
[Kurczę, te powodzie są straszne :-(Jak oglądam w telewizji i widzę tych ludzi *walczących z żywiołem*.......:-(*a z nim ciężko wygrać*:-(]
'Oh dear, those floods are horrible :-(when I watch TV and I see those people *fighting with the forces of nature*........:-(and *it's hard to win with them* :-('
(fresh83 22-05-2010, 15:30,
http://www.babyboom.pl/forum/mamuskowo-f313/mamusie-i-ich-malenstwa-2009-a-35002-print/index47.html?pp=40)

Spring (*wiosna*) in (108) is animated and has the ability to walk.

(108) no tak *przyszla wiosna* i pusto:-(Milan przeszedl trzydniówke, M zdrowieje i ta piekna pogoda za oknem:-):-):-)
[No tak, *przyszła wiosna* i pusto:-(Milan przeszedł trzydniówkę, M zdrowieje i ta piękna pogoda za oknem:-):-):-)]

lit. 'Well *spring has come* and empty :-(Milan went through a 3-day'er, M is getting better and that beautiful weather out the window:-):-):-)'
'Well *spring has come* and there is no one here :-(Milan had a three-day virus, M is getting better and that beautiful weather out the window:-):-):-)'
(fresh83 25-04-2010, 18:44,
http://www.babyboom.pl/forum/mamuskowo-f313/mamusie-i-ich-malenstwa-2009-a-35002-print/index41.html?pp=40)

The sun (*słońce*) in example (109) is personified because it is able to feel pity.

(109) słoneczko by wyszło to od razu by nam było lepiej ;) musimy czekać, aż się zlituje i wylezie ....
[Słoneczko by wyszło, to od razu by nam było lepiej ;) Musimy czekać, aż się zlituje i wylezie ....]
'If the sun came out, immediately we would feel better ;) we have to wait *until it feels pity and comes out*'
(alek 30-04-2006, 19:17,
http://www.babyboom.pl/forum/staramy-sie-f66/1-dziecko-po-30-stce-7471-print/index21.html?pp=40)

3.2.14.2 Metaphors of computers and Internet-related phenomena

This subsection presents metaphorical expressions used to talk about computers and discussion threads.

Sentence (110) describes a thread as *hot*, meaning that there are many participants and conversations are emotional.

(110) Cześć dziewczyny, nie było mnie kilka dni, a tu *wątek stał się gorący*.
'Hi girls I haven't been here in for a few days and *the thread has got hot.*'
(anusieńka 22-08-2005, 23:49,
http://www.babyboom.pl/forum/staramy-sie-f66/1-dziecko-po-30-stce-7471-print/index2.html?pp=40)

In (111), the *quick progress* of a thread is compared to a steam train which moves fast. The common knowledge of the speed of a moving train is the experiential basis for the metaphorical expression *iść całą parą na przód* 'to go full steam ahead'.

(111) Widze ze watek idzie cala para na przod
[Widzę, że wątek idzie całą parą naprzód.]
'I can see *that the thread is going full steam ahead*'
(KINDZIA100 30-03-2006, 00:39,
http://www.babyboom.pl/forum/staramy-sie-f66/1-dziecko-po-30-stce-7471-print/index12.html?pp=40)

In example (112), a computer is personified. A computer *being on strike* equals to 'not working properly'.

(112) U mnie klopoty z *kompem troszke strajkowal* ale mam nadzieje, ze juz bedzie dzialac bez zarzutu
[U mnie kłopoty z *komputerem, troszkę strajkował*, ale mam nadzieję, że już będzie działać bez zarzutu.]
'I had problems with the computer, *which was on strike for a while*, but I hope that it will work okay now.'
(porzeczkas 17-05-2010, 10:25,
http://www.babyboom.pl/forum/mamuskowo-f313/mamusie-i-ich-malenstwa-2009-a-35002-print/index45.html?pp=40)

3.2.14.3 Metaphors of the world, life, fate and nature

In the following set of examples, the world, life, fate and nature are treated metaphorically. In most cases, they are understood as living beings who are *contrary* (113) or *cruel* (116). They can *fool and play tricks on people* (117), and *go crazy* (118).

In example (113), an interesting metaphor is presented, namely LIFE IS A STORY. Nature is portrayed as *a negative character of the story* (*negatywny bohater historii*).

(113) Chcemy być kochane i pragniemy tego, co każda dziewczynka, być księżniczką, której wszystko się udaje. Tutaj pojawia się *negatywny bohater historii – natura, która niestety często bywa przekorna.*
'We want to be loved and we wish like every little girl, to be a princess for whom everything works out. And here the *negative character of the story* appears – *nature, which unfortunately often tends to be contrary*.'
(moniolek 28-02-2006, 23:20,
http://www.babyboom.pl/forum/staramy-sie-f66/1-dziecko-po-30-stce-7471-print/index4.html?pp=40)

In example (114), life is described as an object a person can hold; however, it can escape. In this situation, when life is out of the author's control, a metaphorical expression is used.

(114) Dziękuje za wsparcie w dzień jeszcze jakoś funkcjonuje ale wieczorami czuję potężnego doła tak jak by mi się *życie wymykało z rąk*.
[Dziękuję za wsparcie, w dzień jeszcze jakoś funkcjonuję, ale wieczorami czuję potężnego doła, tak jakby mi się *życie wymykało z rąk*.]
lit. 'Thank you for your support. During the day I somehow function but in the evenings I feel a great depression just as if *my life were escaping out of my hands*.'

'Thank you for your support. During the day I somehow function but in the evenings I feel a great depression just as if *my life is out of control*.'
(jamajka* 24-06-2009, 22:24,
http://www.babyboom.pl/forum/mamuskowo-f313/czuje-ze-jestem-zla-matka-28058-print/?pp=40)

Metaphorical expressions in which objects or abstract concepts are animated are numerous in Polish. Animization, as a certain type of metaphor, is described by Rejakowa as "the most conspicuous metaphor" (2008: 73, translation mine). Samsel comments on the aim of using animization: "The use of animisation in communication is motivated by the desire to create in the receiver an illusion that certain elements of our everyday lives are not just objects but they are "alive" and thus can – in some miraculous way – affect reality" (2011: 188, translation mine). Personification is also widely used. It consists in endowing inanimate beings or abstract concepts with human qualities. Maćkiewicz sees personification as "a way of familiarizing the world deeply rooted in our thinking" (Maćkiewicz 1995: 234, translation mine).

(115) Majeczko skarbie bardzo mocno Cię przytulam… już nie wiem co sądzić… czasami wydaje mi się, że *los nierówno dzieli radościami i smutkami*.
'Majeczka darling, I am hugging you tightly… I don't know what to think anymore…sometimes it seems to me that *fate divides its joys and sorrows unevenly*.'
(moniolek 30-03-2006, 09:39,
http://www.babyboom.pl/forum/staramy-sie-f66/1-dziecko-po-30-stce-7471-print/index12.html?pp=40)

(116) *Natura jest okrutna-skubana nie poczeka!*
'*Nature is cruel – the villain doesn't wait!*'
(ewan 28-02-2006, 01:26,
http://www.babyboom.pl/forum/staramy-sie-f66/1-dziecko-po-30-stce-7471-print/index3.html?pp=40)

(117) Nawet *jeśli natura płata nam figla*, to postęp medycyny jest tak duży..*że można ją trochę oszukać, albo raczej pomóc :)*
'Even if *nature plays tricks on us*, the progress of medicine is so big that *you can fool it a little, or rather help :)*'
(kasia_2005 03-03-2006, 12:54,
http://www.babyboom.pl/forum/staramy-sie-f66/1-dziecko-po-30-stce-7471-print/index4.html?pp=40)

(118) Nie wiem- być *może świat zwariował*. Kiedyś ktoś mądry powiedział mi że założenie rodziny dla zony i matki, to tak jak założenie firmy i prowadzenie jej. Chyba trochę w tym prawdy. Tylko czasami kiepskie wynagrodzenie…'

> [Nie wiem – być *może świat zwariował*. Kiedyś ktoś mądry powiedział mi, że założenie rodziny dla żony i matki to tak, jak założenie firmy i prowadzenie jej. Chyba trochę w tym prawdy. Tylko czasami kiepskie wynagrodzenie…]
> 'I don't know – *maybe the world has gone crazy*. A smart person once told me that establishing a family for a wife and a mother is like establishing a company and running it. I think there's some truth in that. Only sometimes the salary is meagre…'
> (ahonka75 08-07-2009, 11:55,
> http://www.babyboom.pl/forum/mamuskowo-f313/czuje-ze-jestem-zla-matka-28058-print/index2.html?pp=40)

In (119) the world and life *turn upside down*. The metaphorical expression *wywrócić świat do góry nogami* 'to turn the world upside down' is used to illustrate how rapid and drastic changes influence people's lives.

> (119) spokojnie…wszystko będzie jak dawniej:-D teraz jesteś zajęta maluszkiem, zmęczona, dopiero co weszłaś w rolę mamy, *cały Twój świat wywrócił sie do góry nogami…*
> 'easy… everything will be just like before:-D Now you are busy with the little one, tired, you've just taken on the role of a mum, *your whole world has turned upside down…*'
> (xandii 30-12-2008, 12:08,
> http://www.babyboom.pl/forum/troche-intymnosci-f15/czy-ochota-na-seks-po-porodzie-jeszcze-kiedys-nadejdzie-11-print/index4.html?pp=40)

Example (120) presents the metaphor LIFE IS A PATH. Describing life as a path is common in Polish, for instance, when people get married, everybody wishes them *good luck on the new path of life* (*powodzenia na nowej drodze życia*).

> (120) Na początku mówiłam sobie – znów dziecko, jak ja sobie dam radę, ledwo za jednym nadążam – ale na szczęście *na swej drodze spotkałam osoby*, które ciagle mi powtarzały silna jesteś, dasz radę.
> lit. 'At the beginning I would tell myself – another baby, how I will cope, I could barely keep up with one – but fortunately *on my path I met people*, who always tell me that I'm strong, I'll manage.'
> 'At the beginning I would tell myself – another baby, how I will cope, I could barely keep up with one – but fortunately *in my life I met people* who always tell me that I'm strong, I'll manage.'
> (AgaMP 31-12-2005, 11:22,
> http://www.babyboom.pl/forum/troche-intymnosci-f15/13-pytan-o-antykoncepcje-3119-print/?pp=40)

3.2.14.4 Metaphors of freedom and patience

In example (121) the author comments on late parenthood. She and her partner are glad that they waited until their mid-thirties with the decision to become parents. They enjoy their time with the baby very much and they do not think of what they missed out in their lives. In this case, freedom is animated.

(121) I bardzo sie ciesze, ze poczekalismy bo teraz cieszymy sie nasza pociecha bez zadnych wyrzutow ze nam *"wolnosc" uciekla*
[I bardzo się cieszę, że poczekaliśmy, bo teraz cieszymy się naszą pociechą bez żadnych wyrzutów, że nam „*wolność*" *uciekła.*]
lit. 'I'm so happy that we waited because now we can enjoy our little one without any remorse that our *freedom escaped*'
'I'm so happy that we waited because now we can enjoy out little one without remorse that our *freedom was wasted.*'
(Anna28 14-05-2010, 03:37,
http://www.babyboom.pl/forum/mamuskowo-f313/mamusie-i-ich-malenstwa-2009-a-35002-print/index44.html?pp=40)

In example (122) patience is presented as a weapon.

(122) Mysle ze na wszystko przychodzi odpowiedni czas niestety trzeba sie *uzbroic w cierpliwosc.*
[Myślę, że na wszystko przychodzi odpowiedni czas, niestety trzeba się *uzbroić w cierpliwość.*]
lit. 'I think that everything comes at the right time unfortunately you have to *arm yourself with patience.*'
'I think that everything comes at the right time unfortunately you have *to be patient.*'
(Figa 28-10-2004, 15:05,
http://www.babyboom.pl/forum/troche-intymnosci-f15/czy-ochota-na-seks-po-porodzie-jeszcze-kiedys-nadejdzie-11-print/?pp=40)

Example (123) presents the metaphor PATIENCE IS FABRIC.

(123) No właśnie!!! A nam czasem głupoty wpadną do głowy, czy jesteśmy złymi matkami, bo po 6 godzinach płaczu, lub 33 zmianie ciuszków od ulewania zaczyna się *kurczyć cierpliwość* a rosnąć ból głowy;-)
[No właśnie!!! A nam czasem głupoty wpadną do głowy, czy jesteśmy złymi matkami, bo po 6 godzinach płaczu, lub 33. zmianie ciuszków od ulewania, zaczyna się kurczyć cierpliwość, a *rosnąć ból głowy;*-)]
lit. 'Exactly!!! Sometimes foolish thoughts fall into our heads that we are bad mothers because after 6 hours of crying or the 33rd change of clothing from bringing up food our patience starts shrinking and the *headache starts growing*;-)'

'Exactly!!! Sometimes foolish thoughts come to us that we are bad mothers because after 6 hours of crying or the 33rd change of clothing from bringing up food our patience is frayed and we *get headaches*;-)'
(saly 05-07-2009, 00:06,
http://www.babyboom.pl/forum/mamuskowo-f313/czuje-ze-jestem-zla-matka-28058-print/?pp=40)

3.3 Concluding remarks

The aim of Chapter Three has been to present metaphorical expressions found on Polish Internet forums for mothers.

In ten thousand analyzed posts, metaphorical expressions have been found. They have been categorized into 24 groups, namely: metaphors of emotions (anger, aggitation and nerves, depression, happiness and sadness, and other emotions); relationships; sex; conception; bringing up children; children's progress; human body; teeth; illnesses; everyday life; pregnancy, shopping; problems and hardship; people, their behaviour and attitudes; time; weather; computer and Internet-related phenomena; world, life, fate and nature; freedom and patience.

Numerous metaphorical expressions have been identified in discussions involving emotions, especially depression, problems and hardship as well as relationships.

It is also important to note that there are certain discussion threads which do not contain a single metaphorical expression despite their length. These included *Czy można i jak zaplanować płeć dziecka?? chłopiec/dziewczynka?:)* 'How can you plan the baby's sex?? boy/girl?:)'; *kolczyki u niemowlaka* 'earrings for a toddler'; *maluszki i mamusie z Kaszub* 'Babies and mammies from Kaszuby'; *Wakacje z maluszkiem* 'Holidays with the baby'; *żony marynarzy..integujmy się:)* 'sailors' wives..let's get together:)'. What is surprising is the fact that only one discussion thread connected with sex, *Kiepski małżeński sex...* 'Poor marital sex...', contained metaphorical expressions. The remaining threads about sex contained simple instructive posts. These included *Czy twój mężczyzna ogląda strony pornograficzne???* 'Does your man watch pornographic websites???'; *Najlepsze pozycje, aby zajść w ciążę?* 'Best positions to get pregnant?'; *sex analny* 'anal sex'; *sex w ciąży* 'pregnant sex'; *Ulubiona pozycja ;-)* 'Favourite position ;-)'.

Chapter Four Metaphors employed by American users of Internet forums for mothers

4.1 Introductory remarks

In this chapter the posts to be presented are taken from various American Internet forums for parents. All of them contain metaphorical expressions used in various thematic areas. The metaphors they represent will be classified by target domain.

4.1.1 Data collection

For the purpose of this work, ten thousand posts from various American Internet forums in the time frame August 2012–January 2013 have been analyzed. The topics of threads are as various as the ones presented in the previous chapter. It was impossible to find exactly the same topics of Polish and American Internet forums but some of them are very similar. All the examples are presented in their original versions, including mistakes and abbreviations. Some of the most frequently used abbreviations are listed in Table 16.

Table 16: Abbreviations used on American forums for mothers

Abbreviation	Meaning
AAS	All About Surrogacy.com
AFM	as for me
bc	because
bday	birthday
Bfing	breast feeding
BFP	beloved first pregnancy
DD	dear daughter
DH	dear husband
DW	dear wife
ES	elementary school
FIM	first in vitro mother
HS	high school
IF	in vitro father
IM	in vitro mother
IMO	in my opinion
IVF	in vitro fertilization
KUP	keep us posted
mcps	municipal school
OMG	oh my god
OP	original poster
PG	pregnancy
PP	previous poster
rap or rep	reputation
SAHM	stay at home mom
TTC	trying to conceive
wks	weeks

The list of the examined Internet forums and topics is provided below.

1. am i a bad mom?
   http://www.circleofmoms.com/welcome-to-circle-of-moms/am-i-a-bad-mom-444657/2#replies
   204 posts analyzed and only one metaphorical expression found.
2. Can I choose my baby's sex?
   http://www.babycenter.com/404_can-i-choose-my-babys-sex_1933.bc?questionId=1933
   41 posts analyzed and only one metaphorical expression found.
3. crazy stuff your in-laws feed your kids
   http://www.dcurbanmom.com/jforum/posts/list/276495.page
   108 posts analyzed and no metaphorical expressions found.

4. Diaper Fairy
   http://americanpregnancy.org/forums/printthread.php?t=155834&pp=30
   113 posts analyzed and no metaphorical expressions found. The topic of this forum was natural diapers.
5. Do you love your kids more than your wife?
   http://www.dcurbanmom.com/jforum/posts/list/71936.page;jsessionid=67D87A8D3C03F4CFE250F38F70CEC846
   153 posts analyzed and two metaphorical expressions found.
6. Early Pregnancy signs/symptoms
   http://americanpregnancy.org/forums/printthread.php?t=38327&pp=30&page=2
   305 posts analyzed and several metaphorical expressions from various thematic areas found.
7. Found out my husband has account at Ashley Madison
   http://www.dcurbanmom.com/jforum/posts/list/87950.page
   229 posts analyzed and no metaphorical expressions found.
8. gender disappointment
   http://americanpregnancy.org/forums/printthread.php?t=389011&pp=30;
   37 posts analyzed and no metaphorical expressions found. The topic contained short and simple answers to the question of disappointment with the child's gender.
9. Girlfriends, Fiancés, and Wives of Sailors
   http://www.navyformoms.com/group/girlfriendsfianceswivesofsailors?groupUrl=girlfriendsfianceswivesofsailors&id=1971797%3AGroup%3A24811&page=1#comments
   2098 posts analyzed and several metaphorical expressions found.
10. Having babies after 30:Yes or no?
    http://www.circleofmoms.com/welcome-to-circle-of-moms/having-babies-after-30-yes-or-no-630803
    28 posts analyzed and no metaphorical expressions found.
11. How awful – nurse who answered prank call about Princess Kate commits suicide
    http://www.dcurbanmom.com/jforum/posts/list/277176.page
    101 posts analyzed and no metaphorical expressions found.
12. Husband not interested in sex
    http://www.dcurbanmom.com/jforum/posts/list/284651.page
    32 posts analyzed and no metaphorical expressions found.

13. Husband ruined Christmas
    http://www.dcurbanmom.com/jforum/posts/list/279831.page
    94 posts analyzed and several metaphorical expressions from different thematic areas found.
14. I blame Adam Lanza's mother
    http://www.dcurbanmom.com/jforum/posts/list/278508.page
    212 posts analyzed and several metaphorical expressions found.
15. I once knew someone so cheap
    http://www.dcurbanmom.com/jforum/posts/list/281222.page
    391 posts analyzed and no metaphorical expressions found.
16. I want to have an affair – can't pull it off for some reason
    http://www.dcurbanmom.com/jforum/posts/list/284187.page
    134 posts analyzed and several metaphorical expressions found.
17. If I had know this was the case, I probably wouldn't have married you
    http://www.dcurbanmom.com/jforum/posts/list/277971.page
    567 posts analyzed and numerous metaphorical expressions found.
18. I'm Jewish. Ask me anything
    http://www.dcurbanmom.com/jforum/posts/list/276147.page
    320 posts analyzed and several metaphorical expressions found.
19. in tears
    http://forums.llli.org/printthread.php?t=76260&pp=40
    65 posts analyzed and one metaphorical expression found.
20. Interracial sex…
    http://www.dcurbanmom.com/jforum/posts/list/90/174699.page
    195 posts analyzed and one metaphorical expression found.
21. IVF – Sisters
    http://americanpregnancy.org/forums/printthread.php?t=272141&pp=30&page=2
    510 posts analyzed and numerous metaphorical expressions found.
22. Just curious – how many would carry for a gay couple?
    http://www.allaboutsurrogacy.com/forums/index.php?showtopic=35196&st=0
    107 posts analyzed and numerous metaphorical expressions found.
23. Let's Talk About (Pregnant) Sex
    http://www.fitpregnancy.com/pregnancy/sex-relationships/lets-talk-about-pregnant-sex
    77 posts analyzed and one metaphorical expression found.

24. My husband is fucking our au pair and I am ok with it.
    http://www.dcurbanmom.com/jforum/posts/list/256308.page
    58 posts analyzed and no metaphorical expressions found.
25. New to Surrogacy
    http://www.allaboutsurrogacy.com/forums/index.php?showtopic=55519&st=0&s=d7e42e78c7b875a7ae647238dded9485
    93 posts analyzed and numerous metaphorical expressions found.
26. Oh Holy Heck
    http://americanpregnancy.org/forums/showthread.php?355862-Oh-Holy-Heck
    25 posts analyzed and no metaphorical expressions found. This thread contained wishes of good health for a woman pregnant with triplets.
27. Paying 32K and my DD's teacher has NO idea what she's doing
    http://www.dcurbanmom.com/jforum/posts/list/275848.page
    156 posts analyzed and several metaphorical expressions found.
28. Please take off your shoes!!!
    http://www.dcurbanmom.com/jforum/posts/list/284256.page
    281 posts analyzed and several metaphorical expressions found.
29. Post your TTC story and diagnosis here
    http://americanpregnancy.org/forums/printthread.php?t=175&pp=30&page=2
    301 posts analyzed and several metaphorical expressions found.
30. Roll Call!!!
    http://americanpregnancy.org/forums/printthread.php?t=18963&pp=30&page=2
    109 posts analyzed and no metaphorical expressions found.
31. Share your story
    http://www.womenshealth.gov/pregnancy/childbirth-beyond/returning-to-work/index.html
    9 posts analyzed and one metaphorical expression found.
32. Should I feel guilty about going back to work?
    http://www.babycenter.com/400_should-i-feel-guilty-about-going-back-to-work_500239_1.bc?startIndex=100&sortFieldName=createDate
    106 posts analyzed and one metaphorical expression found.
33. S/o "foreigners" what have your found most interesting about USA
    http://www.dcurbanmom.com/jforum/posts/list/30/277136
    360 posts analyzed and several metaphorical expressions found.

34. The dreaded pumping… tips, advice, and recommendations
    http://americanpregnancy.org/forums/printthread.php?t=96&pp=30
    65 posts analyzed and no metaphorical expressions found. It was a purely informative thread.
35. Things I wish I'd known about BFing before Baby Came
    http://americanpregnancy.org/forums/printthread.php?t=537&pp=30
    117 posts analyzed and two metaphorical expressions found.
36. Vent – DD's classmate's mother just called to ask me to invite her kid to my kid's bday party
    http://www.dcurbanmom.com/jforum/posts/list/278038.page
    136 posts analyzed and several metaphorical expressions found.
37. What do all you working mamas do for a living?
    http://forums.llli.org/printthread.php?t=7303&pp=40
    175 posts analyzed and no metaphorical expressions found, a purely informative thread.
38. What does anal sex feel like?
    http://www.dcurbanmom.com/jforum/posts/list/172189.page
    241 posts analyzed and no metaphorical expressions found, a purely informative thread.
39. What to tell child who is product of an affair?
    http://www.dcurbanmom.com/jforum/posts/list/285748.page
    201 posts analyzed and one metaphorical expression found.
40. What were your early pregnancy symptoms?
    http://americanpregnancy.org/forums/printthread.php?t=60&pp=30
    552 posts analyzed and one metaphorical expression found.
41. When to pierce ears?
    www.dcurbanmom.com/jforum/posts/list/288940.page
    37 posts analyzed and no metaphorical expressions found, another purely informative thread.
42. Who Are You?
    http://americanpregnancy.org/forums/printthread.php?t=20212&pp=30
    276 posts analyzed and no metaphorical expressions found. This thread was for mothers of multiple children to get to know each other.
43. Would You Be Upset if We Take Our Three Year Old With Us to Dinner Tonight for New Years Eve?
    http://www.dcurbanmom.com/jforum/posts/list/280828.page
    249 posts analyzed and no metaphorical expressions found.

44. Why do you own a gun?
http://www.dcurbanmom.com/jforum/posts/list/278571.page
332 posts analyzed and several metaphorical expressions found.

4.2 An analysis of selected examples of conceptual metaphors

4.2.1 Metaphors of emotions

This subsection presents metaphors of emotions which are based mainly on physical and cultural experiences of language users. The examples of metaphorical expressions connected with emotions are numerous and they are divided into several groups.

4.2.1.1 Metaphors of anger

This subsection presents metaphors of ANGER. References to war are not as numerous as in Polish, but similarly, the words *attack* and *fight* are most commonly used in association with anger. The metaphorical expressions presented below emphasize strength with which some things are done or said.

In example (124) there are five cases of the word *attack* used metaphorically meaning 'to criticize or criticism'.

> (124) *I'm not the PP you're attacking*, but I too am irritated (not threatened) by the repeated *attacks on private schools* generally by people who prefer public schools. Why the constant need *to attack private schools*? This thread – and many threads on the private schools forum – get unnecessarily littered with *off-topic attacks* from public school parents. I'm not saying some private school posters don't ever criticize public schools, because that definitely happens too. But IMO any fair counting of *attacks* would find many more from the public school parents than from the private school parents.
> (Anonymous 30-11-2012, 09:10,
> http://www.dcurbanmom.com/jforum/posts/list/45/275848.page)

In example (125), the author, instead of using the word *aggressive*, employs a stronger word, *combative*.

> (125) Just throwing out statements and *being combative* is not very constructive (at least to me)
> (Anonymous 12-04-2012, 09:56,
> http://www.dcurbanmom.com/jforum/posts/list/120/275848.page)

Post (126) exemplifies the metaphor ANGER IS HOT FLUID IN A CONTAINER and similar posts make use of the same verb, *to vent*, meaning 'to let go of negative emotions'.

(126) I am trying not to cry in front of our kids but I'm so sad and mad. Thanks for *letting me vent*.
(Anonymous 23-12-2012, 09:25,
http://www.dcurbanmom.com/jforum/posts/list/279831.page)

In example (127), the human body is treated as a container which may explode when full of anger.

(127) There were a couple of times I felt so much rage over something little, I thought *my body would explode!*
(alaskagirl 23-01-2009, 14:22,
http://americanpregnancy.org/forums/printthread.php?t=60&pp=30&page=11)

The author of example (128) uses the expression *to cool off* meaning 'to calm oneself down'.

(128) This whole forum change STINKS!!!! I wish everyone the best in their individual journies. AFM: It'll be a while before *I cool off*, goodbye!!
(Southern Belle 20-08-2010, 20:08,
http://americanpregnancy.org/forums/printthread.php?t=272141&pp=30&page=2)

The author of example (129) uses the phrase *heated discussion* meaning 'discussion full of anger and emotions'. This post is an answer to a rather delicate question: *Would you carry for a gay couple*?

(129) I would answer "Probably not." I've attempted to post why, but it's not coming out right and *I'm not up for a heated discussion*.
(Nicole 30-10-2007, 13:32,
http://www.allaboutsurrogacy.com/forums/index.php?showtopic=35196&st=0)

4.2.1.2 Metaphors of happiness and sadness

Examples (130)–(132) present the highly conventionalized metaphorical expressions *keep one's head up*, *keep one's chin up* and *keep one's spirits up* meaning 'be optimistic'. The metaphor presented in these examples is HAPPY IS UP. In (130), the clause *follow your heart* is an example of the metonymy THE HEART FOR FEELINGS, and the clause *distance makes the heart grow fonder* contains another metonymy, THE HEART FOR THE HUMAN BEING.

(130) for all of you navy girlfriends and fiance's that have familys that dont approve….
follow your heart! distance makes the heart grow fonder and my husband and i are living proof of that. so please just *keep your heads up* !
(Shae*LOVIN MY SAILOR* 02-02-2009, 23:40,

(131) Keep writing him letters and *keep your chin up*!!!
(Amanda 29-01-2009, 14:15,
http://www.navyformoms.com/group/girlfriendsfianceswivesofsailors?groupUrl=
girlfriendsfianceswivesofsailors&id=1971797%3AGroup%3A24811&page=1232#
comments)

(132) so writting as many letters as possible to your sailor will really *keep their spirits up*
(Kellie 28-01-2009, 16:37,
http://www.navyformoms.com/group/girlfriendsfianceswivesofsailors?groupUrl=
girlfriendsfianceswivesofsailors&id=1971797%3AGroup%3A24811&page=1233#
comments)

Example (133) makes use of the metaphorical expression *be on the top of the world* which means 'to be extremely happy'.

(133) I got a call from him today. OMG It was so nice to hear his voice again. This is the first time in 34 days. *I am on top of the world right now.*
(Danielle (Casey's Wife) 22-02-2009, 17:35,
http://www.navyformoms.com/group/girlfriendsfianceswivesofsailors?groupUrl=
girlfriendsfianceswivesofsailors&id=1971797%3AGroup%3A24811&page=1214#
comments)

Metaphorical expressions used in posts (134)–(136) depict worse days as *downs, down days, down cycles* or *low points*. The metaphor illustrated by these examples is SAD IS DOWN.

(134) EKZZS-we all know how your feeling right now and we all battle with those same feelings from time to time. IF is truly a rollercoaster battle, you'll have *your up days down days*, your *really up days and your really down days*....
(Armylovin 26-10-2007, 02:26,
http://americanpregnancy.org/forums/printthread.php?t=175&pp=30&page=3)

(135) I think an affair is a silly thing to do a wife on a *"down cycle."* Marriage ebbs and flows. Get some patience, get in to counseling, whatever.
(Anonymous 17-01-2013, 17:22,
http://www.dcurbanmom.com/jforum/posts/list/30/284187.page)

(136) We've *hit a really low point in our marriage* that I'm not sure we're going to survive because of this kind of disconnect.
(Anonymous 12-12-2012, 09:52,
http://www.dcurbanmom.com/jforum/posts/list/15/277971.page)

The author of post (137) uses a highly conventionalized metaphorical expression, *to feel blue*, which means 'to be sad'.

(137) I feel *so blue* right now. I think it is hormonal, but it has been a long hard road.
(baby2008 30-05-2007, 10:30,
http://americanpregnancy.org/forums/printthread.php?t=175&pp=30&page=2)

4.2.1.3 Metaphors of other feelings and emotions

Three metaphorical expressions in which *heart* means 'feelings' are presented in this subsection. In example (138) the heart is animated as it *goes out to somebody*. The use of the noun *heart* may be treated as a case of the metonymy THE HEART FOR FEELINGS (or, alternatively, THE HEART FOR THE HUMAN BEING, with the metaphorical reading of the phrase *go out to* 'sympathize with').

(138) After everything you have been through, four separate losses with two of them outside of the 1st trimester, *my heart goes out to you* and your husband.
(nostoppingme 28-09-2010, 12:14,
http://americanpregnancy.org/forums/printthread.php?t=272141&pp=30&page=11)

In (139) the heart is personified as it is pictured as a being with the ability to *shout and cry for joy*. The use of *heart* in (139) can also be treated as an example of the metonymy THE HEART FOR THE HUMAN BEING.

(139) WOW *My heart doesn't know whether it wants to shout for joy or cry*!
(KMyers 23-09-2010, 17:36,
http://americanpregnancy.org/forums/printthread.php?t=272141&pp=30&page=10)

In example (140) the heart is pictured as a cold object which is melted by kind words and well wishes which are treated as warm objects.

(140) There were days when I thought I would loose it, but when I would log on and see the well wishes and kind words *it just melted my heart*.
(Southern Belle 23-09-2010, 18:06,
http://americanpregnancy.org/forums/printthread.php?t=272141&pp=30&page=10)

Self esteem in (141) is treated as a human being.

(141) Sure, I can take care of myself so I don't cheat or divorce. But it won't stop *my self esteem from going in the toilet*, or *flirting with guy friends* to make up for the lack of attention at home.
(Anonymous 13-12-2012, 16:16,
http://www.dcurbanmom.com/jforum/posts/list/345/277971.page)

4.2.2 Metaphors of relationships

In the following subsection we concentrate on examples in which relationships are described metaphorically. Example (142) treats marriage as a hotel where people *check into* or *out*.

> (142) I don't know the answer, but if you are still reading OP, it sounds like both you and your wife have *checked out of the marriage*.
> (Anonymous 13-12-2012, 18:20,
> http://www.dcurbanmom.com/jforum/posts/list/360/277971.page)

The metaphorical expression used in (143) is used to describe marriage as *being rocky*, which suggests that there are problems in the marriage.

> (143) If your *marriage was rocky*, would this end it for you?
> (Anonymous 18-01-2010, 16:58,
> http://www.dcurbanmom.com/jforum/posts/list/87950.page)

In the examples below, marriage is pictured as a *device* in which *something can be off* (144), which needs *fixing* (145) and which *can be broken* (146).

> (144) My feelings: if you are in a sexless marriage, *something is off* with how your wife is perceiving you.
> (Anonymous 12-12-2012, 09:54,
> http://www.dcurbanmom.com/jforum/posts/list/30/277971.page)

> (145) "Not OP, but this strikes me as awfully judgmental. Having been on the other side of this, your "*fix the marriage*" comment seems ill-informed to me.
> (Anonymous 13-12-2012, 14:06,
> http://www.dcurbanmom.com/jforum/posts/list/270/277971.page)

> (146) We are in counseling and have uncovered, after months of work, a lot of what we've both contributed to our *broken marriage and broken sex life*.
> (Anonymous 12-12-2012, 13:54,
> http://www.dcurbanmom.com/jforum/posts/list/150/277971.page)

In example (147) marriage is pictured as liquid as it *ebbs and flows*.

> (147) Whatever floats your boat. I think an affair is a silly thing to do a wife on a "down cycle." *Marriage ebbs and flows*. Get some patience, get in to counseling, whatever.
> (Anonymous 17-01-2013, 17:22,
> http://www.dcurbanmom.com/jforum/posts/list/30/284187.page)

4.2.3 Metaphors of sex

In (148), *dry spell* is used metaphorically to mean 'a period of time without sex', which exemplifies the metaphor SEX IS RAIN.

(148) He said things weren't good before child #2. So, to blame the current *dry spell* on child #2 and changes to the body is ignoring past history.
(Anonymous 12-12-2012, 10:44,
http://www.dcurbanmom.com/jforum/posts/list/60/277971.page)

4.2.4 Metaphors of pregnancy

In this subsection, examples concerning PREGNANCY are presented. Post (149) describes the process of trying to conceive and being pregnant as a journey. Post (150) pictures surrogacy as a journey. The metaphorical expressions are highly conventionalized.

(149) *It is not an easy journey*, but you have come to the right place for love & supprot!! Best of luck and KUP *on your journey*.
(nostoppingme 24-09-2010, 15:32,
http://americanpregnancy.org/forums/printthread.php?t=272141&pp=30&page=11)

(150) believe it or not, when i began my search for IPs for my *next journey*, i had a on-tario-based couple refuse to consider me as their surro….AFTER i told them that i had carried for and was again carrying for 2 men.
(jennkelly72 26-05-2009, 07:59,
http://www.allaboutsurrogacy.com/forums/index.php?showtopic=35196&st=45)

4.2.5 Metaphors of everyday life

This subsection presents various metaphors connected with everyday life issues. Example (151) shows a situation in which a woman struggles with morning sickness. The use of the metaphorical expression *fight a battle* suggests how hard and tiresome this process is.

(151) AFM: *I'm fighting a bit of a battle with morning sickness.* No vomiting yet… but so much dry wretching!
(Ourou 13-09-2010, 17:21,
http://americanpregnancy.org/forums/printthread.php?t=272141&pp=30&page=8)

In example (152), the metaphorical expression *pull one's weight* is used to mean 'do as much as possible'. The author of the post explains that his wife does not accept his help; *shoot something down* means 'decline something'.

(152) Anyhow, I feel ling *I'm pulling my weight around the house.* Volunterred to go do the groceries but she *shot that down.*
(Anonymous 12-12-2012, 12:05,
http://www.dcurbanmom.com/jforum/posts/list/90/277971.page)

The phrase *to get all ducks in a row*, used in (153), means 'to get all things organized'.

> (153) Been sending all my insurance and medical stuff *to get all our ducks in a row*.
> (Lilly 29-08-2012, 13:48,
> http://www.allaboutsurrogacy.com/forums/index.php?showtopic=55519&st=0&s=d7e42e78c7b875a7ae647238dded9485)

In (154), the word *shit* is used metaphorically to mean 'the housework'.

> (154) The "*do more shit* to make her life easier" solution can probably work sometimes.
> (Anonymous 12-12-2012, 10:07,
> http://www.dcurbanmom.com/jforum/posts/list/30/277971.page)

In (155), *shit* is used to mean 'problems and everyday worries'.

> (155) *We have enough shit to worry about* on a daily basis, really. I am as aware of my surroundings/alert as I can be to keep myself and my family out of harm's way. *Bad shit obviously could still happen to us*, and no level of preparation can protect against a lot of it.
> (Anonymous 16-12-2012, 08:44,
> http://www.dcurbanmom.com/jforum/posts/list/135/278571.page)

To be a pain is a commonly used phrase to mean that 'somebody or something is a nuisance'. This particular metaphorical expression is used very frequently, also in modified versions, like *to be a pain in the backside, to be a pain in the neck, to be a pain in the ass* as in (156), or *to be a royal pain in the ass*.

> (156) Hardwood is relatively easy to clean (although I wouldn't say it's something I enjoy spending my weekend on), but these *carpets are a royal pain in the ass*.
> (Anonymous 18-01-2013, 22:02,
> http://www.dcurbanmom.com/jforum/posts/list/225/284256.page)

4.2.6 Metaphors of people, their actions and attitudes

In this subsection various metaphors of people are presented. In example (157), people who are called *hired gun* always criticize public schools. The same people are pictured as hunting animals in (158). The metaphorical expressions are used to stress the strength with which the criticism of public schools is made.

> (157) A few weeks ago on a different thread, another poster, not me, suggested that there is an independent school "*hired gun*" here, just waiting to blast away at parents who suggest even mixed experience at any independent school. One thing militating against the "*hired gun*" theory is the sheer crassness and stupidity of whoever is doing these "concerted" or maybe *sock puppetted attacks*.
> (Anonymous 12-03-2012, 09:45,
> http://www.dcurbanmom.com/jforum/posts/list/120/275848.page)

(158) I am trying to glean information but, it is pretty clear the independent school boosters are *lying in wait on these forums for their prey.*
(Anonymous 02-12-2012, 21:45,
http://www.dcurbanmom.com/jforum/posts/list/120/275848.page)

In example (159) two metaphorical expressions are used. The first one, *be an asshole*, is a highly conventionalized and commonly used offensive way of saying that somebody is mean. The other expression in (159), *witch hunt* (misspelled in the original post), refers to 'constant criticism'.

(159) DW here, why can't people just accept that in SOME relationships the spouses have different levels of amount of sexual desire. It doesn't mean the world will end. It doesn't mean the *OP is an asshole*. It doesn't mean YOU will have a divorce. Give it a rest, OP said he was posting his title to get more people to click – so *relax your which hunt.*
(Anonymous 12-12-2012, 12:28,
http://www.dcurbanmom.com/jforum/posts/list/105/277971.page)

Example (160) is taken from a discussion in which a man complains about his wife's low sex drive. The author of (160) portrays this man's wife as a *cold bitch*. The word *cold* suggests that this person is devoid of any feelings and of sex drive. The phrase *cold bitch* is a commonly used and highly conventionalized offensive phrase.

(160) Either *she is a cold bitch* (doubtful and if so, you need to ask yourself why you married her) or you guys have issues.
(Anonymous 12-12-2012, 13:54,
http://www.dcurbanmom.com/jforum/posts/list/150/277971.page)

In post (161), children are pictured as birds since they *grow their own wings* and home as a nest.

(161) For kids: *provide a safe nest*, make best effort to raise them to the best of our ability, teach them to be the best they can be, encourage them when they have self-doubt, guide them, love them, be there for them - help them to *grow their own wings* and take off on their life's journey.
(Anonymous 03-03-2012, 00:25,
http://www.dcurbanmom.com/jforum/posts/list/120/71936.page)

The author of (162) depicts herself as *a broken record*, which means that she 'repeats herself'.

(162) Hire a babysitter and make some plans *I feel like a broken record* but really, go read 12:02 again.
(Anonymous 12-12-2012, 14:22,
http://www.dcurbanmom.com/jforum/posts/list/150/277971.page)

People are also pictured as machines which, when not functioning right, *miss screws* (163), are *broken* and *wired wrong* (164).

(163) I also don't know what happened in their home, but my priors are that a) a ten year old girl couldn't convince a mom to do something like that, and only a *mom missing screws* would ever agree and b) most ten year olds would cry about being excluded but have enough social sense not to push it.
(Anonymous 12-12-2012, 21:57,
http://www.dcurbanmom.com/jforum/posts/list/45/278038.page)

(164) *Some people are just broken and wired wrong.*
(Anonymous 15-12-2012, 19:39,
http://www.dcurbanmom.com/jforum/posts/list/278571.page)

To look down on somebody used in (165) means 'to despise, to consider someone as of a lesser value'. This metaphor has an experiential basis. People who are tall and literally look down on people are usually considered powerful and successful.

(165) I am a child of immigrants. It's my perception that *Americans look down on people of color* in general and people of color with accents.
(Anonymous 14-12-2012, 11:00,
http://www.dcurbanmom.com/jforum/posts/list/300/277136.page)

In example (166) *to have shit in a pile* is used to mean 'to have an organized and stable life'.

(166) A happy, stable guy is attractive to us bc *he seems to have his shit in a pile*. Nothing about your situation says "*I have my shit in a pile*". It's just a pile of… well, you get the point.
(Anonymous 20-01-2013, 11:53,
http://www.dcurbanmom.com/jforum/posts/list/120/284187.page)

Example (167) makes use of two different phrases with the word *shit*. The first one, *not to give shit*, means 'not to care', the second one is used as an offense.

(167) *I don't give shit* about being educated about guns since I never plan to have one. Is that good enough for you, you *sorry piece of shit*?
(Anonymous 17-12-2012, 18:32,
http://www.dcurbanmom.com/jforum/posts/list/270/278571.page)

Shit in example (168) refers to 'lies'.

(168) Your steadfast refusal to identify which country leads me to believe that if you post it you know full well that there are enough of your flavor of Europeans here to point out how *full of shit you are*.
(Anonymous 07-12-2012, 14:46,
http://www.dcurbanmom.com/jforum/posts/list/150/277136.page)

The person *carrying the torch* in post (169) is a leader, a person who makes decisions. This metaphorical expression is associated with the fact that while marching at night, the most important person is the one in the front carrying the source of light.

> (169) Now that I look back, I think I understand why He made this road so easy for us…it forced me to let go of control an trust in Him… I have such high expectations of myself in all aspects of life and this has been a learning experience and I now know *I don't have to be the one always carrying the torch*…
> (nostoppingme 25-08-2010, 11:04,
> http://americanpregnancy.org/forums/printthread.php?t=272141&pp=30&page=4)

The phrase *to jump ship* in (170) is used to mean 'to leave a company, to quit a job and move to competition'.

> (170) One of the best teachers in my kid's mcps *jumped ship* to a private school.
> (Anonymous 04-12-2012, 19:54,
> http://www.dcurbanmom.com/jforum/posts/list/135/275848.page)

The phrase *sticks up their butts* used in (171) is a metaphorical expression based on the opinion that people who have perfectly straight postures are usually arrogant and conceited.

> (171) People on the East coast *have giant sticks up their butts* and are major clean freak germophobes.
> (Anonymous 17-01-2013, 21:13,
> http://www.dcurbanmom.com/jforum/posts/list/45/284256.page)

Example (172) makes use of the metaphorical expression *rock the boat* which means 'make trouble'.

> (172) She's a SAHM and hate my dad. She stays in the marriage because she doesn't want to work and *doesn't want to rock the boat*.
> (Anonymous 12-13-2012, 10:26,
> http://www.dcurbanmom.com/jforum/posts/list/210/277971.page)

Example (173) makes use of the metaphor A HUMAN BEING IS A PIG, which is a resemblance metaphor. It is not the physical appearance that is ascribed to a person, but rather the qualities ascribed to the pig, like being dirty, smelly or messy.

> (173) *So if one of the two persons is* selfish, or lazy, or *a pig*, s/he is only going to have a damaged self to give – if they are capable of giving at all.
> (Anonymous 12-12-2012, 21:17,
> http://www.dcurbanmom.com/jforum/posts/list/195/277971.page)

The metaphorical expression used in (174) depicts some children as cannibals and other children as food.

> (174) While it is certainly true that no school can compare to TJ and Blair for a certain kind of kid (driven, healthy self esteem, wicked smart), *most kids would be eaten alive there* by the kids that are meant to be there.
> (Anonymous 02-12-2012, 09:06,
> http://www.dcurbanmom.com/jforum/posts/list/90/275848.page)

To be out of line (175) is a metaphorical expression based on the observation that people standing in a line are obedient and follow the orders, while a person who crosses the line is a rebel.

> (175) The mom *was out of line*.
> (Anonymous 12-12-2012, 23:20,
> http://www.dcurbanmom.com/jforum/posts/list/45/278038.page)

In post (176), the father is treated as a human being but of a specific kind. He is called *a drama queen*, to illustrate how emotional he is and how much he likes to be in the centre of attention.

> (176) we havent done ANY planning yet…we wanted to have the entire thing at my house..but my dad said that if the wedding is at our house then he won't be able to live there anymore…*he's being a drama queen* about the whole thing
> (Margaret (New Navy Wife!) 5-03-2009, 00:26,
> www.navyformoms.com/group/girlfriendsfianceswivesofsailors?groupUrl=girlfr iendsfianceswivesofsailors&id=1971797%3AGroup%3A24811&page=1210#com ments)

In example (177), the metaphorical expression *go out of one's way* is used to mean 'do as much as possible'.

> (177) Bolded PP above sure does seem to be *going out of his or her way* to apologize for a woman who owned military assault rifles.
> (Anonymous 18-12-2012, 09:30,
> http://www.dcurbanmom.com/jforum/posts/list/195/278508.page)

4.2.7 Metaphors of the human body

In this subsection metaphorical expressions of the human body are presented. In (178) the human body is pictured as food.

> (178) *His body is a feast to my senses and my soul*, and there is nothing hotter for either of us than giving the other pleasure.
> (Anonymous 12-12-2012, 14:55,
> http://www.dcurbanmom.com/jforum/posts/list/165/277971.page)

In example (179) a woman's body is depicted as a car in which hormones are able to *kick into high gear*.

(179) Apparently, my hormones *kicked into high gear* with bf'ing dd.
(queenj919 30-12-2008, 20:02,
http://americanpregnancy.org/forums/printthread.php?t=537&pp=30&page=3)

4.2.8 Metaphors of experiences

In this subsection metaphorical expressions of experience are presented. In example (180), the metaphorical expression *be in the same boat* is used, which exemplifies the metaphor LIFE IS A JOURNEY and means 'to share the same experience'.

(180) Well, *all of us on here seems to be in the same boat* so I'll just put my input too.
(CUAfterDark 17-06-2008, 18:30,
http://americanpregnancy.org/forums/printthread.php?t=38327&pp=30&page=2)

The author of (181) makes use of the metaphorical expression *walk the same path* meaning 'share experience'.

(181) I guess what I'm saying is that reading the snippets of lives here is going to give me so much hope as so many of you are either *walking the same path* or finding their dreams to be moms finally coming true.
(KMyers 23-09-2010, 17:36,
http://americanpregnancy.org/forums/printthread.php?t=272141&pp=30&page=10)

Examples (183)–(185) picture difficult times and unpleasant experiences as *long, rocky* or *bumpy roads* or *rides*, or even as *a roller coaster ride*, as in the case of (182).

(182) DH says when *the roller coaster ride is over* he's going to have a few words with RE about our experience. And you were right, my hormones where completely in overdrive.
(Southern Belle 01-10-2010, 10:55,
http://americanpregnancy.org/forums/printthread.php?t=272141&pp=30&page=12)

(183) Hi Nicola, My daughter will be three in march and is just getting out of nappies, we only put them on her when we go out and at night time now.
But its been a long hard road- we almost had her trained when my twin daughters came along and she reverted, and she is now the only one in our mums group who still wears nappies at all (all same age)
(Louise 01/07/2010, 16:21,

      http://www.circleofmoms.com/welcome-to-circle-of-moms/am-i-a-bad-mom-444657/2#replies)

(184) *I had a really bumpy ride for my PG.* My son was born at 27wks gest.
(tylers_mom29 22-06-2008, 20:40,
http://americanpregnancy.org/forums/printthread.php?t=175&pp=30&page=5)

(185) Im trying not to get too excited because *its been a rocky road* for my DH and I, but man, I cant help it!
(Rix Ride729 19-07-2008, 20:07,
http://americanpregnancy.org/forums/printthread.php?t=38327&pp=30&page=2)

Example (186) presents a metaphorical expression in which education is described as a journey.

(186) Every one of us wants to one day graduate, but these *journeys are long and hard for many.*
(nostoppingme 21-08-2010, 10:36,
http://americanpregnancy.org/forums/printthread.php?t=272141&pp=30&page=3)

The author of post (187) pictures being on duty in the navy as a journey.

(187) your boyfriends finishing his 6 years while mines *just starting his journey* in the navy.
(Minerva 02-03-2009, 22:27,
http://www.navyformoms.com/group/girlfriendsfianceswivesofsailors?groupUrl=girlfriendsfianceswivesofsailors&id=1971797%3AGroup%3A24811&page=1211#comments)

As can be easily seen, all these examples make use of the examples make use of the source domain JOURNEY.

4.2.9 Metaphors of criticism

Examples (188) and (189) contain the highly conventionalized phrase *something stinks* or *sucks* meaning 'something is of a poor quality or bad'.

(188) *Disrespecting women stinks* even if she, the woman, is a racist jerk. I don't know what teh cousin was thinking, but his brain is not wired right.
(Anonymous 05-12-2012, 15:34,
http://www.dcurbanmom.com/jforum/posts/list/270/276147.page)

(189) I agree. I think sometimes middle schools get a bad rap because frankly *middle school sucks*, but the idea that you would be fine for public ES and public HS, but you can't bear to send your kids to Pyle is a little hard to wrap my head around.

(Anonymous 11-29-2012, 23:28,
http://www.dcurbanmom.com/jforum/posts/list/30/275848.page)

The author of (190) compares a heated discussion of public versus private schools to *an arms race*.

(190) You guys totally *play a part in the arms race* when you clip off the relevant part o f that PP's post and just leave the part about TJ/Blair.
(Anonymous 02-12-2012, 10:27,
http://www.dcurbanmom.com/jforum/posts/list/90/275848.page)

The author of (191) uses the verb *butcher* which is an emotionally-loaded equivalent of the verb *criticise*.

(191) It's obvious *you wouldn't have butchered 22:21's post* in a way that makes Blair-TJ parents look bad, if you're actually a Blair parent yourself.
(Anonymous 12-02-2012, 12:12,
http://www.dcurbanmom.com/jforum/posts/list/90/275848.page)

4.2.10 Metaphors of choosing an option

In this subsection metaphorical expressions of choosing an option are presented. All of them are highly conventionalized as they appear in everyday language quite frequently.

Posts (192)–(194) make use of the metaphorical expressions *go a certain route/way/road* and *take a certain route/way/road*, to refer to options.

(192) Also I have a friend who is carrying for IF's and there has been alot of drama for her in the first few months so I just thought it would be easiest *not to go that route*.
(luvmykids 02-11-2011, 20:37,
http://www.allaboutsurrogacy.com/forums/index.php?showtopic=35196&st=60)

(193) Good luck making your decision and *let us know which way you go!*
(HighHopesMama 22-10-2010, 15:47,
http://americanpregnancy.org/forums/printthread.php?t=272141&pp=30&page=17)

(194) OP, good luck to you. *You have taken the hard road* for the benefit of your child, you are a good mother.
(Anonymous 25-01-2013, 22:46,
http://www.dcurbanmom.com/jforum/posts/list/45/285748.page)

The phrase *take the high road* in example (195) means 'do the right things even if it is not easy'.

(195) I would want my *daughter to take the high road*.
(Anonymous 12-12-2012, 18:53,
http://www.dcurbanmom.com/jforum/posts/list/30/278038.page)

The posts presented in this subsection exemplify the metaphor LIFE IS A JOURNEY.

4.2.11 Metaphors of time

4.2.11.1 Metaphors of time in general

Subsection 4.2.11.1 presents three conventional metaphors of time. In example (196) time is presented as a creature that is able to walk. The author of (197) treats time as an object which can be given to somebody. In (198), time is personified and it has an ability to talk.

(196) End of the day, its your soul mate you are left with when *time comes* to end your journey.
(Anonymous 03-03-2012, 00:25,
http://www.dcurbanmom.com/jforum/posts/list/120/71936.page)

(197) I just want to be a mommy again, but I have to *give my body some time.*
(Rebecca_08 03-08-2008, 13:23,
http://americanpregnancy.org/forums/printthread.php?t=175&pp=30&page=4)

(198) *Time will tell!*
(nostoppingme 09-03-2010, 13:19,
http://americanpregnancy.org/forums/printthread.php?t=272141&pp=30&page=7)

4.2.11.2 Metaphors of future

In this subsection metaphors of future are presented. Future is depicted as *a way* or a *road*. Example (199) makes use of the metaphorical expression *go a long way* meaning 'to have a positive effect in the future'.

(199) Do you pull your weight as much as you can with the kids and everything else in the house? *That will go a long way.*
(Anonymous 12-12-2012, 09:37,
http://www.dcurbanmom.com/jforum/posts/list/15/277971.page)

Examples (200) and (201) make use of the metaphor LIFE IS A JOURNEY and picture *future* as a certain point *down the road*. A road ahead in (200) means 'future', or, 'future experiences'.

(200) Just nervous and scared about this *road ahead of us.*
(jli 24-10-2011, 00:46,
http://americanpregnancy.org/forums/printthread.php?t=175&pp=30&page=7)

Down the road in (201) corresponds to 'at the end' or 'eventually'.

(201) The baby is four MONTHS old. SIXTEEN WEEKS. Who are you to predict anything *seven years down the road?*
(Anonymous 13-12-2012, 13:48,
http://www.dcurbanmom.com/jforum/posts/list/270/277971.page)

4.2.12 Metaphors of weapons

In this subsection two metaphors of weapons are presented. In example (202), a gun is pictured as *poison*. In (203) a gun is depicted as a man's *surrogate penis*.

(202) Oh yes, I understand. I guess by that I meant the assault-rifles. Really, anything that can fire X number of rounds (*pick your poison*, 5, 8, 10, 12) without being reloaded.
(Anonymous 17-12-2012, 16:28,
http://www.dcurbanmom.com/jforum/posts/list/270/278571.page)

(203) You will never have some movie worthy intruder come sneaking into your house at night whereby your stupid husband *loads his surrogate penis* and shoots the intruder.
(Anonymous 15-12-2012, 19:56,
http://www.dcurbanmom.com/jforum/posts/list/15/278571.page)

4.3 Concluding remarks

This chapter has aimed to present metaphorical expressions found on American Internet forums.

In ten thousand analyzed posts, only 143 metaphorical expressions were found. They were categorized into 17 groups, namely: emotions (anger, happiness and sadness, other feelings and emotions), metaphors of relationships, sex, pregnancy, everyday life, people, their actions and attitudes, experiences, criticism, choosing an option, time in general, future and weapon.

It is worth noting that there are certain discussion threads which despite their length did not contain a single metaphorical expression. These were: *crazy stuff your in-laws feed your kids*; *Diaper Fairy*; *Found out my husband has account at Ashley Madison*; *gender disappointment*; *Having babies after 30:Yes or no?*; *How awful – nurse who answered prank call about Princess Kate commits suicide*; *Husband not interested in sex*; *I once knew someone so cheap…*; *My husband is fucking our au pair and I am ok with it.*; *Oh Holy Heck*; *Roll Call!!!*; *The dreaded pumping… tips, advice, and recommendations*; *What do all you working mamas do for a living?*; *What does anal sex feel like?*; *When to pierce ears?*; *Who Are You?* and

Would You Be Upset if We Take Our Three Year Old With Us to Dinner Tonight for New Years Eve?

Numerous metaphorical expressions have been found in discussions involving emotions, which would corroborate other findings concerning the metaphoricity of the language of emotions, e.g. Apresjan (1997), Bamberg (1997), Cichmińska (2010), Ekman (1992, 1996), Esenova (2008), Kövecses (1986, 1990, 1998, 2000, 2002, 2006), Malewska (2010), Ortony (1980), Oster (2010) and Wierzbicka (1999).

Chapter Five A comparative analysis of metaphors used on Polish and American Internet forums

5.1 Introductory remarks

The aim of this chapter is to compare the use of metaphors on the Polish and American Internet forums for parents.

Each section in Chapters Three and Four was devoted to an individual thematic area, and each of them was illustrated with examples of metaphorical expressions. There are features that all the presented metaphorical expressions share. First of all, the metaphors the expressions exemplify are based on cultural, bodily and biological experiences which are shared by the Internet forum users. Barcelona highlights the importance of both cultural background and physical experiences in metaphor usage:

> Metaphors [...] are to a large extent culture-specific, because the domains of experience are not necessarily the same in all cultures, but the most abstract, overarching metaphors [...] seem to have as input or 'source' domains universal physical notions like 'verticality', 'container', etc., known as 'image schemas', which are acquired on the basis of our earliest bodily experiences (Barcelona 2000: 6).

Conventionality is another characteristic feature of conceptual metaphor that can be identified in most of the examples presented in Chapters Three and Four.

Many of the presented posts contain examples of personification. Kövecses (2010: 39) claims that personification is a form of ontological metaphor. Lakoff and Johnson comment on personification in following words:

> The point here is that personification is a general category that covers a very wide range of metaphors, each picking out different aspects of a person or ways of looking at a person. What they all have in common is that they are extensions of ontological metaphors and that they allow us to make sense of phenomena in the world in human terms – terms that we can understand on the basis of our own motivations, goals, actions, and characteristics. Viewing something as abstract as inflation in human terms has an explanatory power of the only sort that makes sense to most people. When we are suffering substantial economic losses due to complex economic and political factors that no one really understands, the INFLATION IS AN ADVERSARY metaphor at least gives us a coherent account of why we're suffering these losses (Lakoff and Johnson 1980: 34).

There are numerous examples that picture nonhuman entities, parts of the human body or physiological and emotional states as human beings, to mention just a few:

- (19)   *nerwowka cie dopadla* 'nerves get somebody'
- (27)   *postawic psychike na nogi* 'psyche is to be put on its legs'
- (37)   *zwiazek jest chory* 'relationship is sick'
- (46)   *libido poszlo na urlop* 'libido goes on vacation'
- (138) *the heart goes out to somebody*
- (199) *time will tell*

On the basis of the examples presented in Chapters Three and Four, it is also possible to observe in which discussion threads metaphorical language was used and from which it was absent.

5.2 A qualitative analysis of metaphorical language used on various discussion threads

One of the aims of this study is to investigate which subjects of the Internet discussions contain the most and which the fewest metaphorical expressions. The choice of threads for the analysis is extremely wide: the investigated topics range from *I feel I am a bad mother* to *anal sex*. Some discussions contain only short informative answers, as in the case of *What do all you working mamas do for a living?* or *When to pierce ears?*

It is obvious that not all topics on Polish and American forums were similar. Out of 28 Polish discussion threads and 44 American ones only 15, presented in Table 17, have corresponding subjects.

Table 17: Corresponding discussion threads

1	*Czuję że jestem złą matką* 'I feel I am a bad mother' 90 posts analyzed and **numerous metaphorical expressions** found	*am i a bad mom?* 204 posts analyzed and only **one metaphorical expression** found
2	*1 DZIECKO PO 30-STCE* '1 child after 30' 1200 posts analyzed and **numerous metaphorical expressions** found	*Having babies after 30: Yes or no?* 28 posts analyzed and **no metaphorical expressions** found
3	*Czy można i jak zaplanować płec dziecka?? chłopiec/dziewczynka?:)* 'How can you plan the baby's sex?? boy/girl?:)' 525 posts analyzed and **no metaphorical expressions** found	*Can I choose my baby's sex?* 41 posts analyzed and only **one metaphorical expression** found

4	*kolczyki u niemowlaka* 'earrings for a toddler' 258 posts analyzed and **no metaphorical expressions** found	*When to pierce ears?* 37 posts analyzed and **no metaphorical expressions** found
5	*sex analny* 'anal sex' 292 posts analyzed and **no metaphorical expressions** found	*What does anal sex feel like?* 241 posts analyzed and **no metaphorical expressions** found
6	*sex w ciąży* 'pregnant sex' 954 posts analyzed and **no metaphorical expressions** found	*Let's Talk About (Pregnant) Sex* 77 posts analyzed and **one metaphorical expression** found
7	*Mąż nie ma ochoty na sex* 'Husband doesn't want sex' 236 posts analyzed and **several metaphorical expressions** found	*Husband not interested in sex* 32 posts analyzed and **no metaphorical expressions** found
8	*Zdrada* 'Cheating' 373 posts analyzed and **numerous metaphorical expressions** found	*I want to have an affair – can't pull it off for some reason* 134 posts analyzed and **several metaphorical expressions** found
9	*Kiepski małżeński sex…* 'Poor marital sex…' 122 posts analyzed and **numerous metaphorical expressions** found	*If I had know this was the case, I probably wouldn't have married you* 567 posts analyzed and **numerous metaphorical expressions** found
	Czy ochota na seks po porodzie jeszcze kiedyś nadejdzie? 'Will the desire to have sex come back after giving birth?' 320 posts analyzed and **numerous metaphorical expressions** found	
10	*dramatyczny powrót do pracy* 'Dramatic return to work' 17 posts analyzed and **one metaphorical expression** found	*Should I feel guilty about going back to work?* 106 posts analyzed and **one metaphorical expression** found
11	*Mamusie i ich maleństwa 2009* 'Mammies and their babies 2009' 2399 posts analyzed and **numerous metaphorical expressions** found	*Roll Call!!!* 109 posts analyzed and **no metaphorical expressions** found
12	*maluszki i mamusie z Kaszub* 'Babies and mammies from Kaszuby' 66 posts analyzed and **no metaphorical expressions** found	*Who Are You?* 276 posts analyzed and **no metaphorical expressions** found

13	*żony marynarzy..integujmy się:)* 'sailors' wives..let's get together:)' 81 posts analyzed and **no metaphorical expressions** found	*Girlfriends, Fiances, and Wives of Sailors* 2098 posts analyzed and **several metaphorical expressions** found
14	*Starania po raz pierwszy :)* 'Trying (to conceive) for the first time :)' 840 posts analyzed and **several metaphorical expressions** found	*Post your TTC story and diagnosis here* 301 posts analyzed and **several metaphorical expressions** found Share your story 9 posts analyzed and **one metaphorical expression** found
15	*Zakłopotanie...* 'Embarrassment...' 56 posts analyzed and **several metaphorical expressions** found	*crazy stuff your in-laws feed your kids* 108 posts analyzed and **no metaphorical expressions** found

In the case of the first pair of topics, there is a considerable difference in the number of metaphorical expressions, even though the Polish thread was much shorter. The metaphors SAD IS DOWN and BRINGING UP CHILDREN IS A FIGHT are mainly used.

In the second pair of topics, the discrepancy is easily explainable by the fact that there were only 28 posts in the American discussion and 1200 posts in the Polish one. *Having babies after 30:Yes or no?* was a thread with simple yes/no answers, while the Polish thread contained stories of women who wanted to have babies. It was a very emotional discussion where depression and joy were intertwining.

Cases 3 and 4 were purely informative threads with simple yes/no answers mostly. There were short posts, no longer than four sentences.

Discussion threads connected with sex are an interesting case. Discussions about anal and pregnant sex, 5 and 6, were purely informative; there were no metaphorical expressions, despite the length of these conversations. Also other topics, like *Najlepsze pozycje, aby zajść w ciążę?* 'Best positions to get pregnant?', *Ulubiona pozycja ;-)* 'Favourite position ;-)', *Czy twój mężczyzna ogląda strony pornograficzne???* 'Does your man watch pornographic websites???', *Found out my husband has account at Ashley Madison*, *My husband is fucking our au pair and I am ok with it*, did not contain any metaphorical expressions. On the other hand, online conversations about sex which included emotions, such as anger, disappointment, embarrassment and depression, 8 and 9, are rich in metaphors. Calling spouses names is very metaphorical, examples of such expressions are quoted in sections 3.2.2, 3.2.12 and 4.2.6 presenting metaphors of relationships, people, their behaviour and attitudes.

Topics related to returning to work after maternity leave contain no or just one metaphorical expression, even though the subject is rather emotional.

There are many subjects of online discussions which are initiated by mothers who want to get to know other people. There are 83 "local groups" on Babyboom.pl, to name just a few: *mamy z Bradford* 'moms from Bradford', *Szczecin*, *Mamusie z Leszna* 'Mommies from Leszno' etc. These threads differ in content, some of them (pairs 12 and 13), as well as *Roll Call!!!, Oh Holy Heck, What do all you working mamas do for a living?* and *Diaper Fairy*, consist mostly of greetings and introductions. On the other hand, the topic *Mamusie i ich maleństwa 2009* 'Mommies and their babies 2009' was one of the longest analyzed threads which enabled women to befriend each other. The bonds built on this forum grew so strong that some of its users and their families spent holidays together. There were few such topics, for example the ones about surrogacy, that created such a safe environment that people openly discussed their emotions, fears and frustrations with the help of numerous metaphorical expressions representing various target domains.

Topics 14 and 15 were mainly about sharing stories either of trying to conceive or about problems with parents-in-law; they contained several metaphorical expressions connected mostly with emotions.

The topics of online discussions may be divided into three groups, depending on the number on metaphorical expressions found.

The first set of discussion threads contains topics where no metaphorical expressions were found. It includes the following topics:

- *Najlepsze pozycje, aby zajść w ciąże?* 'Best positions to get pregnant?'
- *Ulubiona pozycja ;-)* 'Favourite position ;-)'
- *Czy twój mężczyzna ogląda strony pornograficzne???* 'Does your man watch pornographic websites???'
- *Wakacje z maluszkiem* 'Holidays with the baby'
- *Found out my husband has account at Ashley Madison*
- *My husband is fucking our au pair and I am ok with it.*
- *How awful – nurse who answered prank call about Princess Kate commits suicide*
- *I once knew someone so cheap…*
- *Oh Holy Heck*
- *The dreaded pumping… tips, advice, and recommendations*
- *What do all you working mamas do for a living?*
- *Would You Be Upset if We Take Our Three Year Old With Us to Dinner Tonight for New Years Eve?*

- *Diaper Fairy*
- *gender disappointment*

The second group presents topics where one or several metaphorical expressions have been found. The following topics belong to this set:

- *Apel o życzliwość dla małych brzuszków* 'Call for kindness for small (pregnant) bellies'
- *Więcej życzliwości dla kobiet w ciąży* 'More kindness for pregnant women'
- *Życzliwość dla mam z dziećmi – tak czy nie?* 'Kindness for mums with children – yes or no?'
- *Ludzie mnie zaskakują :) Jak traktuje się kobiety ciężarne?* 'People surprise me :) How are pregnant women treated?'
- *13 pytań o antykoncepcję* '13 questions about contraception'
- *Dotykanie brzuszka* 'Touching the (pregnant) belly'
- *Husband ruined Christmas*
- *I blame Adam Lanza's mother*
- *I'm Jewish. Ask me anything*
- *in tears*
- *Paying 32K and my DD's teacher has NO idea what she's doing*
- *Please take off your shoes!!!*
- *S/o "foreigners" what have your found most interesting about USA*
- *Things I wish I'd known about BFing before Baby Came*
- *Vent – DD's classmate's mother just called to ask me to invite her kid to my kid's bday party*
- *Why do you own a gun?*
- *What to tell child who is product of an affair?*
- *Do you love your kids more than your wife?*
- *What were your early pregnancy symptoms?*
- *Early Pregnancy signs/symptoms*
- *Interracial sex….*

Online discussion topics which contain numerous metaphorical expressions are found in the third set:

- *Więcej życzliwości dla Cycusiów!!!* 'More kindness for (feeding) Breasts!!!'
- *CIĄŻA TO NIE CHOROBA – Ja to wiem!!* 'Pregnancy is not a disease – I know that!!'
- *IVF – Sisters*
- *Just curious – how many would carry for a gay couple?*
- *New to Surrogacy*

Analyzing the results of the research, it is visible that online discussion topics which involve emotions are the ones with the highest numbers of metaphorical expressions. The first two pairs of corresponding topics listed in Table 17 show that there are large discrepancies between Polish and American use of metaphorical expressions. The Polish participants employ metaphors to discuss being a bad mother and having babies after 30, whereas the American participants use plain language to talk about these issues.

Metaphors used by the Polish Internet forum users listed below are grouped according to the target domains.

Metaphors of emotions:
ANGER IS A HOT FLUID IN A CONTAINER
ANGER IS A FLOOD OF BLOOD
NERVES ARE OBJECTS
NERVES ARE LIVING BEINGS
NERVES ARE FOOD
DEPRESSED IS DOWN
HAPPINESS IS UP
LACK OF EMOTIONS IS ICE
LOVE IS FIRE
THE PSYCHE IS A LIVING CREATURE
PANIC IS A PLANT
FEELINGS ARE FLUIDS

Metaphors of relationships:
RELATIONSHIPS ARE LIVING ORGANISMS
RELATIONSHIPS ARE BUILDINGS

Metaphors of people:
PEOPLE ARE ANIMALS
PEOPLE ARE CLOTHES
PEOPLE ARE BRITTLE OBJECTS
PEOPLE ARE MACHINES

Metaphors of sex:
THE LIBIDO IS A HUMAN BEING
SPERM IS AMMUNITION
SPERM IS SOLDIERS

Metaphors of conception:
GETTING PREGNANT IS HITTING THE TARGET

Metaphors of bringing up children:
BRINGING UP CHILDREN IS WAR
WAILING OF A CHILD IS A SIREN

Metaphors of progress:
RAPID PROGRESS IS AN EXPLOSION
QUICK PROGRESS IS A STEAM TRAIN

Metaphors of the human body:
PARTS OF THE BODY ARE LIVING BEINGS
HEADS ARE CONTAINERS INTO WHICH ONE CAN PUT OBJECTS
THE HEART IS A CONTAINER
TEETH ARE LIVING BEINGS

Metaphors of illnesses and health:
ILLNESSES ARE OBJECTS ONE CATCHES
ILLNESSES ARE PLACES
FEVER IS A LIVING BEING
DISEASE IS AN ENEMY
A HEADACHE IS A PLANT
IMMUNITY IS AN OBJECT ONE CATCHES

Metaphors of everyday life:
CHAOS IS A CIRCUS
REMORSE IS AN OBJECT
IDEAS/THOUGHTS ARE OBJECTS
STAINS ARE LIVING BEINGS
CHOICES ARE EXITS
SNORING IS PERFORMING A CONCERT
HEALTH SERVICE IS A LIVING BEING
SUFFERING IS WALKING
POWER IS UP
STRESS IS A LIVING BEING
QUEUE IS A CONTAINER

Metaphors of shopping:
SHOPPING IS HUNTING
SHOPPING IS FISHING

Metaphors of problems:
OVERCOMING PROBLEMS IS FIGHTING
PROBLEMS ARE OBJECTS
PROBLEMS ARE RIDES

Metaphors of time:
TIME PASSING IS MOTION OF AN OBJECT
TIME IS A LIVING BEING
TIME IS A VALUABLE COMMODITY

Metaphors of weather:
THE SEASONS OF THE YEAR ARE LIVING BEINGS
THE SUN IS A LIVING BEING

Metaphors of computers and Internet-related phenomena:
COMPUTERS ARE PEOPLE
THE INTERNET IS A PLACE

Metaphors of world, life, fate and nature:
THE WORLD IS A LIVING BEING
LIFE IS A PATH
LIFE IS A STORY
LIFE IS AN OBJECT
FATE IS A HUMAN BEING
NATURE IS A HUMAN BEING

Metaphors of freedom and patience:
FREEDOM IS A LIVING BEING
PATIENCE IS A WEAPON
PATIENCE IS FABRIC

Metaphors used by the American Internet forum users listed below are also grouped according to the target domains.

Metaphors of emotions:
ANGER IS A HOT FLUID IN A CONTAINER
HAPPINESS IS UP
SAD IS DOWN

Metaphors of criticism:
CRITICISM IS AN ATTACK
CRITICISM IS A WITCH HUNT
TO CRITICISE IS TO BUTCHER

Metaphors of the human body and body parts:
THE HUMAN BODY IS FOOD
THE HUMAN BODY IS A CAR
THE HEART IS A LIVING BEING
THE HEART IS A HUMAN BEING

Metaphors of relationships:
RELATIONSHIPS ARE HOTELS
RELATIONSHIPS ARE ROADS
RELATIONSHIPS ARE DEVICES
RELATIONSHIPS ARE FLUIDS

Metaphors of sex:
SEX IS RAIN
LACK OF SEX DRIVE IS COLDNESS

Metaphors of pregnancy and conception:
PREGNANCY IS A JOURNEY
TRYING TO CONCEIVE IS A JOURNEY
SURROGACY IS A JOURNEY

Metaphors of problems:
PROBLEMS/WORRIES ARE SHIT

Metaphors of everyday life:
DOING CHORES IS PULLING ONE'S WEIGHT
CHORES ARE SHIT
ANNOYING THINGS ARE A PAIN
SELF ESTEEM IS AN OBJECT
HOME IS A NEST
LIES ARE SHIT
TO CHANGE A JOB IS TO JUMP SHIP
TO MAKE TROUBLES IS TO ROCK THE BOAT
TO DESPISE IS TO LOOK DOWN
DOING EVERYTHING IN ONE'S MIGHT IS GOING OUT OF ONE'S WAY
EDUCATION IS A JOURNEY
MILITARY DUTY IS A JOURNEY
A DISCUSSION IS AN ARMS RACE
OPTIONS ARE ROUTES/WAYS/ROADS
BAD IS SMELLY

Metaphors of people:
PEOPLE ARE GUNS
PEOPLE ARE MACHINES
PEOPLE ARE ANIMALS
PEOPLE ARE PIGS
PEOPLE ARE CANNIBALS
PEOPLE ARE FOOD
MEAN PEOPLE ARE ASSHOLES/ASSES
CHILDREN ARE BIRDS
EMOTIONAL PEOPLE ARE DRAMA QUEENS

Metaphors of life:
LIFE IS A JOURNEY

Metaphors of experience:
SHARING EXPERIENCE IS BEING IN THE SAME BOAT
SHARING EXPERIENCE IS WALKING THE SAME PATH
EXPERIENCE IS A ROAD
EXPERIENCE IS A (ROLLER COASTER) RIDE

Metaphors of time:
TIME IS A LIVING BEING
TIME IS AN OBJECT
TIME IS A HUMAN BEING
FUTURE IS A WAY/ROAD

Metaphors of weapons:
A GUN IS POISON
A GUN IS A PENIS

5.3 A quantitative analysis of metaphorical expressions

One of the aims of this study has been to examine the differences and similarities between the metaphors used by Polish and American mothers on Internet forums. Table 18 presents thematic areas to which the identified metaphorical expressions belong, as well as the numbers of such expressions.

Table 18: Metaphorical expressions: Thematic areas

Metaphors		Polish Forums				American Forums			
		Number of Occurrences		% of Occurrences (N = 205)		Number of Occurrences		% of Occurrences (N = 171)	
Metaphors of emotions	Metaphors of anger	4	44	2.0%	21.5%	19	36	11.1%	21.0%
	Metaphors of aggitation and nerves	6		2.9%		-		0.0%	
	Metaphors of depression	22		10.7%		-		0.0%	
	Metaphors of happiness and sadness	4		2.0%		13		7.6%	
	Metaphors of panic	1		0.5%		-		0.0%	
	Metaphors of other feelings and emotions	7		3.4%		4		2.3%	
Metaphors of relationships		28		13.7%		10		5.8%	
Metaphors of sex		4		2.0%		1		0.6%	
Metaphors of pregnancy		-		0.0%		35		20.5%	
Metaphors of conception		4		2.0%		-		0.0%	
Metaphors of bringing up children		2		1.0%		-		0.0%	
Metaphors of children's progress		8		3.9%		-		0.0%	
Metaphors of parts of the body	Metaphors of teeth	22	26	10.7%	12.7%	-	2	0.0%	1.2%
	Metaphors of other parts of the body	4		2.0%		2		1.2%	
Metaphors of illnesses		12		5.9%		-		0.0%	
Metaphors of everyday life		24		11.7%		9		5.3%	
Metaphors of shopping		2		1.0%		-		0.0%	
Metaphors of problems and hardship		24		11.7%		-		0.0%	
Metaphors of people, their behaviour and attitudes		6		2.9%		35		20.5%	
Metaphors of experiences		-		0.0%		16		9.4%	

Metaphors		Polish Forums		American Forums	
		Number of Occurrences	% of Occurrences (N = 205)	Number of Occurrences	% of Occurrences (N = 171)
Metaphors of criticism		-	0.0%	10	5.8%
Metaphors of choosing an option		-	0.0%	7	4.1%
Metaphors of time	Metaphors of time (in general)	11	5.4%	3	1.8%
	Metaphors of the future	-	0.0%	5	2.9%
	Total			8	4.7%
Metaphors of the weather		4	2.0%	-	0.0%
Metaphors of computers and Internet-related phenomena		3	1.5%	-	0.0%
Metaphors of the world, life, fate and nature		12	5.9%	-	0.0%
Metaphors of freedom and patience		3	1.5%	-	0.0%
Metaphors of weapons		-	0.0%	2	1.2%

The data in Table 18 show that there are quite large differences in the choice of thematic areas used as well as in the numbers of metaphorical expressions employed within the same thematic areas.

In the analyzed discussion threads on American forums, despite the fact that many topics involved emotions, there are no metaphors of depression. In the Polish online conversations, there are numerous instances of metaphorical expressions connected with depression. There are, however, examples of realizations of the metaphor SAD IS DOWN.

On the one hand, metaphors of pregnancy are present only on American forums, especially the ones about surrogacy. Polish discussion threads contain metaphorical expressions referring to conception, bringing up children and children's progress.

Metaphorical expressions connected with everyday life also differ in number. Moreover, the Polish users of Internet forums employed numerous metaphors of problems and hardship as well as of illnesses. Metaphors of teeth are so deeply entrenched in the Polish language that it is hard to think of other ways of talking about teething than *zęby idą* 'teeth are coming'.

The American users of Internet forums for mothers use many more metaphorical expressions of people, their behavior and attitudes. The ratio is approximately 1 to 6. Calling other people names is quite metaphorical in English. Also, metaphorical expressions related to experience, criticism and choosing options are found in the posts written by the American users.

Complaining about the fate, world, life and nature as well as about the weather and devices is encountered only in posts written by Polish parents.

Table 19 presents a ranking list of Polish and American metaphorical expressions according to the thematic areas.

Table 19: Use of metaphors in thematic areas: Ranking lists

Polish Forums				American Forums			
Rank	Thematic Area	Number of Occurences	% of Occurrences (N = 205)	Rank	Thematic Area	Number of Occurrences	% of Occurrences (N = 171)
1	Relationships	28	13.7%	1–2	Pregnancy	35	20.5%
2	Problems and hardship	24	11.7%	1–2	People. their behaviour and attitudes	35	20.5%
3–4	Teeth	22	10.7%	3	Anger	19	11.1%
3–4	Depression	22	10.7%	4	Experiences	16	9.4%
5–6	Illnesses	12	5.9%	5	Happiness and sadness	13	7.6%
5–6	Everyday life	24	11.7%	6–7	Relationships	10	5.8%
5–6	The world, life, fate and nature	12	5.9%	6–7	Criticism	10	5.8%
7	Time	11	5.4%	8	Everyday life	9	5.3%
8	Children's progress	8	3.9%	9	Choosing an option	7	4.1%
9	Other feelings and emotions	7	3.4%	10	Future	5	2.9%
10–11	Aggitation and nerves	6	2.9%	11	Other feelings and emotions	4	2.3%
10–11	People, their behaviour and attitudes	6	2.9%	12	Time	3	1.8%
12–13	Anger	4	2.0%	15	Parts of the body	2	1.2%

	Polish Forums				American Forums		
Rank	Thematic Area	Number of Occurences	% of Occurrences (N = 205)	Rank	Thematic Area	Number of Occurences	% of Occurrences (N = 171)
12–13	Happiness and sadness	4	2.0%	-	Weapons	2	1.2%
12–13	Conception	4	2.0%		Sex	1	0.6%
12–13	Parts of the body	4	2.0%	15			
12–13	Sex	4	2.0%	-	-	-	-
12–13	Weather	4	2.0%	-	-	-	-
14–15	Computers and Internet-related phenomena	3	1.5%	-	-	-	-
14–15	Freedom and patience	3	1.5%	-	-	-	-
16–17	Bringing up children	2	1.0%	-	-	-	-
16–17	Shopping	2	1.0%	-	-	-	-

The data in Table 19 show that the Polish Internet forum users employed the largest number of metaphorical expressions referring to relationships (28 instances). 24 metaphorical expressions were used to talk about everyday life as well as about problems and hardship. 22 expressions were used to talk about depression and teething. In the fourth position, with 12 metaphorical expressions each, 3 thematic areas are placed: (1) illnesses, (2) the world, life, fate and nature and (3) everyday life.

The largest number of metaphorical expressions used by the American Internet forum users was in the areas of pregnancy and people, their behaviour and attitudes (35 instances in each area). 19 metaphorical expressions were employed in to refer to anger and 16 to talk about experience. 13 metaphorical expressions were used to discuss happiness and sadness.

The data in Table 20 show that there are large differences in the popularity of the thematic areas.

Table 20: Use of metaphors in thematic areas: Ranking lists (2)

Thematic Area	Polish Forums		American Forums	
	Rank	% of Occurrences (N = 205)	Rank	% of Occurrences (N = 171)
Relationships	1	13.7%	6–7	5.8%
Problems and hardship	2–3	11.7%	-	-
Everyday life	2–3	11.7%	8	5.3%
Teeth	4–5	10.7%	-	-
Depression	4–5	10.7%	-	-
Illnesses	6–7	5.9%	-	-
The world, life, fate and nature	6–7	5.9%	-	-
Time	8	5.4%	12	1.8%
Children's progress	9	3.9%	3	11.1%
Other feelings and emotions	10	3.4%	-	
Metaphors of aggitation and nerves	11–12	2.9%	11	2.3%
People, their behaviour and attitudes	11–12	2.9%		
Anger	13–18	2.0%	1–2	20.5%
Happiness and sadness	13–18	2.0%	5	7.6%
Conception	13–18	2.0%	-	-
Parts of the body	13–18	2.0%	13	1.2%
Sex	13–18	2.0%	15	0.6%
Weather	13–18	2.0%	-	-
Computers and Internet-related phenomena	19–20	1.5%	-	-
Freedom and patience	19–20	1.5%	-	-
Bringing up children	21–22	1.0%	-	-
Shopping	21–22	1.0%	-	-
Pregnancy	-	-	1–2	20.5%

Thematic Area	Polish Forums		American Forums	
	Rank	% of Occurrences (N = 205)	Rank	% of Occurrences (N = 171)
Experiences	-	-	4	9.4%
Criticism	-	-	6–7	5.8%
Choosing an option	-	-	9	4.1%
Future	-	-	10	2.9%
Weapons	-	-	14	1.2%

The data in Table 20 show that out of 28 thematic areas in the discussion of which metaphorical expressions were employed only 9 occurred on both Polish and American forums, namely relationships (rank 1 on Polish, 6–7 on American), everyday life (rank 2–3 on Polish, 8 on American), time (rank 8 on Polish, 12 on American), anger (rank 13–18 on Polish, 3 on American), people, their behaviour and attitudes (rank 11–12 on Polish, 1–2 on American), other feelings and emotions (rank 13–18 on Polish, 6–7 on American) and happiness and sadness (rank 13–17 on Polish, 5 on American). Only 2 however had the same rank, namely parts of the body (rank 13–18 on Polish, 13 on American) and sex (rank 13–18 on Polish, 15 on American).

Table 21 and Table 22 present classification of the most popular metaphors by target domains and source domains.

Table 21: Target domains of the most popular metaphors: Quantitative data (No. – number of occurrences, % – percentage of occurrences)

Target Domain	Source Domain	Polish Forums (N = 205)				American Forums (N = 171)			
		No.	%	No.	%	No.	%	No.	%
ANGER	HEATED FLUID IN A CONTAINER	1	0.48%	3	1.46%	9	5.26%	9	5.26%
	FLOOD OF BLOOD	2	0.97%			0	0.0%		
DEPRESSION	PIT	19	9.3%	19	9.3%	0	0.0%	0	0.0%
NERVES	LIVING BEING	1	0.48%	4	1.95%	0	0.0%	0	0.0%
	OBJECT	2	0.97%			0	0.0%		
	FOOD	1	0.48%			0	0.0%		
HAPPINESS	SPACE (UP)	4	1.95%	4	1.95%	6	3.51%	6	3.51%
SAD	SPACE (DOWN)	0	0.0%	0	0.0%	5	2.92%	5	2.92%
LACK OF EMOTIONS	ICE	2	0.97%	2	0.97%	0	0.0%	0	0.0%
LOVE	FIRE	3	1.46%	3	1.46%	0	0.0%	0	0.0%
EDUCATION	JOURNEY	0	0.0%	0	0.0%	1	0.58%	1	0.58%
MILITARY DUTY	JOURNEY	0	0.0%	0	0.0%	1	0.58%	1	0.58%
NERVES	FOOD	1	0.48%	1	0.7%	0	0.0%	0	0.0%
SELF ESTEEM	OBJECT	0	0.0%	0	0.0%	1	0.58%	1	0.58%
RELATIONSHIPS	LIVING ORGANISMS	2	0.97%	3	1.46%	0	0.0%	10	5.85%
	BUILDINGS	1	0.48%			0	0.0%		
	HOTELS	0	0.0%			2	1.17%		
	ROADS	0	0.0%			3	1.75%		
	DEVICES	0	0.0%			4	2.34%		
	FLUIDS	0	0.0%			1	0.58%		
SEX	RAIN	0	0.0%	0	0.0%	1	0.58%	1	0.58%
LACK OF SEX DRIVE	COLD	0	0.0%	0	0.0%	1	0.58%	1	0.58%
GETTING PREGNANT	HITTING THE TARGET	1	0.48%	1	0.48%	0	0.0%	0	0.0%
BRINGING UP CHILDREN	WAR	2	0.97%	2	0.97%	0	0.0%	0	0.0%
PROGRESS	EXPLOSION	1	0.48%			0	0.0%		
	STEAM TRAIN	1	0.48%			0	0.0%		
PARTS OF BODY	LIVING BEINGS	1	0.48%	1	0.48%	0	0.0%	0	0.0%

Target Domain	Source Domain	Polish Forums (N = 205)				American Forums (N = 171)			
		No.	%	No.	%	No.	%	No.	%
HEADS	CONTAINERS INTO WHICH ONE CAN PUT THINGS	2	0.97%	2	0.97%	0	0.0%	0	0.0%
TEETH	LIVING BEINGS	21	10.4%	21	10.4%	0	0.0%	0	0.0%
ILLNESSES	OBJECTS ONE CATCHES	3	1.46%	9	4.39%	0	0.0%	0	0.0%
	ENEMIES	1	0.48%			0	0.0%		
	LIVING BEINGS	1	0.48%			0	0.0%		
	PLACES	3	1.46%			0	0.0%		
	PLANTS	1	0.48%			0	0.0%		
REMORSE	OBJECT WITH WEIGHT	1	0.48%	1	0.48%	0	0.0%	0	0.0%
STAINS	LIVING BEINGS	2	0.97%	2	0.97%	0	0.0%	0	0.0%
CHOICE	EXIT	1	0.48%	1	0.48%	0	0.0%	0	0.0%
SNORING	PERFORMING A CONCERT	1	0.48%	1	0.48%	0	0.0%	0	0.0%
HEALTH SERVICE	LIVING BEING	1	0.48%	1	0.48%	0	0.0%	0	0.0%
THE INTERNET	PLACE	1	0.48%	1	0.48%	0	0.0%	0	0.0%
DOING CHORES	PULLING ONE'S WEIGHT	0	0.0%	0	0.0%	2	1.17%	3	1.75%
	SHIT	0	0.0%			1	0.58%		
PROBLEMS/ WORRIES	SHIT	0	0.0%	0	0.0%	1	0.58%	1	0.58%
ANNOYING THINGS	PAIN	0	0.0%	0	0.0%	1	0.58%	1	0.58%
SHOPPING	HUNTING/FISHING	2	0.97%	2	0.97%	0	0.0%	0	0.0%
SUFFERING	WALKING	4	1.95%	4	1.95%	0	0.0%	0	0.0%
POWER	SPACE (UP)	1	0.48%	1	0.48%	0	0.0%	0	0.0%
STRESS	LIVING BEING	1	0.48%	1	0.48%	0	0.0%	0	0.0%
WAILING OF A CHILD	SIREN	1	0.48%	1	0.48%	0	0.0%	0	0.0%
QUEUE	CONTAINER	18	8.78%	18	8.78%	0	0.0%	0	0.0%
OVERCOMING PROBLEMS	FIGHTING	6	4.5%	6	2.93%	0	0.0%	0	0.0%
PROBLEMS	OBJECTS	3	1.46%	4	1.95%	0	0.0%	0	0.0%
	RIDES	1	0.48%			0	0.0%		
FREEDOM	LIVING BEING	1	0.48%	1	0.48%	0	0.0%	0	0.0%

Target Domain	Source Domain	Polish Forums (N = 205)				American Forums (N = 171)			
		No.	%	No.	%	No.	%	No.	%
HOME	NEST	0	0.0%	0	0.0%	1	0.58%	1	0.58%
CHILDREN	BIRDS	0	0.0%	0	0.0%	1	0.58%	1	0.58%
CRITICISM	WITCH HUNT	0	0.0%	0	0.0%	1	0.58%	1	0.58%
TO DESPISE	TO LOOK DOWN	0	0.0%	0	0.0%	1	0.58%	1	0.58%
TO CHANGE JOB	TO JUMP SHIP	0	0.0%	0	0.0%	1	0.58%	1	0.58%
LIES	SHIT	0	0.0%	0	0.0%	1	0.58%	1	0.58%
TO MAKE TROUBLE	TO ROCK THE BOAT	0	0.0%	0	0.0%	1	0.58%	1	0.58%
DOING EVERYTHING IN ONE'S MIGHT	GOING OUT OF ONE'S WAY	0	0.0%	0	0.0%	3	1.75%	3	1.75%
EMOTIONAL PEOPLE	DRAMA QUEENS	0	0.0%	0	0.0%	1	0.58%	1	0.58%
MEAN PEOPLE	ASSHOLES/ASSES	0	0.0%	0	0.0%	3	1.75%	3	1.75%
PEOPLE	BRITTLE OBJECTS	1	0.48%	3	1.46%	0	0.0%	9	5.26%
	MACHINES	2	0.97%			4	2.34%		
	GUNS	0	0.0%			1	0.58%		
	ANIMALS	0	0.0%			1	0.58%		
	PIGS	0	0.0%			1	0.58%		
	CANNIBALS	0	0.0%			1	0.58%		
	FOOD	0	0.0%			1	0.58%		
TIME PASSING	MOTION OF AN OBJECT	9	4.39%	9	4.39%	0	0.0%	0	0.0%
TIME	VALUABLE COMMODITY	1	0.48%	2	0.97%	0	0.0%	3	1.75%
	LIVING BEING	1	0.48%			1	0.58%		
	OBJECT	0	0.0%			1	0.58%		
	HUMAN BEING	0	0.0%			1	0.58%		
SHARING EXPERIENCE	BEING IN THE SAME BOAT	0	0.0%	0	0.0%	3	1.75%	4	2.34%
	WALKING THE SAME PATH	0	0.0%			1	0.58%		
LIFE	STORY	1	0.48%	3	2.2%	0	0.0%	1	0.58%
	PATH	1	0.48%			0	0.0%		
	OBJECT	1	0.48%			0	0.0%		
	JOURNEY	0	0.0%			1	0.58%		

Target Domain	Source Domain	Polish Forums (N = 205)				American Forums (N = 171)			
		No.	%	No.	%	No.	%	No.	%
PATIENCE	WEAPON	1	0.48%	2	0.97%	0	0.0%	0	0.0%
	FABRIC	1	0.48%			0	0.0%		
PREGNANCY	JOURNEY	0	0.0%	0	0.0%	2	1.17%	2	1.17%
TRYING TO CONCEIVE	JOURNEY	0	0.0%	0	0.0%	8	4.68%	8	4.68%
SURROGACY	JOURNEY	0	0.0%	0	0.0%	23	13.45%	23	13.45%
HEART	CONTAINER	2	1.97%	2	0.97%	0	0.0%	2	1.17%
	LIVING BEING	0	0.0%			1	0.58%		
	HUMAN BEING	0	0.0%			1	0.58%		
EXPERIENCE	ROAD	0	0.0%	0	0.0%	7	5.0%	10	5.85%
	(ROLLER COASTER) RIDE	0	0.0%			3	2.2%		
COMPUTERS	PEOPLE	1	0.48%	1	0.48%	0	0.0%	0	0.0%
SEASONS OF THE YEAR	LIVING BEINGS	1	0.48%	1	0.48%	0	0.0%	0	0.0%
SUN	LIVING BEING	1	0.48%	1	0.48%	0	0.0%	0	0.0%
WORLD	LIVING BEING	3	1.46%	3	1.46%	0	0.0%	0	0.0%
FATE	HUMAN BEING	1	0.48%	1	0.48%	0	0.0%	0	0.0%
NATURE	HUMAN BEING	3	1.46%	3	1.46%	0	0.0%	0	0.0%
TO CRITICISE	TO BUTCHER	0	0.0%	0	0.0%	1	0.58%	1	0.58%
DISCUSSION	ARMS RACE	0	0.0%	0	0.0%	1	0.58%	1	0.58%
BAD	SMELLY	0	0.0%	0	0.0%	7	4.09%	7	4.09%
OPTIONS	ROUTES/WAYS/ROADS	0	0.0%	0	0.0%	7	4.09%	7	4.09%
FUTURE	WAY/ROAD	0	0.0%	0	0.0%	5	2.92%	5	2.92%
WEAPONS	POISON	0	0.0%	0	0.0%	1	0.58%	2	1.17%
	PENIS	0	0.0%			1	0.58%		
OTHER DOMAINS		71	34.6%	71	34.6%	32	18.71%	32	18.71%

The data in Table 21 shows which target domains were the most popular among the Polish and American forum users. Among the Poles, these were TEETH (10.4%) pictured as living beings with the ability to walk, DEPRESSION (9.3%) depicted as a PIT or valley, QUEUE (8.78%) pictured as a CONTAINER and TIME PASSING (4.39%) as a motion of an object.

Among the Americans, these were SURROGACY (13.45%) pictured as a journey, EXPERIENCE (5.85%) depicted as a road and a roller coaster ride,

RELATIONSHIPS (5.85%) pictured as hotels, roads, devices and fluids, PEOPLE (5.26%) depicted as machines, guns, animals, pigs, cannibals and food and ANGER (5.26%) realized by the metaphor A HEATED FLUID IN A CONTAINER.

Out of 70 target domains presented in Table 21, only 8 were used by both Poles and Americans. These are ANGER, HAPPINESS, RELATIONSHIPS, PEOPLE, TIME, LIFE and HEART.

Table 22: Source domains of the most popular metaphors: Quantitative data (No. – number of occurrences, % – percentage of occurrences)

Source Domain	Target Domain	Polish Forums (N = 205)				American Forums (N = 171)			
		No.	%	No.	%	No.	%	No.	%
HEATED FLUID IN A CONTAINER	ANGER	1	0.48%	1	0.48%	9	5.26%	9	5.26%
FLOOD OF BLOOD	ANGER	2	0.97%	2	0.97%	0	0.0%	0	0.0%
LIVING BEING	TIME	1	0.48%	38	18.53%	1	0.58%	1	0.58%
	TOOTH	21	10.24%			0	0.0%		
	HEART	2	0.97%			0	0.0%		
	NERVES	1							
	PART OF BODY	1	0.48%			0	0.0%		
	HEALTH SERVICE	1	0.48%			0	0.0%		
	STRESS	1	0.48%			0	0.0%		
	ILLNESS	1	0.48%			0	0.0%		
	WORLD	3	1.46%			0	0.0%		
	FREEDOM	1	0.48%			0	0.0%		
	SEASONS	1	0.48%			0	0.0%		
	STAIN	2	0.97%			0	0.0%		
	SUN	1	0.48%			0	0.0%		
	RELATIONSHIP	2	0.97%			0	0.0%		
FOOD	NERVES	1	0.48%	1	0.48%	0	0.0%	1	0.58%
	PEOPLE	0	0.0%			1	0.58%		
WAY/ROAD/ROUTE/PATH	FUTURE	0	0.0%	1	0.48%	5	2.92%	22	12.86%
	OPTIONS	0	0.0%			7	4.09%		
	LIFE	1	0.48%			0	0.0%		
	RELATIONSHIP	0	0.0%			3	1.75%		
	EXPERIENCE	0	0.0%			7	4.09%		

Source Domain	Target Domain	Polish Forums (N = 205)				American Forums (N = 171)			
		No.	%	No.	%	No.	%	No.	%
PLACE	ILLNESS	3	1.46%	4	1.95%	0	0.0%	0	0.0%
	INTERNET	1	0.48%			0	0.0%		
FIRE	LOVE	3	1.46%	3	1.46%	0	0.0%	0	0.0%
CONTAINER	HEAD	2	0.97%	22	10.73%	0	0.0%	0	0.0%
	HEART	2	0.97%			0	0.0%		
	QUEUE	18	8.78%			0	0.0%		
HUMAN BEING	HEART	0	0.0%	5	2.44%	1	0.58%	2	1.17%
	TIME	0	0.0%			1	0.58%		
	FATE	1	0.48%			0	0.0%		
	NERVES	1							
	NATURE	3	1.46%			0	0.0%		
	COMPUTER	1	0.48%			0	0.0%		
OBJECT	LIFE	1	0.48%	19	9.27%	0	0.0%	2	1.17%
	TIME	9	4.39%			1	0.58%		
	ILLNESS	3	1.46%			0	0.0%		
	SELF ESTEEM	0	0.0%			1	0.58%		
	PROBLEM	3	1.46%			0	0.0%		
	NERVES	1	0.48%						
	THOUGHT/ IDEA	1	0.48%			0	0.0%		
	REMORSE	1	0.48%			0	0.0%		
	PEOPLE	1	0.48%			0	0.0%		
MACHINE/ DEVICE	PEOPLE	2	0.97%	2	0.97%	4	2.34%	8	4.68%
	RELATIONSHIP	0	0.0%			4	2.34%		
JOURNEY	PREGNANCY	0	0.0%	0	0.0%	2	1.17%	36	21.05%
	TRYING TO CONCEIVE	0	0.0%			8	4.68%		
	SURROGACY	0	0.0%			23	13.45%		
	LIFE	0	0.0%			1	0.58%		
	EDUCATION	0	0.0%			1	0.58%		
	MILITARY DUTY	0	0.0%			1	0.58%		
BUILDING/ HOTEL	RELATIONSHIP	1	0.48%	1	0.48%	2	1.17%	2	1.17%
FLUID	RELATIONSHIP	0	0.0%	0	0.0%	1	0.58%	1	0.58%
RAIN	SEX	0	0.0%	0	0.0%	1	0.58%	1	0.58%

Source Domain	Target Domain	Polish Forums (N = 205)				American Forums (N = 171)			
		No.	%	No.	%	No.	%	No.	%
PLANT	ILLNESS	1	0.48%	1	0.48%	0	0.0%	0	0.0%
ENEMY	ILLNESS	1	0.48%	1	0.48%	0	0.0%	0	0.0%
ANIMALS	PEOPLE	0	0.0%	0	0.0%	1	0.58%	1	0.58%
PIGS	PEOPLE	0	0.0%	0	0.0%	1	0.58%	1	0.58%
BIRDS	PEOPLE	0	0.0%	0	0.0%	1	0.58%	1	0.58%
STORY	LIFE	1	0.48%	1	0.48%	0	0.0%	0	0.0%
POISON	WEAPON	0	0.0%	0	0.0%	1	0.58%	1	0.58%
PENIS	WEAPON	0	0.0%	0	0.0%	1	0.58%	1	0.58%
FABRIC	PATIENCE	1	0.48%	1	0.48%	0	0.0%	0	0.0%
WEAPON	PATIENCE	1	0.48%	1	0.48%	0	0.0%	0	0.0%
NEST	HOME	0	0.0%	0	0.0%	1	0.58%	1	0.58%
SPACE (DOWN)	SADNESS	0	0.0%	0	0.0%	5	2.92%	5	2.92%
FIGHTING/ WAR	TRYING	0	0.0%	8	3.90%	1	0.58%	1	0.58%
	OVERCOMING PROBLEMS	6	2.93%			0	0.0%		
	BRINGING UP CHILDREN	2	0.97%			0	0.0%		
SHIT	LIES	0	0.0%	0	0.0%	1	0.58%	3	1.75%
	CHORES	0	0.0%			1	0.58%		
	PROBLEMS/ WORRIES	0	0.0%			1	0.58%		
(ROLLER COASTER) RIDE	EXPERIENCE	0	0.0%	1	0.48%	3	1.75%	3	1.75%
	PROBLEM	1	0.48%			0	0.0%		
SPACE (UP)	HAPPINESS	4	1.95%	4	1.95%	6	3.51%	6	3.51%
	POWER	0	0.0%			0	0.0%		
OTHER DOMAINS		106	51.70%	106	51.70%	62	36.35%	62	36.35%

As regards source domains (Table 22), the most popular domain among the Polish mothers was LIVING BEINGS (18.53%) used to metaphorically describe teeth, parts of body, time, stress, illnesses, relationships, stains, the sun, the world etc. The second place is occupied by the domain of CONTAINER (10.73%) which was used to talk about head, heart and especially about queues. The third place belongs to OBJECTS (9.27%) employed to talk about time, illnesses, problems, people, ideas and life. Overcoming problems and bringing up children was pictured as FIGHTING/WAR (3.90%). The American mothers, on the other hand, most frequently used the domains of JOURNEY (21.05%) to describe surrogacy, being pregnant or the process of trying to conceive, WAY/ROAD/ROUTE/PATH (12.86%) to talk about the future, options, experience and relationships, and A HEATED FLUID IN A CONTAINER (5.26%) to describe the state of being angry. In the case of some posts containing Polish *serce* and English *heart*, it is possible to provide alternative interpretations. These nouns may be seen as examples of metonymies, THE HEART FOR THE HUMAN BEING or THE HEART FOR FEELINGS. Additionally, such posts may contain metaphtonymies, combining e.g. the metonymy THE HEART FOR THE HUMAN BEING and the metaphor THE HEART IS A CONTAINER.

Out of 31 source domains presented in Table 22, 11 were used by both Poles and Americans. These are A HEATED FLUID IN A CONTAINER, LIVING BEINGS, FOOD, WAY/ROAD/ROUTE/PATH, HUMAN BEING, OBJECT, MACHINE/DEVICE, BUILDING, FIGHTING/WAR, (ROLLER COASTER) RIDE and SPACE (UP).

5.4 Concluding remarks

The thematic areas occurring in the posts with metaphorical expressions written by the Polish and American mothers varied considerably. Out of 27 thematic areas only 10 appeared on both Polish and American forums, namely relationships, everyday life, time, anger, sex, parts of the body, people, their behaviour and attitudes, happiness, sadness and other emotions.

The most popular thematic areas among the Polish mothers were relationships, problems and hardship, depression and teething. The most frequently used metaphors in the area of relationships were OVERCOMING PROBLEMS IS FIGHTING and LIFE IS A PATH. Relationships were also depicted as buildings and living organisms. In the area of problems and hardship, the metaphor OVERCOMING PROBLEMS IS FIGHTING was also most frequently used. Apart from that, problems were pictured as objects and rides. To talk about depression mothers used the metaphor DEPRESSION IS A PIT. To talk about teething the metaphor TEETH ARE LIVING BEINGS was most commonly employed.

Among the American mothers, the most popular thematic areas were pregnancy and people, their behaviour and attitudes, as well as anger and experience. In the area of pregnancy, the most frequently used metaphor was PREGNANCY/SURROGACY IS A JOURNEY. People were depicted as machines, animals and guns. There were many metaphorical expressions used to insult people, like *assholes*, *asses*, *drama queens* etc. The metaphors ANGER IS A HEATED FLUID

IN A CONTAINER and ARGUMENT IS WAR were the most popular. To talk about experience, the American mothers used the metaphors EXPERIENCE IS A ROAD and EXPERIENCE IS A (ROLLER COASTER) RIDE.

The most popular target domains among the Polish forum users were TEETH depicted as living beings, DEPRESSION pictured as a PIT and QUEUE depicted as a CONTAINER.

In the American posts, the most frequently used target domains were SURROGACY described as a journey, EXPERIENCE pictured as a road and RELATIONSHIPS depicted as hotels, roads, devices and fluids.

Only 8 target domains were used by both Poles and Americans. These are ANGER, HAPPINESS, RELATIONSHIPS, PEOPLE, TIME, LIFE and HEART. As regards source domain, 11 were used by both Poles and Americans. These include A HEATED FLUID IN A CONTAINER, LIVING BEINGS, FOOD, WAY/ROAD/ROUTE/PATH, HUMAN BEING, OBJECT, MACHINE/DEVICE, BUILDING, FIGHTING/WAR, (ROLLER COASTER) RIDE and SPACE (UP).

The most popular source domain among the Polish mothers was the domain of LIVING BEINGS used to talk about teeth, parts of body, time, stress, illnesses, relationships, stains, the sun, the world etc. Also the domain of OBJECTS, employed to talk about time, illnesses, problems, people, ideas and life, and the domain of CONTAINER were frequently used.

The most popular source domains among the American mothers were the domain of JOURNEY used to talk about surrogacy, being pregnant or the process of trying to conceive and the domain of WAY/ROAD/ROUTE/PATH used to metaphorically describe future, options, experience and relationships.

Conclusions

The present study has attempted to analyze conceptual metaphors occurring in the language of the Internet forum users. The purpose has been to collect metaphorical expressions in two languages of different cultural backgrounds in order to examine to what extent the used mappings differ or show similarities, as well as to check which topics of online discussions involve the largest number of metaphors.

Metaphorical expressions are conceptual in nature because they are based on cultural and bodily experiences of the sender and the receiver. It has been proved that the interconnectedness between the source and target domains was based mostly on these experiences. Conventionality, as another characteristic of conceptual metaphors, could be identified in most of the examples presented in Chapters Three and Four. Animization and personification, which are forms of ontological metaphor, are frequently used by the Polish and American users of the researched forums. The data collected allow us to draw the general conclusion that the language used in online discussions shares features of ordinary spoken language and is used spontaneously, which creates a perfect environment for the use of conceptual metaphors.

The other objectives of the study have been to show which topics of Internet discussions are and which are not expressed metaphorically. The analysis allows us to state that online discussion topics which involve emotions are the ones with the highest numbers of metaphorical expressions.

In the Polish online discussions, there were numerous instances of metaphorical expressions connected with relationships, problems and hardship, depression and teething. Complaining about the fate, world, life and nature was also frequently observed on the Polish forums. On the American forums, there were numerous metaphors in the thematic areas of pregnancy, people, their behaviour and attitudes as well as of anger and experience.

To conclude, thematic areas which were the most frequently used by the Polish mothers were relationships, problems and hardship, depression and teething. The metaphors employed to talk about these subjects were OVERCOMING PROBLEMS IS FIGHTING, LIFE IS A PATH, RELATIONSHIPS ARE BUILDINGS, RELATIONSHIPS ARE LIVING ORGANISMS, OVERCOMING PROBLEMS IS FIGHTING, PROBLEMS ARE OBJECTS, PROBLEMS ARE RIDES, DEPRESSION IS A PIT and TEETH ARE LIVING BEINGS.

The American mothers most frequently talked metaphorically about pregnancy, anger, experience, as well as about people, their behavior and attitudes. The metaphors employed within these thematic areas were PREGNANCY/SURROGACY IS A JOURNEY, ANGER IS A HEATED FLUID IN A CONTAINER, ARGUMENT IS WAR, EXPERIENCE IS A ROAD, EXPERIENCE IS A (ROLLER COASTER) RIDE, PEOPLE ARE MACHINES and PEOPLE ARE GUNS.

The target domains most frequently used by the Polish mothers were TEETH pictured as living beings, DEPRESSION depicted as a pit and TIME PASSING pictured as a motion of an object. The American mothers most frequently used the target domains of SURROGACY pictured as a journey, EXPERIENCE depicted as a road and RELATIONSHIPS described as hotels, roads, devices, and fluids. The target domains of ANGER, HAPPINESS, RELATIONSHIPS, PEOPLE, TIME, LIFE and HEART were the only ones which were used by both Poles and Americans.

The source domains used by both Polish and American mothers were the following: A HEATED FLUID IN A CONTAINER, LIVING BEINGS, FOOD, WAY/ROAD/ROUTE/PATH, HUMAN BEING, OBJECT, MACHINE/DEVICE, BUILDING, FIGHTING/WAR, (ROLLER COASTER) RIDE and SPACE (UP). The Polish mothers most frequently employed the source domains of LIVING BEINGS and OBJECTS. Among the American mothers, the most popular source domains were JOURNEY and WAY/ROAD/ROUTE/PATH.

It is hoped that the arguments presented in this study, along with the results of the research project, will be a useful contribution to a better understanding of conceptual metaphors used in online discussions as this is an interesting and still not fully investigated topic, especially from the comparative perspective.

References

Apresjan, Valentina (1997). Emotion metaphors and cross-linguistic conceptualisation of emotion. *Lingüística cognitiva aplicada al estudio del inglés: Número monográfico de Cuadernos de Filología Inglesa* 6/9: 179–195.

Aouil, Bassam, Maria Kajdasz-Aouil (2007). Internet jako środowisko komunikacyjne. In: Tanaś Maciej (ed.), *Kultura i język mediów*, Kraków: Oficyna Wydawnicza „Impuls", 61–89.

Aouil, Bassam (2008). Komunikowanie się w Internecie – narzędzia, specyfika i właściwości. In: Wawrzak-Chodaczek Mirosława (ed.), *Komunikacja społeczna w świecie wirtualnym*. Toruń: Wydawnictwo Adam Marszałek, 1–40.

Badyda, Ewa (2013). *„Upadły anioł zmysłów"? Metaforyka zapachu i percepcji węchowej we współczesnej polszczyźnie*. Gdańsk: Wydawnictwo Uniwersytetu Gdańskiego.

Bakuła, Kordian (2003). Poglądy językoznawców angielskich i amerykańskich na to, co mówione, i to, co pisane. In: *Kształcenie Językowe* 4: 49–78

Bakuła, Kordian (2008). *Mówione = pisane: komunikacja, język, tekst*. Wrocław: Wydawnictwo Uniwesytetu Wrocławskiego.

Bamberg, Michael (1997). Language, concepts and emotions: The role of language in the construction of emotions. *Language Sciences* 19/4: 309–340.

Barcelona, Antonio (2000). The cognitive theory of metaphor and metonymy. In: Barcelona Antonio (ed.), *Metaphor and Metonymy at the Crossroads: A Cognitive Perspective*. Berlin – New York: Mouton de Gruyter, 1–30.

Baron, Naomi S. (1998). Letters by phone or speech by other means: The linguistics of email. *Language and Communication* 18: 133–170.

Baron, Naomi S. (2003). Language of the Internet. In: Farghali Ali (ed.), *The Stanford Handbook for Language Engineers*. Stanford: CSLI Publications, 59–127.

Barsalou, Lawrence W. (1999). Perceptual symbol systems. *Behavioral and Brain Sciences* 22: 577–609.

Barsalou, Lawrence W., Wenchi Yeh, Barbara J. Luka, Karen L. Olseth, Kelly S. Mix, Ling-Ling Wu (1993). Concepts and meaning. In: Beals Katharine, Gina Cooke, David Kathman, Sotaro Kita, Karl-Erik McCullough, David Testen (eds.), *Chicago Linguistics Society* 29: *Papers from the Parasession on Conceptual Representations*. Chicago: Chicago Linguistics Society, 23–61.

Bartmiński, Jerzy (2009). *Językowe podstawy obrazu świata*. Lublin: Wydawnictwo Uniwersytetu Marii Curie-Skłodowskiej.

Bartmiński, Jerzy (2012 [2009]). *Aspects of Cognitive Ethnolinguistics*. Sheffield: Equinox Publishing Ltd. Tans. Adam Glaz.

Ben-Ze'ev, Aaron (2005). *Miłość w sieci: Internet i emocje*. Trans. Anna Zdziemborska. Poznań: Dom Wydawniczy Rebis.

Biel, Łucja (2010). Proxemic motivation in language: Relational metaphors and registers. In: Danuta Stanulewicz, Tadeusz Z. Wolański, Joanna Redzimska (eds.), *Lingua Terra Cognita II: A Festschrift for Roman Kalisz*. Gdańsk: Wydawnictwo Uniwersytetu Gdańskiego, 183–203.

Bielenia, Magdalena (2009a). The role of metaphors in the language of investment banking. *Special Issue of Iberica 2009*: 139–155.

Bielenia, Magdalena (2009b). Metaforyczność nazw bankowości inwestycyjnej, czyli świat byków, niedźwiedzi, rycerzy i odstraszaczy rekinów. In: Katarzyna Jarosińska-Buriak (ed.), *Metafora w kulturze. Część I (Literatura, Teoria, Język, Przekład)*. Elbląg: Wydawnictwo PWSZ, 259–268.

Bralczyk Jerzy, Katarzyna Mosiołek-Kłosińska (eds.) (2000). *Język w mediach masowych*. Warszawa: Upowszechnianie Nauki – Oświata „UN-O".

Cameron, Lynne (2009). A Discourse Dynamics Framework for Metaphor. Available at <http://creet.open.ac.uk/projects/metaphor-analysis/theories.cfm?paper=ddfm>. Accessed 22 November 2012.

Cameron, Lynne, Robert Maslen, Zazie Todd, John Maule, Peter Stratton, Neil Stanley (2009). The discourse dynamics approach to metaphor and metaphor-led discourse analysis. *Metaphor and Symbol* 24/2: 63–89.

Camp, Elisabeth (2006). Metaphor in the mind: The cognition of metaphor. *Philosophy Compass* 1/2: 154–170.

Castells, Manuel (2003). *Galaktyka Internetu: Refleksje nad Internetem, biznesem i społeczeństwem*. Trans. Tomasz Horonowski. Poznań: Dom Wydawniczy Rebis.

Castells, Manuel (2011). *Społeczeństwo sieci*. Trans. Kamila Pawluś, Mirosława Marody, Janusz Stawiński, Sebastian Szymański. Warszawa: Wydawnictwo Naukowe PWN.

Cherny, Lynn (1999). *Conversation and Community: Chat in a Virtual World*. Stanford, CA: CSLI Publications.

Chilton, Paul A. (1996). *Security Metaphors: Cold War Discourse from Containment to Common House*. New York: Peter Lang International Academic Publishers.

Chilton, Paul A. (2006 [2004]). *Analysing Political Discourse: Theory and Practice*. Abingdon: Routledge.

Chilton, Paul A., Christina Schäffner (eds.) (2002). *Politics as Text and Talk: Analytic Approaches to Political Discourse*. Amsterdam – Philadelphia, PA: John Benjamins.

Cieślicka, Anna (2002). Metaphors of teaching and learning: Investigating bilingual metaphorical competence. In: Danuta Stanulewicz (ed.), *PASE Papers in Language Studies: Proceedings of the Ninth Annual Conference of the Polish Association for the Study of English, Gdańsk, 26–28 April 2000*. Gdańsk: Wydawnictwo Uniwersytetu Gdańskiego, 383–392.

Cieślicka Anna (2008). Are conceptual metaphors activated on-line during processing of figurative expressions? In: Maria Jodłowiec, Anna Niżegorodcew (eds.), *Metaphor and Cognition*. Frankfurt am Main: Peter Lang, 99–116.

Cichmińska, Monika (2010). Sadness and fear: A study into the negative emotions. In: Stanisław Puppel, Marta Bogusławska-Tafelska (eds.), *New Pathways in Linguistics*. Olsztyn: Wydawnictwo Uniwersytetu Warmińsko-Mazurskiego w Olsztynie, 39–58.

Cortazzi, Martin, Lixian Jin (1999). Bridges to learning: Metaphors of teaching, learning and language. In: Lynne Cameron, Graham Low (eds.), *Researching and Applying Metaphor*. Cambridge: Cambridge University Press, 149–176.

Coulson, Seana (2006). Conceptual blending in thought, rhetoric, and ideology. In: Glen Kristiansen, René Dirven (eds.), *Cognitive Linguistics: Current Applications and Future Perspectives*. Berlin – New York: Mouton de Gruyter, 187–210.

Coulson Seana, Todd Oakley (2005). Blending and coded meaning: Literal and figurative meaning in cognitive semantics. *Journal of Pragmatics* 37: 1510–1536.

Collot, Milena, Nancy Belmore (1996). Electronic language: A new variety of English. In: Susan C. Herring (ed.), *Computer-mediated Communication: Linguistic, Social, and Cross-cultural Perspectives*. Amsterdam: John Benjamins, 13–28.

Croft, William, Alan D. Cruse (2004). *Cognitive Linguistics*. Cambridge: Cambridge University Press.

Crystal, David (1995). *The Cambridge Encyclopedia of the English Language*. Cambridge: Cambridge Univeristy Press.

Crystal, David (2004). *Language and the Internet*. Cambridge: Cambridge University Press.

Danet, Brenda (2001). *Cyberpl@y: Communicating Online*. London: Berg.

Davis, Boyd H., Jeutonne P. Brewer (1997). *Electronic Discourse: Linguistic Individuals in Virtual Space*. Albany, NY: State University of New York Press.

Deignan Alice, Liz Potter (2004). A corpus study of metaphors and metonyms in English and Italian. *Journal of Pragmatics* 36: 1231–1252.

Dirven, René, Ralf Pörings (2002). *Metaphors and Metonymy in Comparison and Contrast*. Berlin – New York: Mounton de Gruyter.

Dixon, Izabela (2011). Fear – aspects of the language of control and manipulation. In: Stanisław Puppel, Marta Bogusławska-Tafelska (eds.), *New Pathways in Linguistics*. Olsztyn: Wydawnictwo Uniwersytetu Warmińsko-Mazurskiego w Olsztynie, 41–66.

Dixon, Izabela (2012). The game of cricket as a source of metaphors. *Beyond Philology* 9: 7–23. Available at <http://fil.ug.edu.pl/sites/default/files/_nodes/strona-filologiczny/33797/files/beyond_philology_9_2012.pdf>. Accessed 19 April 2014.

Dixon, Izabela (2013a). Fear is evil and other fear metaphors. In: Oleksij Prokopczuk, Klaudiusz Bobowski (eds.), *Wschód–Zachód: Sprachliche Einheiten in System und Text/Language Units in System and Text*. Słupsk: Wydawnictwo Naukowe Akademii Pomorskiej w Słupsku, 47–55.

Dixon, Izabela (2013b). Punishment or state sponsored execution? Moral principles of the war on terror as seen through the language of on-line press. In: Bhavana Mahajan, Raja Bagga (eds.), *Reframing Punishment: Reflections of Culture, Literature and Morals*, Oxford: Inter-Disciplinary Press, United Kingdom, 81–93.

Dixon, Izabela, Martyna Gibka (2013). Fear as a mind trap: Monsters and demons to which fears have given life. Paper presented at *7th Global Interdisciplinary Conference on Fear, Horror and Terror*, Oxford, 5–7 September 2013. Available at <http://www.inter-disciplinary.net/at-the-interface/wp-content/uploads/2013/07/dixonfhtpaper.pdf>. Accessed 22 October 2014.

Ekman, Paul (1992). An argument for basic emotions. *Cognition and Emotion* 6/3-4: 169–200. Available at <https://www.paulekman.com/wp-content/uploads/2013/07/An-Argument-For-Basic-Emotions.pdf>. Accessed 18 May 2012.

Ekman, Paul (1998). Universality of emotional expression? A personal history of the dispute: Afterword. In: Paul Ekman (ed.), *Charles Darwin's the Expression of the Emotions in Man and Animals. Third edition. With introduction, Afterword and Commentaries*. New York – Oxford: Oxford University Press, 363–393.

Esenova, Orazgozel (2008). Plant metaphors for the expression of emotions in the English language. *Beyond Philology* 5: 7–21. Available at <http://fil.ug.edu.pl/sites/default/files/_nodes/strona-filologiczny/33797/files/beyond_philology_5.pdf>. Accessed 22 February 2012.

Ess, Charles (1996). *Philosophical Perspectives on Computer-mediated Communication*. Albany: State University of New York Press.

Ess, Charles (2001). *Culture, Technology, Communication: Towards an Intercultural Global Village*. Albany: State University of New York Press.

Evans, Vyvyan (2006). Lexical concepts, cognitive models and meaning-construction. *Cognitive Linguistics* 17/4: 491–534.

Evans, Vyvyan (2010). *Leksykon językoznawstwa kognitywnego*. Trans. Magdalena Buchta, Małgorzata Cierpisz, Joanna Podhorodecka, Agnieszka Gicala, Justyna Winiarska. Kraków: Universitas.

Evans, Vyvyan (2008). Lexical concepts and cognitive models theory and metaphor. Available at <http://creet.open.ac.uk/projects/metaphor-analysis/theories.cfm?paper=lccm>. Accessed 11 December 2012.

Evans, Vyvyan, Melanie Green (2006). *Cognitive Linguistics: An Introduction*. Edinburgh: Edinburgh University Press.

Fabiszak, Małgorzata (2005). Kognitywna teoria metafory: nowe terminy, stare pojecia? In: Henryk Kardela, Zbysław Muszyński, Maciej Rajewski (eds.), *Kognitywistyka: Problemy i perspektywy*. Lublin: Wydawnictwo Uniwersytetu Marii Curie-Skłodowskiej, 137–147.

Fabiszak, Małgorzata (2007). *A Conceptual Metaphor Approach to War Discourse and Its Implications*. Poznań: Wydawnictwo Naukowe UAM.

Fabiszak, Małgorzata (2010). Vilification of the enemy: Different enemies, the same linguistic strategies. In: Danuta Stanulewicz, Tadeusz Z. Wolański, Joanna Redzimska (eds.), *Lingua Terra Cognita II: A Festschrift for Roman Kalisz*. Gdańsk: Wydawnictwo Uniwersytetu Gdańskiego, 73–97.

Fauconnier, Gilles, Mark Turner (2003). *The Way We Think*. New York: Basic Books.

Gabryś, Danuta (1994). On teaching non-literal English: The case of metaphor. In: *Papers in Linguistics and Language Acquisition*. Katowice: Wydawnictwo Uniwersytetu Śląskiego, 64–77.

Garrett, R. Kelly, James N. Danziger (2007). IM = Interruption managment? Instant messaging and disruption in the workplace. *Journal of Computer-Mediated Communication* 13/1. Available at <http://jcmc.indiana.edu/vol13/issue1/garrett.html>. Accessed 03.05.2016.

Geeraerts Dirk, Hubert Cuyckens (2007). Introducing Cognitive Linguistics. In: Dirk Geeraerts, Hubert Cuyckens (eds.), *The Oxford Handbook of Cognitive Linguistics*. Oxford: Oxford University Press, 3–24.

Gibbs, Raymond W. Jr. (ed.). (2008). *The Cambridge Handbook of Metaphor and Thought*. New York: Cambridge University Press.

Gibbs, Raymond W. Jr., Paula Lenz Costa Lima, Edson Francozo (2004). Metaphor is grounded in embodied experience. *Journal of Pragmatics* 36: 1189–1210.

Giddens, Anthony (2006). *Sociology*. Cambridge: Polity.

Gierczyńska, Marta (2009). Cognitive nature of metaphors in the language of American and Polish politicians. In: Zofia Jancewicz (ed.), *W dialogu języków i kultur. II Międzynarodowa Konferencja Naukowa*. Warszawa: Lingwistyczna Szkoła Wyższa w Warszawie, 73–82.

Gierczyńska-Kolas, Marta (2013). 'Monsters-in-law': An analysis of conceptual metaphors in comments about mothers-in-law. In: Oleksij Prokopczuk, Klaudiusz Bobowski (eds.), *Wschód–Zachód: Sprachliche Einheiten in System und Text: Language Units in System and Text*. Słupsk: Wydawnictwo Naukowe Akademii Pomorskiej w Słupsku, 56–60.

Glucksberg, Sam (2001). *Understanding Figurative Language: From Metaphor to Idioms*. New York: Oxford University Press US.

Glucksberg, Sam (2008). How metaphors create categories – quickly. In: Raymond W. Gibbs, Jr. (ed.), *The Cambridge Handbook of Metaphor and Thought*. New York: Cambridge University Press, 67–83.

Goban-Klas, Tomasz (2001). *Media i komunikowanie masowe: Teorie i analizy prasy, radia, telewizji i Internetu*. Warszawa – Kraków: Wydawnictwo Naukowe PWN.

Goddard, Cliff (2002). Explicating emotions across languages and cultures: A semantic approach. In: Susan R. Fussell (ed.), *The Verbal Communication of Emotions: Interdisciplinary Perspectives*. New York: Psychology Press, 19–52.

Gogołek, Włodzimierz (2010). *Komunikacja sieciowa: Uwarunkowania kategorie i paradoksy*. Warszawa: Oficyna Wydawnicza ASPRA-JR.

Golus, Beata (2003). Fenomen rozmów internetowych i ich języka. Paper presented at the conference *Druga Internetowa Konferencja Naukowa Dialog a nowe media*, Katowice, Uniwersytet Śląski, March – April 2003. Available at <http://uranos.cto.us.edu.pl/~dialog/archiwum/referaty.html>. Accessed 12 May 2007.

Goossens, Lois (1990). Metaphtonymy: The interaction of metaphor and metonymy in expressions for linguistic action. *Cognitive Linguistics* 1/3: 323–342.

Gorczyńska, Ilona (2002). Experiential grounding of metaphors underlying selected phrases of biblical origin in contemporary English. *Beyond Philology* 2: 53–69.

Gorczyńska, Ilona (2010). Expressing the inexpressible and cognising the incognisable: On the role of metaphor in the Bible. In: Danuta Stanulewicz, Tadeusz Z. Wolański, Joanna Redzimska (eds.), *Lingua Terra Cognita II: A Festschrift for Roman Kalisz*. Gdańsk: Wydawnictwo Uniwersytetu Gdańskiego, 281–298.

Grady, Joseph E. (1999). A typology of motivation for conceptual metaphor: Correlation vs. resemblance. In: Raymond W Gibbs, Jr., Gerard J. Steen (eds.), *Metaphor in Cognitive Linguistics*. Amsterdam: John Benjamins, 101–124.

Grady, Joseph E. (2005). Primary metaphors as inputs to conceptual integration. *Journal of Pragmatics* 37: 1595–1614.

Grady, Joseph E. (1999). Metaphor. In: Dirk Geeraerts, Hubert Cuyckens (eds.), *The Oxford Handbook of Cognitive Linguistics*. Oxford: Oxford University Press, 188–212.

Gruszczyński, Włodzimierz (2001a). Czy normy językowe obowiązują w internecie? In: Jerzy Bralczyk, Katarzyna Mosiołek-Kłosińska (eds.), *Zmiany w publicznych zwyczajach językowych*. Warszawa: Rada Języka Polskiego przy Prezydium PAN, 183–190.

Gruszczyński, Włodzimierz, (2001b): Czaty w sieci, czyli o polskich zwyczajach językowych w Internecie. *Dialog* 2: 137–145.

Grzenia, Jan (2003a). Strona WWW jako forma dialogowa. Paper presented at the conference *Druga Internetowa Konferencja Naukowa Dialog a nowe media*, Katowice, Uniwersytet Śląski, March – April 2003. Available at <http://uranos.cto.us.edu.pl/~dialog/archiwum/referaty.html> Accessed 12 May 2007.

Grzenia, Jan (2003b). Komunikacja językowa w Internecie – przegląd publikacji mało znanych w Polsce. Paper presented at the conference *Druga Internetowa Konferencja Naukowa Dialog a nowe media*, Katowice, Uniwersytet Śląski, March-April 2003. Available at <http://uranos.cto.us.edu.pl/~dialog/archiwum/referaty.html>. Accessed 12 May 2007.

Grzenia, Jan (2006). *Komunikacja językowa w Internecie*. Warszawa: Wydawnictwo Naukowe PWN.

Gut, Dorota (1999). Piszę, więc jestem: O języku Internetu. *Polska Sztuka Ludowa: Konteksty* 1–2: 164–168.

Habrajska, Grażyna (1997). Wpływ internetu na typologizację w języku. In: Irena Kamińska-Szmaj, Tomasz Piekot, Monika Zaśko-Zielińska (eds.), *Oblicza komunikacji 1. Perspektywy badań nad tekstem, dyskursem i komunikacją*. Kraków: Teritum.

Habrajska, Grażyna (2002). Strategie konwersacyjne w internetowych grupach dyskusyjnych. In: Grzegorz Szpila (ed.), *Język a komunikacja: Język trzeciego tysiąclecia II, tom 1. Nowe oblicza komunikacji we współczesnej polszczyźnie*. Kraków: Tertium, 161–173.

Habrajska, Grażyna, Joanna Ślósarska (2006). *Kognitywizm w poetyce i stylistyce*. Kraków: Universitas.

Hale, Constance, Jessie Scanlon (1999). *Wired Style: Principles of English Usage in the Digital Age*. New York: Broadway Books.

Hård af Segerstad, Ylva (2002). *Use and Adaptation of Written Language to the Conditions of Computer-mediated Communication*. Gothenburg: Department of Linguistics University of Gothenburg.

Herring, Susan C. (1999). Interactional coherence in CMC. *Journal of Computer-Mediated Communication* 4/4. Available at <http://jcmc.indiana.edu/vol4/issue4/herring.html>. Accessed 1 July 2005.

Herring, Susan C. (2001). Computer-mediated discourse. In: Deborah Schiffrin, Deborah Tannen, H. Hamilton (eds.), *The Handbook of Discourse Analysis*. Malden, MA: Blackwell, 612–634.

Herring, Susan, C. (2002). Computer-mediated communication on the Internet. *Annual Review of Information Science and Technology* 36/1: 109–168.

Hiraga, Masako K. (2005). *Metaphor and Iconicity: A Cognitive Approach to Analysing Texts*. New York: Palgrave McMillan.

Hiraga, Masako (2006). Wzajemna zależność metafory i ikoniczności – podejście kognitywne do tekstów poetyckich. Trans. Karolina Bałłaban, Olga Sokołowska. In: Olga Sokołowska, Danuta Stanulewicz (eds.), *Językoznawstwo kognitywne III: Kognitywizm w świetle innych teorii*. Gdańsk: Wydawnictwo Uniwersytetu Gdańskiego, 356–395.

Holme, Randal (2004). *Mind, Metaphor and Language Teaching*. Basingstoke: Polgrave Macmillan.

Huang, Yan (2012). *The Oxford Dictionary of Pragmatics*. Oxford: Oxford University Press.

Jagodzińska, Joanna (2000). Uśmiech i śmiech w dyskusjach internetowych – o sposobach zapisu uczuć towarzyszących wypowiedzi. *Poradnik Językowy* 3: 38–49.

Jakubowska, Ewa. (2009). Metaphors of femininity. In: Maria Wysocka (ed.), *On Language Structure, Acquisition and Teaching: Studies in Honour of Professor Janusz Arabski on the Occasion of His 70th Birthday*. Katowice: Wydawnictwo Uniwersytetu Śląskiego, 143–153.

Jasińska, Małgorzata (2001). Językowy savoir-vivre w Internecie. In: Grażyna Habrajska (ed.), *Język w komunikacji* 3. Łódź: Wydawnictwo Wyższej Szkoły Humanistyczno-Ekonomicznej, 119–125.

Jindo, Job Y. (2010). *Biblical Metaphor Reconsidered: A Cognitive Approach to Poetic Prophecy in Jeremiah 1–24*. Winona Lake, Indiana: Eisenbrauns.

Kalisz, Roman (1990). A cognitive approach to spatial terms represented by 'in front of' and 'behind' in English and their metaphorical extensions. In: Jerzy Tomaszczyk, Barbara Lewandowska-Tomaszczyk (eds.), *Meaning and Lexicography*. Amsterdam – Philadelphia: John Benjamins, 167–179.

Kalisz, Roman (1999). Some linguistic aspects of evil. In: Michał Post (ed.), *Anglica Wratislaviensia XXXV. Festschrift for Profesor Jan Cygan on the Occasion of his 70th Birthday*. Wrocław: Wydawnictwo Uniwersytetu Wrocławskiego, 61–67.

Kalisz, Roman (2001). Types of metaphors: A cognitive view. In: Olga Kubińska, David Malcolm (eds.), *Paradoksy humanistyki: Księga pamiątkowa ku czci Profesora Andrzeja Zgorzelskiego*. Gdańsk: Wydawnictwo Uniwersytetu Gdańskiego, 159–165.

Kalisz, Roman (2008). Metaphors, blends and predicate-argument structure. In: Zdzisław Wasik, Tomasz Komendziński (eds.), *Metaphor and Cognition*. Frankfurt am Main: Peter Lang, 27–34.

Kalisz, Roman, Wojciech Kubiński (1998). Dwadzieścia lat językoznawstwa kognitywnego w USA i w Polsce – próba bilansu. In: Wojciech Kubińska, Roman Kalisz, Ewa Modrzejewska (eds.), *Językoznawstwo kognitywne: Wybór tekstów*. Gdańsk: Wydawnictwo Uniwersytetu Gdańskiego, 7–27.

Keysar, Boaz, Shen Yeshayahu, Sam Glucksberg, William S. Horton (2000). Conventional language: How metaphorical is it? *Journal of Memory and Language* 43: 576–593.

Kloch, Zbigniew (2006). Metafora w dyskursie publicznym; Michnik, Urban, Miller przed komisją sejmową. *Nauka* 1: 65–77.

Kövecses, Zoltán (1986). *Metaphors of Anger, Pride and Love: A Lexical Approach to the Structure of Concepts*. Amsterdam – Philadelphia: John Benjamins.

Kövecses, Zoltán (1990). *Emotion Concepts*. New York: Springer Science & Business Media.

Kövecses, Zoltan (1998). Kognitywny model gniewu na podstawie amerykańskiej angielszczyzny. Trans. Wojciech Kubiński, Ewa Modrzejewska. In: Wojciech Kubińska, Roman Kalisz, Ewa Modrzejewska (eds.), *Językoznawstwo kognitywne: Wybór tekstów*. Gdańsk: Wydawnictwo Uniwersytetu Gdańskiego, 104–137.

Kövecses, Zoltán (2002). *Metaphor: A Practical Introduction*. Oxford: Oxford University Press.

Kövecses, Zoltán (2006). *Language, Mind, and Culture: A Practical Introduction*. Oxford: Oxford University Press.

Kövecses, Zoltán. (2007 [2000]). *Metaphor and Emotion. Language, Culture, and Body in Human Feeling*. Cambridge: Cambridge University Press.

Krzeszowski, Tomasz P. (1991). Metaphor – metaphorization – cognition. *Biuletyn Polskiego Towarzystwa Językoznawczego* 43–45: 83–95.

Krzeszowski, Tomasz P. (1998). Aksjologiczne aspekty metafor. Trans. Roman Kalisz, Wojciech Kubiński. In: Wojciech Kubińska, Roman Kalisz, Ewa

Modrzejewska (eds.), *Językoznawstwo kognitywne: Wybór tekstów*. Gdańsk: Wydawnictwo Uniwersytetu Gdańskiego, 80–103.

Lakoff, George (1982). *Categories: An Essay in Cognitive Linguistics*. Available at <https://georgelakoff.files.wordpress.com/2011/04/categories-an-essay-in-cognitive-linguistics-lakoff-1982.pdf>. Accessed 08 February 2015.

Lakoff, George (1992). Metaphors and war: The metaphor system used to justify the war in the gulf. In: Martin Pütz (ed.), *Thirty Years of Linguistic Evolution: Studies in Honour of René Dirven on the Occasion of His Sixtieth Birthday*. Amsterdam: John Benjamins, 461–482.

Lakoff, George (1993 [1979]). The contemporary theory of metaphor. In: Andrew Ortony (ed.), *Metaphor and Thought*. Cambridge: Cambridge University Press, 202–251.

Lakoff, George (1995). Metaphor, morality, and politics, or, why conservatives have left liberals in the dust. *Social Research* 62/2: 177–214.

Lakoff, George (2002 [1996]). *Moral Politics: How Liberals and Conservatives Think*. Chicago: The University of Chicago Press, Ltd.

Lakoff, George, Mark Johnson (1980). *Metaphors We Live By*. Chicago: The University of Chicago Press, Ltd.

Lakoff, George, Mark Johnson (1999). *Philosophy in the Flesh: The Embodied Mind and Its Challenge to Western Thought*. New York: Basic Books.

Lakoff, George, Mark Johnson (1980). *Metaphors We Live By*. Chicago: The University of Chicago Press, Ltd.

Lakoff, George, Mark Johnson (2003). *Metaphors We Live By*. Chicago: The University of Chicago Press, Ltd.

Lakoff, George, Mark Turner (1989). *More than Cool Reason: A Field Guide to Poetic Metaphor*. Chicago: University of Chicago Press.

Langacker, Ronald, W. (1987). *Foundations of Cognitive Grammar 1: Theoretical Prerequisites*. Stanford: Stanford University Press.

Langacker, Ronald, W. (1999 [1997]). The contextual basis of cognitive semantics. In: Jan Nuyts, Erick Pederson (eds.), *Language and Conceptualisation*. Cambridge: Cambridge University Press, 229–252.

Langacker, Ronald, W. (2008). *Cognitive Grammar: A Basic Introduction*. Oxford: Oxford University Press.

Lisiecki, Michał (2001). Komunikacja przez komputer (CMC). In: *Język w komunikacji* 3. Łódź: Wydawnictwo Wyższej Szkoły Humanistyczno-Ekonomicznej, 106–118.

Liu Wei, Wenyu Liu (2014). Analysis on the word-formation of English netspeak neologism. *Journal of Arts and Humanities*. MIR Centre for Socio-Economic Research, USA, 22–30.

Łuczak, Anna (2010). Figurative language in Business English: The natural world metaphors. *Beyond Philology* 7: 67–75. Available at <http://fil.ug.edu.pl/sites/default/files/_nodes/strona-filologiczny/33797/files/beyond_philology_07.pdf>. Accessed 14 December 2014.

Łuczak, Anna (2011). Figurative language in Business English: Health, sports and marriage metaphors. *Beyond Philology* 8/7–19. Available at http://fil.ug.edu.pl/sites/default/files/_nodes/strona-filologiczny/33797/files/beyond_philology_8_2011.pdf. Accessed 07 December 2014.

Łuczak, Anna (2014). Figurative language in Business English: Metaphors of transport and war. *Beyond Philology* 11: 67–82. Available at https://fil.ug.edu.pl/sites/default/files/_nodes/strona-filologiczny/33797/files/beyond_philology_11_2014.pdf. Accessed 02 May 2015.

Maćkiewicz, Jolanta (1995). Metafora w reklamie. In: Andrzej Maria Lewicki, Ryszard Tokarski (eds.), *Kreowanie świata w tekstach*. Lublin: Wydawnictwo Uniwersytetu Marii Curie-Skłodowskiej, 229–238.

Maćkiewicz, Jolanta (2010). Myśli chodzą po głowie… czyli o pewnej metaforze. In: Danuta Stanulewicz (ed.), *Lingua Terra Cognita I: Księga pamiątkowa ofiarowana Profesorowi Romanowi Kaliszowi*. Gdańsk: Wydawnictwo Uniwersytetu Gdańskiego, 151–162.

Maia, Belinda H.M.S. (1998). The language of emotion – 'metaphors', 'scenarios' or 'metalanguage'? In: Jacek Fisiak (ed.), *Lexical Semantics, Cognition and Philosophy*. Łódź: Wydawnictwo Uniwersytetu Łódzkiego, 203–218.

Malewska, Anna (2010). Expressing emotions in English and Polish in the SLA perspective. *Beyond Philology* 7: 327–350. Available at <http://fil.ug.edu.pl/sites/default/files/_nodes/strona-filologiczny/33797/files/beyond_philology_07.pdf>. Accessed 18 May 2013.

Maliszewska Anna (2002). Wirtualna buźka. Modyfikująca rola znaków graficznych w komunikacji internetowej. In: Kazimierz Michalewski (ed.), *Tekst w mediach*. Łódź: Wydawnictwo Uniwersytetu Łódzkiego, 149–155.

Matuszczyk Bożena, Danuta Stanulewicz (2002). O strukturze internetowych listów reklamowych i informacyjnych. In: Kazimierz Michalewski (ed.), *Tekst w mediach*. Łódź: Wydawnictwo Uniwersytetu Łódzkiego, 156–162.

Matuszczyk, Bożena (2010). Metafory orientacyjne w Lalce Bolesława Prusa jako klucz interpretacyjny powieści. In: Danuta Stanulewicz (ed.), *Lingua Terra Cognita I: Księga pamiątkowa ofiarowana Profesorowi Romanowi Kaliszowi*. Gdańsk: Wydawnictwo Uniwersytetu Gdańskiego, 163–171.

Maynor, Nancy (1994). The language of electronic mail: written speech? In: G.D. Little, M. Montgomery (eds.), *Centennial Usage Studies*. Tuscaloosa: University of Alabama Press, 48–54.

Mazur, Alicja (2011). Conceptualizations of death. *Beyond Philology* 8: 21–55. Available at <http://fil.ug.edu.pl/sites/default/files/_nodes/strona-filologiczny/33797/files/beyond_philology_8_2011.pdf>. Accessed 22 February 2013.

McGlone, Matthew S. (1996). Conceptual metaphors and figurative language interpretation: Food for thought? *Journal of Memory and Language* 35: 544–565.

McGlone, Matthew S. (2007). What is the explanatory value of a conceptual metaphor? *Language & Communication* 27: 109–126.

Murphy, Gregory L. (1996). On metaphoric representation. *Cognition* 60: 173–204.

Murray, Peter J. (1997). *A Rose by Any Other Name*. Available at <http://www.december.com/cmc/mag/1997/jan/murray.html>. Accessed 12 June 2009.

Murray, Knowles, Rosamund Moon (2006). *Introducing Metaphor*. New York: Routledge.

Musiał, Anna (2002). Exploring teacher trainees' metaphors of language teaching. In: Danuta Stanulewicz (ed.), *PASE Papers in Language Studies: Proceedings of the Ninth Annual Conference of the Polish Association for the Study of English, Gdańsk, 26–28 April 2000*. Gdańsk: Wydawnictwo Uniwersytetu Gdańskiego, 463–470.

Musolff, Anreas (2004). *Metaphor and Political Discourse: Analogical Reasoning in Debates about Europe*. New York: Palgrave McMillan.

Nerlich, Brigitte, David D. Clarke (2007). Cognitive linguistics and the history of linguistics. In: Dirk Geeraerts, Hubert Cuyckens (eds.), *The Oxford Handbook of Cognitive Linguistics*. Oxford: Oxford University Press, 589–609.

Notess, Greg R. (2009). Forget not the forums. *Online* 33/2. Available at <https://www.questia.com/magazine/1P3-1646339991/forget-not-the-forums>. Accessed 08 June 2012.

Ortony, Andrew (ed.) (1979). *Metaphor and Thought*. London – New York – Melbourne: Cambridge University Press.

Ortony, Andrew (1980). Some psycholinguistic aspects of metaphor. In: Richard Honeck, Robert Hoffman (eds.), *Cognition and Figurative Language*. Hillsdale, NJ: Erlbaum, 69–83.

Oster, Ulrike (2010). Using corpus methodology for semantic and pragmatic analyses: What can corpora tell us about the linguistic expression of emotions? *Cognitive Linguistics* 21/4: 727–763.

Ożóg, Kazimierz (2002). Metafory potoczne w języku polityki. *Język Polski* 1: 21–24.

Pajdzińska, Anna (1996). Wrażenia zmysłowe jako podstawa metafor językowych. *Etnolingwistyka* 8: 113–130.

Paroń, Katarzyna (2011). Rzeczywistość to metafora – próba kognitywnej analizy metafor w felietonach Jerzego Urbana. *Acta Universitatis Lodziensis. Folia Litteraria Polonica* 14/1: 43–53.

Pawelec, Andrzej (2006). *Metafora pojęciowa a tradycja*. Kraków: Universitas.

Piechota, Ewa (2005). Metafory konwencjonalne w nauczaniu języka obcego. *Języki Obce w Szkole* 49/1: 16–18.

Podracki, Jerzy, Magdalena Trysińska (2006). Metafory a frazeologia w języku polityków (na przykładzie rozmów prowadzonych w TVP i Internecie). *Studia Logopaedica* 1: 429–439.

Podracki, Jerzy, Ewa Wolańska (2008). *Język w mediach elektronicznych*. Warszawa: Semper.

Ponterotto, Diane (1994). Metaphors we can learn by. *English Teaching Forum* 32/3: 2–7.

Reddy, Michael (1979). The conduit metaphor: A case of frame conflict in our language about language. In: Andrew Ortony (ed.), *Metaphor and Thought*. Cambridge: Cambridge University Press, 284–324.

Redzimska, Joanna (2008a). Iconicity in metaphors. In: Nils-Lennart Johannesson, David C. Minugh (eds.), *Selected Papers from the 2006 and 2007 Stockholm Metaphor Festival*. 2nd Edition. Stockholm: Department of English, Stockholm University, 153–162.

Redzimska, Joanna (2008b). The role of metaphors in cross-cultural understanding. In: Katarina Rasulić, Ivana Trbojević Milošević (eds.), *English Language and Literature Studies: Structures across Cultures (ELLSSAC) Proceedings* I. Belgrad: Faculty of Philology, 329–336.

Redzimska, Joanna (2010). Amalgamacja pojęciowa w metaforach Wielkiego Łańcucha Bytów. In: Danuta Stanulewicz (ed.), *Lingua Terra Cognita* I: *Księga pamiątkowa ofiarowana Profesorowi Romanowi Kaliszowi*. Gdańsk, Wydawnictwo Uniwersytetu Gdańskiego, 173–184.

Rejakowa, Bożena (2008). *Kulturowe aspekty języka mody*. Lublin: Wydawnictwo Uniwersytetu Marii Curie-Skłodowskiej.

Rejniewicz, Paulina (2010). Metaphors in the language of music: Classical string music in focus. *Beyond Philology* 7: 103–129. Available at <http://fil.ug.edu.pl/sites/default/files/_nodes/strona-filologiczny/33797/files/beyond_philology_07.pdf>. Accessed 09 July 2014.

Ritchie David L. (2008). Context-Limited Simulation Theory of Metaphor. Available at <http://creet.open.ac.uk/projects/metaphor-analysis/theories.cfm?paper=cls>. Accessed 12 December 2012.

Ritchie, David L. (2008). Gateshead revisited: The integrative function of ambiguous metaphors in a tricky political situation. *Metaphor and Symbol* 23: 24–49.

Rohrer, Tim (2006). Kognitywna nauka o metaforze – od filozofii do neuronauki. Trans. Karolina Bałłaban, Olga Sokołowska. In: Olga Sokołowska, Danuta Stanulewicz (eds.). *Językoznawstwo kognitywne III: Kognitywizm w świetle innych teorii*. Gdańsk: Wydawnictwo Uniwersytetu Gdańskiego, 423–443.

Rumelhart, David E. (1993 [1979]). Some problems with the notion of literal meanings. In: Andrew Ortony (ed.), *Metaphor and Thought*. Cambridge: Cambridge University Press, 71–82.

Rundell, Michael (2002). Conceptual metaphor and its value for language learners. *The Teacher* 7: 18–20.

Samsel, Justyna (2011). Kiedy sukienki urzekają, a bransoletki uwodzą – animizacje wybranych atrybutów kobiecości w czasopismach kobiecych. *Białostockie Archiwum Językowe* 11: 187–198.

Semino, Elena (2008). *Metaphor in Discourse*. Cambridge: Cambridge University Press.

Shea, Virginia (1994). *Netiquette*. San Francisco: Albion Books.

Siek-Piskozub, Teresa, Ariadna Strugielska (2010). Capturing educational change in conceptual metaphors: Implications for teacher education. *The International Journal of Research in Teacher Education* 2/2: 61–69.

Słoń, Anna (2010). Some remarks on the conceptualisation of time by Elves in *The Lord of the Rings*. In: Danuta Stanulewicz, Tadeusz Z. Wolański, Joanna Redzimska (eds.), *Lingua Terra Cognita* II: *A Festschrift for Professor Roman Kalisz*. Gdańsk: Wydawnictwo Uniwersytetu Gdańskiego, 343–357.

Sokołowska, Olga (2008). Metaphor and the schematicity of concepts. In: Zdzisław Wąsik, Tomasz Komendziński (eds.), *Metaphor and Cognition*. Frankfurt am Main: Peter Lang, 35–42.

Sokołowska, Olga (2010). *Conceptualizing Properties Evidence From Language: A Study of Property Imagery on the Basis of Selected Predications in English and Polish*. Gdańsk: Wydawnictwo Uniwersytetu Gdańskiego.

Sorówka, Anna (2001). Komunikowanie przez internet – język reklamowych stron www a przekład. In: Grażyna Habrajska (ed.), *Język w komunikacji* 3. Łódź: Wydawnictwo Wyższej Szkoły Humanistyczno-Ekonomicznej, 126–133.

Stanulewicz, Danuta (2001). Retoryka artykułów prasowych traktujących o języku. In: Wojciech Kubiński, Danuta Stanulewicz (eds.), *Językoznawstwo kognitywne II: Zjawiska pragmatyczne*. Gdańsk: Wydawnictwo Uniwersytetu Gdańskiego, 348–373.

Stanulewicz, Danuta (2008). On some metalinguistic metaphors from a cognitive perspective. In: Zdzisław Wąsik, Tomasz Komendziński (eds.), *Metaphor and Cognition*. Frankfurt am Main: Peter Lang, 63–73.

Stanulewicz, Danuta (2009a). *Colour, Culture and the Language: Blue in Polish*. Gdańsk: Wydawnictwo Uniwersytetu Gdańskiego.

Stanulewicz, Danuta (2009b). Metaphorically speaking, they are travellers, wild animals, clay and *tabula rasa*: How teachers conceptualize learners. In: Maria Wysocka (ed.), *On Language Structure, Acquisition and Teaching: Studies in Honour of Professor Janusz Arabski on the Occasion of His 70th Birthday*. Katowice: Wydawnictwo Uniwersytetu Śląskiego, 474–483.

Stanulewicz, Danuta (2010). Temporal uses of the Polish spatial prepositions przed 'in front of' and za 'behind'. In: Danuta Stanulewicz, Tadeusz Z. Wolański, Joanna Redzimska (eds.), *Lingua Terra Cognita II: A Festschrift for Professor Roman Kalisz*. Gdańsk: Wydawnictwo Uniwersytetu Gdańskiego, 359–386.

Steen, Gerard (2004). Can discourse properties of metaphor affect metaphor recognition? *Journal of Pragmatics* 34: 1295–1313.

Strugielska, Ariadna, Teresa Siek-Piskozub (2008). Conceptual metaphors as a reflection of personal experience in education. In: Zdzisław Wąsik, Tomasz Komendziński (eds.), *Metaphor and Cognition*. Frankfurt am Main: Peter Lang, 117–131.

Strugielska, Ariadna, Teresa Siek-Piskozub (2013). A usage-based model of linguistic metaphors: Inferences for the cognitive theory of metaphor and teacher education. In: Katarzyna Piątkowska, Ewa Kościałkowska-Okońska (eds.), *Correspondences and Contrasts in Foreign Language Pedagogy and Translation Studies*. Cham – Heidelberg – New York – Dordrecht – London: Springer International Publishing Switzerland, 17–30.

Suler, John (1996). *The Psychology of Cyberspace*. Available at <http://users.rider.edu/~suler/psycyber/psycyber.html>. Accessed 12 June 2012.

Sutherland, Kathryn (ed.) (1997). *Electronic Text: Investigations in Method and Theory*. Oxford: Clarendon Press.

Sweetser, Eve (1989). *From Etymology to Pragmatics: Metaphorical and Cultural Aspects of Semantic Structure*. Cambridge: Cambridge University Press.

Szczepańska, Elżbieta (2009). Procesy językowe w komunikacji internetowej, jako przejaw globalizacji języka. *Bohemistyka* 1: 51–62.

Szpunar, Magdalena (2006). Rozważania na temat komunikacji internetowej. In: Jan Mazur, Małgorzata Rzeszutko-Iwan (eds.), *Teksty kultury: Oblicza komunikacji XXI wieku* 2. Lublin: Wydawnictwo Uniwersytetu Marii Curie-Skłodowskiej, 219–231.

Szwedek, Aleksander (2008). Ontological sources of structural and orientational metaphors. In: Zdzisław Wąsik, Tomasz Komendziński (eds.), *Metaphor and Cognition*. Frankfurt am Main: Peter Lang, 9–16.

Szwedek, Aleksander (2009). Ontogenetic and phylogenetic explanations of metaphorization. In: Maria Wysocka (ed.), *On Language Structure, Acquisition and Teaching: Studies in Honour of Professor Janusz Arabski on the Occasion of His 70th Birthday*. Katowice: Wydawnictwo Uniwersytetu Śląskiego, 202–210.

Tabakowska, Elżbieta (2004). *Kognitywizm po polsku – wczoraj i dziś*. Kraków: Universitas.

Tabakowska, Elżbieta (1995). *Gramatyka i obrazowanie: Wprowadzenie do językoznawstwa kognitywnego*. Kraków: Polska Akademia Nauk.

Taras, Bożena (2003). Gall Anonim w Internecie, czyli o komunikacji incognito. Paper presented at the conference *Druga Internetowa Konferencja Naukowa Dialog a nowe media*, Katowice, Uniwersytet Śląski, March – April 2003. Available at <http://uranos.cto.us.edu.pl/~dialog/archiwum/referaty.html>. Accessed 12 May 2007.

Taylor, John R., Jeanette Littlemore (eds.) (2014). *The Bloomsbury Companion to Cognitive Linguistics*. Bloomsbury Publishing.

Taylor, John R. (2007 [2002]). *Gramatyka kognitywna*. Trans. Magdalena Buchta, Łukasz Wiraszka. Kraków: Universitas.

Thurlow, Crispin, Lara Lengel, Alice Tomic (2004). *Computer Mediated Communication: Social Interaction and the Internet*. London: Sage.

Thurlow, Crispin, Kristine Mroczek (eds.) (2011). *Digital Discourse: Language in the New Media*. New York: Oxford University Press.

Turner, Mark (1987). *Death Is the Mother of Beauty: Mind, Metaphor, Criticism*. Chicago: University of Chicago Press.

Turner, Mark (1996). *The Literary Mind*. New York: Oxford University Press.

Turner, Mark (2001). *Cognitive Dimensions of Social Science*. New York: Oxford University Press.

Ungerer, Friedrich, Hans-Jorg Schmid (1996). *An Introduction to Cognitive Linguistics (Learning About Language)*. London – New York: Addison-Wesley Publishing Company.

Wallace, Patricia (2005). *Psychologia Internetu*. Trans. Tomasz Horonowski. Poznań: Dom Wydawniczy Rebis.

Walther, Joseph B. (1996). Computer-mediated communication: impersonal, Interpersonal and hyperpersonal interaction. *Communication Research* 23/1: 3–43.

Warschauer, Mark (2000). Language, identity, and the Internet. In: B. Kolko, L. Nakamura, G. Rodman (eds.), *Race in Cyberspace*. New York: Routledge, 151–170.

Wąsik, Elżbieta (1999). Metafory języka w metodologii badawczej socjolingwistyki. In: Stanisław Puppel (ed.), *Dyskurs naukowy – tradycja i zmiana*. Opole: Wydawnictwo Uniwersytetu Opolskiego, 229–240.

Wąsik, Elżbieta (2008). On the use and cognitive value of metaphors in the sociology of language. In: Zdzisław Wąsik, Tomasz Komendziński (eds.), *Metaphor and Cognition*. Frankfurt am Main: Peter Lang, 75–85.

Wąsik, Zdzisław (2008). Metaphors of form and substance in the academic discourse on language. In: Zdzisław Wąsik, Tomasz Komendziński (eds.), *Metaphor and Cognition*. Frankfurt am Main: Peter Lang, 87–98.

Werry, Christopher C. (1996). Linguistic and interactional features of Internet relay chat. In: Susan C. Herring (ed.), *Computer-mediated Communication: Linguistic, Social, and Crosscultural Perspectives*. Amsterdam: John Benjamins, 47–63.

Wierzbicka, Anna (1999). *Emotions across Languages and Cultures*. Cambridge: Cambridge University Press.

Wilson, John (1990). *Politically Speaking: The Pragmatic Analysis of Political Language*. Oxford: Basil Blackwell.

Wolf, Lilla (1999). Najnowsze tendencje w nauczaniu słownictwa – wszechstronność metafor w języku codziennym. *Języki Obce w Szkole* 43/2: 110–113.

Zawojski, Piotr (2002). Monitory między nami: O byciu razem i osobno w cyberprzestrzeni. Available at <http://www.zawojski.com/2006/04/19/monitory-miedzy-nami-o-byciu-razem-i-osobno-w-cyberprzestrzeni>. Accessed 15 March 2010.

Author Index

A
Apresjan Valentina 137, 167
Aouil Bassam 67, 167

B
Badyda Ewa 43, 167
Bakuła Kordian 59, 60, 67, 167
Bamberg Michael 43, 137, 167
Barcelona Antonio 28, 139, 167
Baron Naomi 67, 167
Barsalou Lawrence 15, 34–37, 167
Bartmiński Jerzy 43, 167, 168
Belmore Nancy 67, 169
Ben-Ze'ev Aaron 54, 168
Biel Łucja 43, 168
Bielenia Magdalena 44, 168
Bralczyk Jerzy 67, 168
Brewer Jeutonne 67, 169

C
Cameron Lynne 15, 37–39, 168
Castells Manuel 47, 67, 168
Cherny Lynn 67, 168
Chilton Paul 43, 168, 169
Cichmińska Monika 43, 137, 169
Cieślicka Anna 44, 169
Clarke David 17, 18, 178
Collot Milena 67, 169
Cortazzi Martin 44, 169
Coulson Seana 169
Croft William 43, 169
Cruse Alan 43, 169
Crystal David 47, 57–60, 64–67, 169
Cuyckens Hubert 18, 19, 171

D
Danet Brenda 67, 169
Danziger James 53, 171

Davis Boyd 67, 169
Deignan Alice 169
Dirven René 18, 169
Dixon Izabela 43, 44, 170

E
Ekman 43, 137, 170
Esenova Orazgozel 43, 167, 170
Ess Charles 43
Evans Vyvyan 15, 18–28, 39, 40, 43, 171

F
Fabiszak Małgorzata 43, 171
Fauconnier Gilles 18, 171
Francozo Edson 33, 34, 171

G
Gabryś Danuta 44, 171
Geeraerts Dirk 18, 19, 171
Gibbs Raymond 33, 34, 43, 74, 171
Gibka Martyna 170
Giddens Anthony 48, 173
Gierczyńska-Kolas Marta 43, 172
Glucksberg Marta 43, 172
Glucksberg Sam 43, 172
Goban-Klas Tomasz 67, 172
Goddard Cliff 43, 172
Gogołek Włodzimierz 59, 172
Golus Beata 67, 172
Goossens Lois 42, 172
Gorczyńska Ilona 44, 172
Grady Joseph 39, 173
Green Melanie 18–23, 25–28, 171
Gruszczyński Włodzimierz 62, 67, 173
Grzenia Jan 54, 67, 173
Gut Dorota 67, 173

185

H

Habrajska Grażyna 60, 67, 173
Hale Constance 67, 173
Hans-Jorg Schmid 67, 182
Hård af Segerstad Ylva 67, 174
Herring Susan C 67, 169
Hiraga Masako 21, 44, 174
Holme Randal 44, 174
Huang Yan 41, 42, 174

J

Jagodzińska Joanna 44, 67, 174
Jakubowska Ewa 43, 67, 174
Jasińska Małgorzata 67, 174
Jindo Job 44, 174
Johnson Mark 13, 15, 17, 23, 25–27, 29, 31, 33, 41, 43, 139, 174

K

Kajdasz-Aouil Maria 67, 167
Kalisz Roman 43, 67, 167
Kelly Garrett R 167
Keysar Boaz 167
Kloch Zbigniew 43, 167
Kövecses Zoltán 24–27, 29–34, 42, 43, 137, 139, 167
Krzeszowski Tomasz 43, 175

L

Lakoff George 13, 15, 17, 18, 22–25, 27–29, 31–33, 41–43, 139, 176
Langacker Ronald 17, 18, 43, 176
Lengel Lara 68, 176
Lenz Paula 171
Lima Costa 33, 34, 171
Lisiecki Michał 176
Littlemore Jeanette 42, 43, 182
Lixian Jin 44, 169
Luka Barbara 167
Łuczak Anna 44, 169

M

Maćkiewicz Jolanta 43, 44, 110, 177
Maia Belinda 43, 177
Malewska Anna 43, 137, 177
Maliszewska Anna 65, 177
Maslen Robert 168, 177
Matuszczyk Bożena 44, 67, 177
Maynor Nancy 67, 177
Mazur Alicja 44, 169
McGlone Matthew 21, 22, 26, 169
Mosiołek-Kłosińska Katarzyna 67, 168
Mroczek Kristine 67, 168
Murphy Gregory 178
Murray Knowles 49, 178
Murray Peter 49, 179
Musiał Anna 44, 179

N

Nerlich Brigitte 17, 18, 178
Notess Greg 55, 56, 178

O

Olseth Karen 167
Orony Andrew 21, 43, 137, 178
Oster Ulrike 43, 62, 137, 178
Ożóg Kazimierz 43, 178

P

Pajdzińska Anna 43, 178
Paroń Katarzyna 178, 179
Pawelec Andrzej 179
Piechota Ewa 44, 179
Podracki Jerzy 43, 179
Ponterotto Diane 44, 179
Pörings Ralf 170, 179
Potter Liz 169, 179

R

Reddy Michael 44, 179
Redzimska Joanna 43, 168
Rejakowa Bożena 110, 168

Rejniewicz Paulina 44, 168
Ritchie David 35–37, 179
Rohrer Tim 43, 179
Rosamund Moon 178, 179
Rumelhart David 33, 43, 178
Rundell Michael 44, 178

S
Samsel Justyna 110, 180
Scanlon Jessie 67, 173
Schäffner Christina 43, 169
Semino Elena 43, 180
Shen Yeshayahu 180
Siek-Piskozub Teresa 43, 44, 180
Słoń Anna 44, 180
Sokołowska Olga 13, 43, 177
Sorówka Anna 180
Stanulewicz Danuta 13, 43, 44, 67, 168–174, 177–180
Steen Gerard 29, 173
Strugielska Ariadna 43, 44, 180, 181
Suler John 49, 181
Sutherland Kathryn 67, 181
Sweetser Eve 43, 181
Szczepańska Elżbieta 67, 181
Szpunar Magdalena 48, 181
Szwedek Aleksander 43, 181

T
Tabakowska Elżbieta 187
Taras Bożena 68, 187

Taylor John 42, 43, 182
Thurlow Crispin 68, 182
Todd Oakley 169
Tomic Alice 68, 182
Trysińska Magdalena 43, 179, 182
Turner Mark 18, 22, 23, 28, 29, 43, 171, 182

U
Ungerer Friedrich 182

W
Wallace Patricia 48, 63, 64, 180
Walther Joseph 68, 182
Warschauer Mark 68, 182
Wąsik Elżbieta 44, 68, 183
Wąsik Zdzisław 44, 68, 179–183
Wei Liu 177
Wenchi Yeh 167, 177
Werry Christopher 68, 182
Wierzbicka Anna 43, 167, 183
Wilson John 43, 182
Wolańska Ewa 179, 182
Wolf Lilla 44, 183

Z
Zawojski Piotr 48, 183
Zazie Todd 168

Subject Index

active communication 53
asynchronous communication 50–52
classification of metaphors 29–34
cognitive function of metaphor 30–33
Cognitive Linguistics 17–19
cognitive processes in metaphor understanding 26
cognitive semantics 19
Conceptual Metaphor Theory 21–24
Context-Limited Simulation Theory of Metaphor 34–37
conventionality of metaphors 29
Discourse Dynamics Framework for Metaphor 37–39
experiential basis of metaphor 27
features of language used in online communication 57–67
forum as a form of communication medium 54–57
hiding and highlighting 25
Internet as a medium stimulating communication 54
Invariance Hypothesis 28
levels of generality of metaphor 34
metaphors of aggitation and nerves 75–55
metaphors of anger 74, 121
metaphors of bringing up children 89
metaphors of children's progress 89
metaphors of choosing an option 134
metaphors of computers and Internet-related phenomena 108
metaphors of conception 88
metaphors of criticism metaphors of depression 77–80
metaphors of emotions 74–83, 121–124
metaphors of everyday life 95–99, 126
metaphors of experiences 132
metaphors of freedom and patience 112
metaphors of future 135
metaphors of happiness and sadness 80, 122–124
metaphors of illnesses 93–95
metaphors of other feelings and emotions 81, 124
metaphors of parts of the body 90–92
metaphors of people, their behaviour and attitudes 105, 127–131
metaphors of pregnancy 126
metaphors of problems and hardship 100–105
metaphors of relationships 83–87, 125
metaphors of sex 87, 125
metaphors of shopping 99
metaphors of teeth 92
metaphors of the human body 90, 131
metaphors of the world, life, fate and nature 109–112
metaphors of time 106, 135
metaphors of weapons 136
metaphors of weather 107
metaphtonymy 41–43
metonymy 41–43
nature of metaphor 33
synchronous communication 52
Theory of Lexical Concepts and Cognitive Models 39–41

Gdańsk Studies in Language

Edited by Danuta Stanulewicz

Vol. 1   Karolina Janczukowicz: Teaching English Pronunciation at the Secondary School Level. 2014.

Vol. 2   Olga Aleksandrowska: The Educational Potential of Texts of Culture in Teaching English to Senior Secondary School Students. 2015.

Vol. 3   Karolina Janczukowicz / Mikołaj Rychło (eds.): General Education and Language Teaching Methodology. The Gdańsk School of ELT. 2015.

Vol. 4   Anna Turula / Beata Mikołajewska / Danuta Stanulewicz (eds.): Insights into Technology Enhanced Language Pedagogy. 2015.

Vol. 5   Maciej Rataj: Attitudes to Standard British English and Standard Polish. A Study in Normative Linguistics and Comparative Sociolinguistics. 2016.

Vol. 6   Zofia Chłopek: Early Bilingualism and Multilingualism. Parents' and Caregivers' Attitudes and Observations. 2016

Vol. 7   Hanna Komorowska / Jarosław Krajka: Monolingualism – Bilingualism – Multilingualism. The Teacher's Perspective. 2016.

Vol. 8   Justyna Giczela-Pastwa / Uchenna Oyali (eds.): Norm-Focused and Culture-Related Inquiries in Translation Research. Selected Papers of the CETRA Research Summer School 2014. 2016.

Vol. 9   Marcin Opacki: Reconsidering Early Bilingualism. A Corpus-Based Study of Polish Migrant Children in the United Kingdom. 2016.

Vol. 10 Danuta Stanulewicz / Karolina Janczukowicz / Małgorzata Rocławska-Daniluk (eds.): Language Education. Controversies, Observations and Proposals. 2016.

Vol. 11 Marta Gierczyńska-Kolas: Metaphors Used on Polish and American Internet Forums for Mothers. A Comparative Analysis. 2017.

Vol. 12 Małgorzata Smentek: Exploring Translation in Language Learning. 2017.

Vol. 13 Martin Blaszk: Happening in Education – Theoretical Issues. 2017.

www.peterlang.com

www.ingramcontent.com/pod-product-compliance
Ingram Content Group UK Ltd.
Pitfield, Milton Keynes, MK11 3LW, UK
UKHW041902230426
12049UKWH00002B/12